Troika!

The Remarkable Ascent of
a Great Global University,
Nanyang Technological University
Singapore,

2003–2017

Troika!

The Remarkable Ascent of a Great Global University, Nanyang Technological University Singapore,

2003–2017

Bertil Andersson
Haresh Shah
Guaning Su
Tony Mayer

Nanyang Technological University, Singapore

World Scientific

NEW JERSEY · LONDON · SINGAPORE · BEIJING · SHANGHAI · HONG KONG · TAIPEI · CHENNAI · TOKYO

Published by

World Scientific Publishing Co. Pte. Ltd.
5 Toh Tuck Link, Singapore 596224
USA office: 27 Warren Street, Suite 401-402, Hackensack, NJ 07601
UK office: 57 Shelton Street, Covent Garden, London WC2H 9HE

Library of Congress Cataloging-in-Publication Data
Names: Andersson, Bertil, author. | Shah, Haresh C., author. | Su, Guaning, author. |
   Mayer, Tony, 1942– author.
Title: Troika! : the remarkable ascent of a great global university, Nanyang Technological University
   Singapore, 2003–2017 / Bertil Andersson, Haresh Shah, Guaning Su, Tony Mayer.
Description: Hackensack : World Scientific Publishing Co. Pte. Ltd., 2021. |
   Includes bibliographical references.
Identifiers: LCCN 2021001633 | ISBN 9789811236051 (hardcover) |
   ISBN 9789811236563 (paperback) | ISBN 9789811236068 (ebook) |
   ISBN 9789811236075 (ebook other)
Subjects: LCSH: Nanyang Technological University--History--21st century. |
   Universities and colleges--Singapore--Administration. | Educational leadership--Singapore.
Classification: LCC LG395.S53 A827 2021 | DDC 378.5957--dc23
LC record available at https://lccn.loc.gov/2021001633

British Library Cataloguing-in-Publication Data
A catalogue record for this book is available from the British Library.

Copyright © 2022 by World Scientific Publishing Co. Pte. Ltd.

All rights reserved. This book, or parts thereof, may not be reproduced in any form or by any means, electronic or mechanical, including photocopying, recording or any information storage and retrieval system now known or to be invented, without written permission from the publisher.

For photocopying of material in this volume, please pay a copying fee through the Copyright Clearance Center, Inc., 222 Rosewood Drive, Danvers, MA 01923, USA. In this case permission to photocopy is not required from the publisher.

For any available supplementary material, please visit
https://www.worldscientific.com/worldscibooks/10.1142/12252#t=suppl

Desk Editor: Tan Boon Hui

Typeset by Stallion Press
Email: enquiries@stallionpress.com

Printed in Singapore

The book tells a fascinating journey from the early history to the future challenges facing one of the most successful young universities in South-East Asia, covering the period of 2003 to 2017. The three influential authors were actively and intimately involved in laying the foundations for restructuring the educational system and turning NTU into a research powerhouse. They offer precious insights into the strategic thinking and the sometimes difficult decisions behind the rise in the world's top university rankings, highlighting the role of a forward-looking global university in the wider context of Singapore's future.

Helga Nowotny
Professor emerita ETH Zurich
Former President of the European Research Council

The narrative of the development of a university in Singapore in this book is like a mirror of the incredible development of Singapore from a city like many others in Asia in the 50's and 60's of the 20th century, poorer than Manila, to today's city state — a powerhouse in financial issues, in ideas, business models and well-being (including the pandemic). Reading and analysing the excellently presented large amount of facts, figures and ideas in this book is a must for all those who are interested to learn how Asia, Europe and the USA might join in common efforts to steer the future of our globe. And be amazed by a lot of interesting additional information which will surprise you: Could you ever believe that such a scientifically and technologically relevant institution, Nanyang Technological University, belongs to the 15 most beautiful campuses in the world? Enjoy reading!

Dr Christian Patermann
Former Director, Directorate-General for Research & Innovation
European Commission, Brussels

This excellent book is a timely review of the short, but dynamic history of Nanyang Technological University. In just 18 years it has gone from young start-up to being one of the top 50 universities in the world. It now sits alongside universities which have been in business for hundreds of years. It has done this by growing and attracting world-renowned researchers and teachers. It has also had a strong focus on new and emerging technologies; NTU is number three in the world for quality publications in Artificial Intelligence. Another thing that makes NTU exceptional and justifies its high score, is a strong focus on business and industry, leading to excellent industrial engagement and a strong thread of "use-inspired research". The Rolls-Royce@NTU Corporate Lab with which I was involved is a typical example and had over 300 top-level researchers and technical experts working on the research programme. It was the first of its kind, but many other major companies have followed this model.

The three drivers give us a fascinating personal insight into their own contribution in each phase of the University's foundation and growth. I am sure you will enjoy reading their wonderful stories and the amazing history of this great, modern university.

Professor Ric Parker
Former Director of Research and Technology, Rolls-Royce Group

Foreword I

Su Guaning and Bertil Andersson, Second and Third President of Nanyang Technological University, requested me in 2017 to write a Foreword for their planned book on the transformation of NTU under their presidencies from 2003 to 2011 and 2011 to 2017, during which they also worked closely with Professor Haresh Shah of Stanford University.

From their diverse origins and cultural backgrounds, a series of close encounters brought Guaning, Bertil and Haresh together in NTU to pursue a common quest. The transformation of NTU is a good illustration how Singapore has made progress. An unbiased assessment of alternative futures and strengths and weaknesses is followed up by strategic planning and injection of suitable talents.

I congratulate the NTU Troika, Guaning, Bertil and Haresh for their achievements and observe with satisfaction the benefits that their offspring, NTU, has brought to Singapore. The Troika executed, with the support of the Singapore government and the NTU Board of Trustees, a major leap in higher education and research resulting in leading edge solutions being developed in Singapore in collaboration with partners around the world. This has helped to strengthen Singapore and bring about a brighter future for our people.

Dr Tony Tan Keng Yam
Seventh President of the Republic of Singapore

Foreword II

NTU's transformation owes a lot to many people, and among them are this book's authors — Su Guaning, second President of NTU, Bertil Andersson, who started as Guaning's Provost and went on to be the third President of NTU, and Haresh Shah, a member of the Board of Trustees and emeritus professor of Stanford University.

While this is not meant to be an official account of the history of NTU, it is nevertheless interesting for those wishing to understand the personal perspectives of those meeting the challenges of that time.

NTU has transformed from being a purely teaching university to one that is focused almost in equal parts on teaching and research. The need for research is founded on the belief that as Singapore progresses, being able to apply technology alone is not enough, Singapore must also be able to create new knowledge and innovations. This change is anything but simple. From relooking at how education should be delivered in today's world e.g. the Blue Ribbon Commission, to learning how to compete for research grants, revamping curriculum to broaden students' perspectives, moving from lectures based on transmitting knowledge to flipped classrooms where professors are facilitators in discussions — these are the myriad challenges they wrestled with.

With the momentous decision to allow the universities to be autonomous came another set of transformations. Autonomy meant that the university and the Board of Trustees had to choose what to focus on, which professors to hire, where to spend more money on and where to spend less, what to build and what to maintain. These simple statements set off the need for new budgeting processes, performance, appointments and tenure processes, salary administration processes, etc. These are continuing changes that are still taking place today as the world does not stand still in terms of how to do things better, whether it is digitalisation, the cloud, greater demands for cyber security, and so on.

Guaning, Bertil and Haresh had ringside seats as NTU initiated its transformation. The success can be seen, not merely in NTU's rise in rankings to being one of the best global universities, but in the expansion of its offering to Singaporeans, starting with engineering and business, but now also science, the humanities, arts and social sciences and medicine.

But a university's work is never done. While NTU has come a long way and many have contributed to this journey, there is still much further to go and more contributors are needed for the future.

Koh Boon Hwee

Preface

This book by Professors Bertil Andersson, Haresh Shah and Su Guaning is the inside story of how a modest Asian university at the turn of the millennium has been able to achieve global prominence. In the space of nearly 15 years, Nanyang Technological University (NTU) has achieved a stature rivalling many older, well-established and celebrated academic institutions in the US, the UK and the rest of the world.

This is the very personal story of the three principal authors who worked hand in glove, taking NTU Singapore on this incredible journey. The transformation of NTU during 2003–2017 is a rare event in the annals of higher education, the improbability of the achievement only matched by the scale of the ambition that it represented. This is also the personal story of three academic leaders who found common cause and worked closely together, taking NTU Singapore on this audacious journey. Engineering this transformation, the three leaders made good use of the opportunities provided by the Singapore government's restructuring of research and higher education governance in the period covered by the book, as well as the generous funding that accompanied it. They were also careful to obtain the support of the Board of Trustees, the faculty, the students, the alumni and parents and the social fabric of Singapore citizens.

About the Authors

Bertil Andersson is a renowned Swedish biochemist within the field of photosynthesis research. In addition, he is a prominent international academic leader with experience from several countries. He completed his PhD in biochemistry in 1978 at the University of Lund, Sweden, followed by a post-doctoral period at the Commonwealth Scientific and Industrial Research Organisation (CSIRO)/Australian National University in Canberra, Australia. In 1986, he became the Professorial Chair of Biochemistry at Stockholm University. In 1999, he was appointed as President of Linköping University, Sweden. Then, in 2004, he took the position as Chief Executive Officer (CEO) of the European Science Foundation (ESF) in Strasbourg, France. In 2007, Andersson was recruited to Singapore as the first Provost of Nanyang Technological University (NTU) and, in 2011, became the President of NTU, a position he held until the end of 2017. In Singapore, he received the President's Science and Technology Medal as well as the prestigious Meritorious Service Medal for his contributions to academia and research in the country.

He is currently a Board member or Advisor to a number of international academic institutions, research foundations, governmental organisations, as well as private companies. During the years 1988–2010, Andersson was a member of the Nobel Committee for Chemistry (Chair in 1997) and Board and Trustees of the Nobel Foundation in Stockholm. He is a member of a number of international learned societies, and the holder of over 20 Honorary Doctorates from universities in 11 countries.

Haresh Shah is a pioneer and international authority on risk analysis, earthquake engineering and probabilistic methods. He received the B.Eng from Poona University and M.S. and Ph.D. from Stanford. At Stanford University, he founded the John A. Blume Earthquake Engineering Center and chaired the Civil and Environmental Engineering Department. While at Stanford, he started up Risk Management Systems, a major supplier of software and methods for risk mitigation for the insurance industry.

In 2005, NTU President Su Guaning sought Professor Shah's advice with a view to restructuring NTU and develop it as a research-intensive university. He took on the challenge first as Senior Academic Advisor to the President and member, Board of Advisors. He was appointed to the Board of Trustees upon its establishment in 2006 and made Chairman, Academic Affairs Committee.

He founded a number of companies and established the Institute of Catastrophic Risk Management while at NTU. He developed the Report of the Blue Ribbon Commission for Undergraduate Education with profound and long lasting impact on generations of NTU students.

Professor Shah is Obayashi Professor of Engineering (Emeritus) at Stanford University; Founding Director and Chairman of World Seismic Safety Initiative; and Founder and Chairman of Asia Risk Transfer Solutions, Inc. (ARTS), Singapore. He is the recipient of the John S. Bickley Gold Medal from the International Insurance Society. On the 100th anniversary of the 1906 San Francisco earthquake, Professor Shah was awarded the "Top Seismic Engineer of the 20th Century" by the Applied Technology Council/Engineering New Record.

Su Guaning is President Emeritus of Nanyang Technological University (NTU) Singapore. He received BSc (Eng.), MS and PhD degrees, all in Electrical Engineering, from the University of Alberta, California Institute of Technology, and Stanford University, respectively. He was also conferred an honorary doctorate by the University of Alberta in 2015.

A pioneer in defence research in Singapore, he was Director, Defence Science Organisation from 1986 to 1997; Deputy Secretary (Technology), Ministry of Defence, Singapore from 1998 to 2001; and Founding Chief

Executive, Defence Science and Technology Agency (DSTA) from 2000 to 2002. He became the 2nd NTU President on 1 January 2003.

President Su expanded NTU into a comprehensive university. He also persuaded Professor Haresh Shah and Professor Bertil Andersson to join him in his quest to transform NTU from a professionally-focused teaching institution into a top-tier research-intensive university. This book documents their work resulting in NTU's dramatic ascent.

Professor Su was conferred the National Science and Technology Medal, the Defence Technology Medal (Outstanding Service), and the Meritorious Service Medal by Singapore; Knighthood of the Legion of Honour by France; and the Friendship Award by China. He is a Life Fellow of the Institute of Electrical and Electronics Engineers and Founding Fellow of the Singapore Academy of Engineering. In February 2020, Professor Su was elected an International Member of the US National Academy of Engineering.

Tony Mayer is a geologist educated at the University of Manchester. He conducted research at the University of Leicester (carbonatites of East Africa) and at University College London (working on gabbroic igneous intrusions). Mayer then pursued a career in research management joining, the UK Natural Environment Research Council (NERC). In 1984, he was seconded to the Joint Oceanographic Institutions for Deep Earth Sampling (JOIDES) science planning office of the international Ocean Drilling Program based in the University of Rhode Island, US. On his return to the UK, he headed North American Electric Reliability Corporation (NERC) international activities, including responsibility for polar sciences and global environmental change research. In 1995, Mayer joined the European Science Foundation (ESF) in Strasbourg, and gained extensive experience in developing research policy in Europe and worked with the European Commission (EC) in a variety of roles. In 2003, he became Director of the European Cooperation in Science and Technology (COST) Office in Brussels. He was the Scientific Secretary of the EC's European Research Advisory Board (EURAB) (industry/academia group). When Andersson became Provost of NTU in 2007, Mayer joined him as Associate Registrar, supporting him in the development of a variety of policy issues. Mayer instituted a research integrity (RI) programme at NTU and became its Research Integrity Officer. He was the founding Co-Chair of three World Conferences on Research Integrity and also developed a national RI network in Singapore. Mayer continues as an advisor on research integrity, working with universities and on various European Framework projects.

Acknowledgements

We especially want to thank Dr. Tony Tan Keng Yam, Seventh President of Singapore, for writing the Foreword and for his leadership and foresight that created the environment for us to do our work. It would not be an understatement to say that the Singaporean universities would not be where they are today without Dr. Tony Tan's guidance and reforms of the Singaporean academic landscape.

With sadness, we acknowledge the contribution of the late President S. R. Nathan, Sixth President of Singapore. President Nathan was very generous with his time in discussions with Haresh and Guaning on matters relating to NTU.

We thank former Minister for Education Tharman Shanmugaratnam (now Senior Minister), who had an unwavering vision of education as the great leveller. His guidance and vision have been most helpful in bringing out the best in NTU. In addition, we wish to thank former Minister for Education Ng Eng Hen, who was responsible for the broadening of the NTU base in adding the natural and life sciences and the arts to the university's portfolio and without whom the Medical School would not have been realised. We also wish to thank former Minister for Education, now Deputy Prime Minister, Heng Swee Keat, for his unstinting support of NTU and its policies.

We thank Chairman of the NTU Board of Trustees, Koh Boon Hwee, for his indulgence of our idiosyncrasies and his wise counsel, always coming at the right moment. As Chairman since 1993, NTU today bears his indelible imprint. We also thank him for his Foreword.

We thank former Permanent Secretary of Education, Lim Chuan Poh. As Chairman of A*STAR, he has been a most valuable colleague. We thank him, in particular, for his crucial contributions towards the establishment of the Lee Kong Chian School of Medicine.

We thank Dr. Lee Seng Tee, Chairman of Lee Foundation, for its most generous gift of S$150 million, which, together with government matching funds, raised S$400 million for the "flying start" given to the establishment of the medical school at NTU.

There are so many people to thank that we risk giving offence by acts of omission. Without the support, the roles played and the contributions of our colleagues and friends at NTU, the ascent of NTU into the ranks of the leading world universities would not have been possible.

In writing this account of the transformation of NTU, we wish to acknowledge the advice and comments of Deputy President and Provost Professor Ling San; former Acting Provost and Vice President (International Affairs) Professor Er Meng Hwa; Senior Vice President (Research) Professor Lam Khin Yong; former Senior Associate Provost Professor Kam Chan Hin; Associate Vice President (Wellbeing) Professor Kwok Kian Woon; former Registrar and Chief Planning Officer Mr. Chan Kwong Lok; Chief Communication Officer Dr Vivien Chiong; and the many other friends and colleagues from NTU who have provided much-needed assistance in the preparation of this book. We are particularly grateful to Professor Michael Khor for his input on rankings, the citation plot, and the lists of Nanyang Assistant Professors and NRF Fellows, and to the NTU Corporate Communications Office for the use of NTU's copyrighted material.

Finally, we wish to thank World Scientific Publishing Co. Pte. Ltd. for making this book a reality. Our thanks go to Phua Kok Khoo (K K Phua) and our desk editors, Tan Boon Hui and Lai Ann.

Contents

Foreword I	vii
Foreword II	ix
Preface	xi
About the Authors	xiii
Acknowledgements	xvii
List of Acronyms and Abbreviations	xxi
Introduction	xxvii
Stage I Base Camp — Setting the Scene	**1**
Chapter 1 The Starting Point for Change	3
Chapter 2 From Third World to First — Singapore's Higher Education and Research	7
Chapter 3 Nanyang Technological University — Its Early History and Evolution	13
Chapter 4 A Farewell to Arms — Guaning's Tale	31
Chapter 5 An "Earth-Shaking" Trajectory from California to Singapore — Haresh's Tale	41
Chapter 6 From the Arctic to the Equator: A Viking's Journey — Bertil's Tale	53

Stage II Plotting the Route   63

Chapter 7 Troika: The Council of Three   65
Chapter 8 Academic Governance Evolution and Reform   83
Chapter 9 Developing the Strategic Plan   95
Chapter 10 The Chinese Connection   113

Stage III The Ascent   119

Chapter 11 Restructuring the University   121
Chapter 12 Finance and Budgetary Reform   141
Chapter 13 Reforming Education — Producing the Graduates
            of the Future   145
Chapter 14 Elephants and Gazelles: The People Factor   173
Chapter 15 A Unique Medical School   189
Chapter 16 The Research Powerhouse Part 1: The Big Picture   207
Chapter 17 The Research Powerhouse Part 2:
            Systems, Structures and Quality   225
Chapter 18 Ranking and Reputation   245
Chapter 19 Communicating with and Serving the Society   253
Chapter 20 The University in a Tropical Garden   259
Chapter 21 A Great Global University: Taking NTU to
            the World   271

Stage IV Peaks Ahead   279

Chapter 22 Unfinished Business — Future Challenges in an
            Uncertain World   281

Appendices   287
Bibliography   303
Index   305

List of Acronyms And Abbreviations

Singapore has a reputation for its propensity to use acronyms and abbreviations and NTU is a non-exception. Below is a list of acronyms and abbreviations divided into three categories: NTU, Singapore and General.

NTU

AAC	Academic Affairs Committee of the Board of Trustees
APT	Appointments, Promotion & Tenure
ARISE	Ageing Research Institute for Society & Education
BRC	Blue Ribbon Commission
CELT	Centre for Excellence in Learning & Teaching
CNYSP	C N Yang Scholars Programme
CRADLE	Centre for Research & Development for Learning
EMB	Experimental Medicine Building
EOS	Earth Observatory of Singapore (RCE)
ERIAN	Energy Research Institute at NTU
IAS	Institute of Advanced Studies
IMI	Institute for Media Innovation
Nantah	Nanyang University
NAP	Nanyang Assistant Professor
NEWRI	Nanyang Environment & Water Research Institute
NIMBELS	Nanyang Integrated Medical, Biological & Environmental Life Sciences
NISB	Nanyang Institute of Structural Biology

NITHM (now HealthTech)	Nanyang Institute of Technology in Health & Medicine
NSS	Nanyang Shared Services
NTSP	NTU/NIE Teaching Scholars Programme
NUE	New Undergraduate Experience
PDG	Provosts & Deans Group
PTI & PT2	Promotion & Tenure reviews
REP	Renaissance Engineering Programme
REIDS	Renewable Energy Integration Demonstrator Singapore (NTU)
RIEO	Research Integrity & Ethics Office
RSO	Research Support Office
SCALE@NTU	Singtel Cognitive & Artificial Intelligence Laboratory for Enterprises
SCELSE	Singapore Centre for Environmental Life Sciences Engineering (RCE)
SC3DP	Singapore Centre for 3D Printing
SRCPT	School Review Committee for Promotion & Tenure
SUG	Start-Up Grant
TPI	The Photonics Institute
UAPB	University Academic Personnel Board
URECA	Undergraduate Research Experience on Campus
USP	University Scholars Programme

Schools and Major Groups of NTU:

ADM	Art, Design & Media
ASE	Asian School of Environment
CEE	Civil & Environmental Engineering
NBS	Nanyang Business School
NIE	National Institute of Education
EEE	Electrical & Electronic Engineering
LKC Medicine	Lee Kong Chian School of Medicine

MAE	Mechanical & Aerospace Engineering
MSE	Material Sciences & Engineering
RSIS	S. Rajaratnam School of International Studies
SBS	School of Biological Sciences
SCBE	School of Chemical & Biomedical Engineering
SCSE	School of Computer Science & Engineering
SCHSS (later SCH & SSS)	School of Humanities & Social Sciences
SPMS	School of Physical & Mathematical Sciences
WKWSCI	Wee Kim Wee School of Communication & Information

Singapore

ARC	Academic Research Council (MOE)
A*STAR	Agency for Science, Technology & Research
ARTC	Advanced Re-Manufacturing & Technology Centre (A*STAR)
CEUS	Committee for the Expansion of the University System in Singapore (MOE)
CPE	College of Physical Education
CPF	Central Provident Fund
CQT	Centre for Quantum Technology (RCE)
CREATE	Campus for Research Excellence & Technological Enterprise (NRF)
CRP	Competitive Research Programme (NRF)
DSO	Defence Science Organisation
DSTA	Defence Science and Technology Agency
EDB	Economic Development Board
ERP	External Review Panel of QAFU (MOE)
IAAP	International Academic Advisory Panel (MOE)
IE	Institute of Education

IMCB	Institute of Molecular & Cell Biology (A*STAR)
IMDA	Infocomm Media Development Authority
JC	Junior College
MBI	MechanoBiology Institute (RCE)
MINDEF	Ministry of Defence
MOE	Ministry of Education
MRT	Mass Rapid Transit
NHG	National Healthcare Group
NMRC	National Medical Research Council
NRF	National Research Foundation
NSTB	National Science & Technology Board
NTI	Nanyang Technological Institute
NUHS	National University Healthcare System
NUS	National University of Singapore
PAP	People's Action Party
PUB	Public Utilities Board
QAFU	Quality Assurance Framework for Universities (MOE)
RCE	Research Centre of Excellence (NRF/MOE)
RIEC	Research, Innovation & Enterprise Council
RSB	Research Scholarship Budget (MOE)
SAB	Scientific Advisory Board (NRF)
SGH	Singapore General Hospital
SINGA	Singapore International Graduate Award
SMA	Singapore–MIT Alliance
SMU	Singapore Management University
SSDSN	Singapore Sustainable Development Solutions Network
SUTD	Singapore University of Technology & Design
TTC	Teachers Training College
TTSH	Tan Tock Seng Hospital

General

ANU	Australian National University, Canberra
ARPANET	Advanced Research Project Agency Network (USA)
ARWU	Academic Ranking of World Universities (SJTU)

ASEAN	Association of Southeast Asian Nations
Caltech	California Institute of Technology
CERN	Conseil Européen pour la Recherche Nucléaire
CIA	Central Intelligence Agency (USA)
CMU	Carnegie-Mellon University, Pittsburgh, USA
CNRS	Centre National de la Recherche Scientifique (France)
COST	European Cooperation in Science & Technology
CSIRO	Commonwealth Science & Industrial Research Organisation (Australia)
DARPA	Defense Advanced Research Projects Agency (USA)
EMBA	Executive Master in Business Administration
EMBC	European Molecular Biology Conference
EMBO	European Molecular Biology Organisation
EPFL	École Polytechnique Fédérale de Lausanne (Switzerland)
ERC	European Research Council
ESF	European Science Foundation
ESSEC	École Supérieure des Sciences Économiques et Commerciales (France/Singapore)
ETH	Eidgenössische Technische Hochschule, Zürich (Switzerland)
EU	European Union
EURYI	European Young Investigators Award
FOA/FOI	Totalförsvarets forskningsinstitut (Swedish Defence Research Institute)
GERD	Gross Domestic Expenditure on Research & Development (GDP)
GDP	Gross Domestic Product
GLOBALTECH	Global Alliance of Technological Universities
HKUST	Hong Kong University of Science & Technology
HOD	Head of Department in a university
HUJ	Hebrew University of Jerusalem
ICSU	International Science Council
IITB	Indian Institute of Technology Bombay

INSEAD	Institut Européen d'Administration des Affaires (France/Singapore)
IP	Intellectual property
IPL	Institute Para Limes
IUPAP	International Union of Pure & Applied Physics (ICSU)
KI	Karolisnka Institutet, Stockholm, Sweden
KPI	Key performance Indicator
LMB	Laboratory for Molecular Biology, Cambridge, UK
MIT	Massachusetts Institute of Technology
MNC	Multi-national Corporation
MOOC	Massive open on-line course
NIH	National Institutes of Health (USA)
NSF	National Science Foundation (USA)
OECD	Organisation for Economic Cooperation & Development
QS	Quacquarelli Symonds
RMB	Renmimbi (Yuan), China
RMS	Risk Management Solutions
RPMS	Royal Postgraduate Medical School, UK
SCUT	South China University of Technology
SJTU	Shanghai Jiao Tong University, China
SSGKC	Sino-Singapore Guangzhou Knowledge City (China)
STEM	Science, technology, engineering and mathematics
TCM	Traditional Chinese medicine
Technion	Israel Institute of Technology, Haifa, Israel
TEL	Technology-enhanced learning
THE	Times Higher Education (UK)
TUM	Technische Universität Munich, Germany
UCLA	University of California, Los Angeles, USA
UMI	Unité Mixte Internationale (CNRS)
UNSW	University of New South Wales, Sydney, Australia

Introduction

Why We Have Written This Book

Look around any big bookstore and you find that there are many books on the histories of universities. For the most part, they chart the long history and development of venerable institutions such as Bologna, Oxford, and Cambridge in Europe or the Ivy League universities of the US. Many are official histories commissioned to celebrate a significant anniversary and so create a story from what may be rather "dry" records of meetings and correspondences or the highlighting of eminent scholars through the centuries.

Instead of a historical treatise, this book tells the story of the ascent of Nanyang Technological University (NTU) in Singapore to the peak of academic excellence in merely 15 years. The way it was done by the combination of three academic leaders from diverse backgrounds makes it even more interesting. Often, when NTU delegations visited academic institutions around the world, we were asked (with some incredulity) how NTU rose so quickly in global rankings of academic excellence in such a short time. The answer is not straightforward. The ascent of NTU is a story of a unique combination of events: a collective leadership team, the enabling Singapore government policies, Singapore society's expectations, faculty and students working with the leadership team and the window of opportunity opened by the university leadership changes during the first decade and a half of 21st century Singapore.

This book is written as a composite personal account of the exploits of the three of us who, together, formed the Troika: Bertil Andersson, Haresh Shah and Su Guaning, as the NTU leadership team that brought about this great leap in quality and reputation of the university. Inevitably, in a change of this magnitude, many questions have been asked. How was this possible? Will it last? What can we learn from the NTU ascent? Is it a useful reference for university leaders around the world? What were the internal and external forces involved in bringing this change about and what were the obstacles that stood in the way and how were they overcome? It is our hope that readers may find some of the answers in this book.

This book charts this remarkable and rapid rise, over a span of just under 15 years (2003 to 2017), of a very young institution, NTU in Singapore, founded as recently as 1991. We describe how the university changed from being, primarily, a good mainstream engineering teaching institution to one of the most highly ranked research-intensive universities — in the top 15 universities according to the QS World University Ranking — as seen through the eyes and recollections of the three prime movers behind this unique and rapid change that has occurred in leading academic circles. Universities are analogous to big ocean tankers because they cannot easily be manoeuvred and can only change direction slowly, and yet, at NTU, rather than an ocean liner, it behaved more like a speedboat.

New Year's Day, 2003, saw the first member of the Troika, Su Guaning, at the helm of this young institution, NTU. Over the first 22 years, (including its predecessor institution Nanyang Technological Institute), NTU had performed well in its mission of producing engineers and other professionals for the burgeoning Singapore economy.

NTU needed to change from a good but rather traditional teaching institution focused on engineering to a first-class research-intensive university making major contributions to Singapore's economy. Guaning saw this as the major challenge and set about doing it with existing resources. But, one person, even as President, is inadequate to succeed in this. What he did was to begin moving in the right direction and at the same time seek external help to climb the mountain. From 2003 to 2006, under his "watch", NTU opened three new schools, expanded enrolment and transformed itself into a more comprehensive university. Guaning brought

Haresh in as Senior Academic Adviser in 2005. The two of them then recruited Bertil in 2006, thus creating the Troika, with its Chinese-Singaporean "orchestrator", a Viking Warrior leading NTU's leap into the future and an Indian-American "sage" providing contemplative guidance and ideological justifications.

The ascent was also the story of the developing friendship among three very different personalities with a common cause. Coming from diverse backgrounds and origins, serendipity brought the three people together in the right place at the right time for this chemistry to work. What we created is a great global institution at the crossroads of East and West. The confluence of imagination, enthusiasm and determination of the Troika has taken a relatively unknown institution to the high peaks of world academic excellence. The remarkable scale of the transformation and the speed with which this happened should be informative for all those interested in the advancement of their own universities.

The result of these changes is the NTU of today. It was research, its weakness in 2003, that was one of the key factors that led the way for NTU to join the leading group of world universities.

Fast forward to 31 December 2017, the last day of Bertil's term as third President of NTU, by which time NTU was among the world's top 15 universities according to the *2017* QS World University Rankings. This was a happy outcome beyond the expectations of the three prime movers behind this rapid ascent when they met and plotted the ascent in the first Troika meeting of February 2007. Among world universities, perhaps the only two comparable cases of such relatively quick ascents to the top tier are the École Polytechnique Fédérale de Lausanne (EPFL) in Switzerland and the Hong Kong University of Science and Technology (HKUST).

Today, NTU ranks, by whatever measure one takes, as one of the world's leading academic institutions challenging the long-established centres of learning, especially in Europe and North America, sitting at the forefront of learning in Asia. At the same time, NTU has become a sought-after and valued partner of a phalanx of global technology-based multinational corporations and a magnet for global talent.

Not only has the rise of NTU been remarkably rapid but it has also mirrored the rise of Singapore, that unique city-state in the global arena, as it moves towards a real knowledge-based economy. Singapore's global pre-eminence is also a story of determination and far-sightedness in order to succeed in an intensely competitive world. Now, many countries in the world, including G20 and G7 countries, try to repeat the Singaporean model.

In this book, we three Troika members reveal where we came from, our passions in life and the growth of our inter-relationship. We describe how we came together with these diverse backgrounds and experiences, complementing each other, and were then woven into the complex tapestry of the university.

A university is one of the most complex organisations to manage. By its very nature, it is difficult to change direction. There are multiple stakeholders such as faculty, staff, students, the public at large and the government in a publicly funded institution, and many others; there is the fine-tuned balance between academic freedom and political "control" deriving from the funding source. After all, he who pays the piper calls the tune. There are collegial decision-making structures, heterogeneous cultures of faculty and students and the balance between teaching/education and research/advancing learning and knowledge. All these factors had to be taken into account in NTU's reform and growth.

To properly reflect the circumstances under which this ascent to academic excellence took place, we felt it imperative to write this book. There was no single ingredient or recipe behind the Troika's campaign. We simply observed the need and seized the opportunities offered in Singapore with the socio-economic, political and academic winds that were upon us. We led the university community in a team effort to scale the mountain of academic excellence. We consider ourselves lucky in that, under a different set of circumstances, this accomplishment may not have been possible. Therefore, this transformation may be a feat that is not duplicable in another place and another time. We happened to be the right people in the right place at the right time.

Our expectation in writing this book is that the reader, especially political and academic leaders, will appreciate the mix of factors as well as our determination to nurture and guide NTU towards its current position as a leading global academic and research powerhouse.

These experiences and the surrounding circumstances are unique to NTU and not repeatable elsewhere. Instead of following in our footsteps, our hope is that others may find our account instructive in studying universities and their evolution. It may also be of interest for academic leaders who may wish to embark on a similar journey.

Stage I

Base Camp — Setting the Scene

Chapter 1

The Starting Point for Change

Singapore is renowned for the rapidity with which it implements decisions, once taken, and for results to quickly become visible, bearing in mind that this rapid response is set against a background of a well-considered and long-term policy. Singaporeans know where they want to get to and rapidly take steps to achieve their goals. The extent and speed of the change that we accomplished in NTU mirrors this national characteristic.

Certainly, much of what was achieved could not have taken place without the active support of the Board of Trustees and the government, through the Ministry of Education, in particular. The government has shown its commitment to making Singapore a real knowledge-based society by its investment in research and in higher education. This was led by Dr. Tony Tan, former Deputy Prime Minister and the originator and chair of the National Research Foundation (NRF) and, later, President of the Republic of Singapore (2011–2017). His role was critical in the research and innovation five-year plan of 2005 that created the NRF and substantially increased investment in research.

In 1991, when NTU was established with degree-granting powers, Singapore had a GERD[1] of 1% supported by a gross domestic product (GDP) much lower than today. The government established the National Science and Technology Board (NSTB) and committed to a five-year

---

[1] GERD: gross domestic product expenditure on research and development (R&D) as a percentage of national gross domestic product.

investment of S$2 billion. The scope included attracting industrial investment in research, co-funding of private sector research, establishing research institutes and promoting graduate education, research and entrepreneurship at universities, with a major part earmarked for the institutes. All this came together in what became known as the Agency for Science, Technology and Research (A*STAR) in 2002.

So, 1991 was an *annus mirabilis* with the establishment of two institutions that have become world-renowned knowledge-generating centres, and with the National University of Singapore (NUS), they are the biggest generators of intellectual property (IP) in Singapore.

Of course, it was not for another 14 years that NTU's rapid transition to its present position really started. The growth of investment in research by the Singapore government over the past 30 years — a remarkable level of constant and consistent commitment to such a far-sighted policy — is shown in Appendix 5.

The remarkable and rapid transformation of NTU started from what went before. NTU was one of Singapore's two universities, at that time, and was primarily a teaching institution centred on engineering. The preeminent academic institution was NUS, which was a traditional comprehensive university, founded in 1905 as the Straits Settlements and Federated Malay States Government Medical School, evolving later into an institution of higher education on the British model. From 1980 onwards, NUS combined teaching and research and rose in world rankings over the period under discussion as it became a research-intensive institution in the modern model. Thus, in comparison, NTU's focus was local rather than international, operating within the narrow confines of the subjects then being offered. This resulted in NTU being seen, within Singapore, as a "poor relation" to NUS and very much a second-choice institution. As Haresh's tale shows, the lack of a wider perspective in the attitudes that prevailed within NTU tended to reinforce this public perception. Research was a "minority taste" and international collaboration tended to be confined to student exchange schemes. In addition, a rather narrow, inward-looking mindset prevailed until 2006 when the Singaporean universities became autonomous institutions. Even then, overseas telephone calls were frowned upon and the administrative departments saw themselves in an administrative controlling role rather than support and facilitating. "Bean counters" tended to prevail, even to the extent of recording the strips of staples being used!

Therefore, this was the challenge — turn NTU into a forward-looking, world-leading, research-intensive academic institution as quickly as possible. From the outset, Guaning, when he became NTU's second president in 2003, recognised the scale of the required change. Taking advantage of his stint as Defence Science and Technology Agency (DSTA) Fellow at Stanford University, he looked into Silicon Valley and Stanford as models. In his and Haresh's tale, they refer to their first real contact at Stanford. Guaning set out his vision in his inaugural speech as President in 2003 when he said that he wanted staff and students to be at a university of "international renown ... and with universal acclaim". He also said that "the twin pillars of any university are teaching and research". This represented the "changing of the guard" from the establishment of NTU as a well-respected teaching institution into something else — the ambition to become a top-class university renowned for both education *and* research.

The initial years of Guaning's presidency were very much taken up with the expansion of the university-going cohort by building three new schools and increasing undergraduate population by 6,300, as well as preparing for autonomous university status. At that time, both universities, as well as the polytechnics, were statutory boards of the Ministry of Education (MOE), with their own governing councils. However, the prevailing mindset was to take instructions from the Ministry. By 2005, the Ministry was increasingly taking a view that, to enable the universities to advance, they needed to be granted autonomy so that their fate and direction of travel was in their own hands. This would then give a strong impetus for senior management to take new initiatives. Of course, with autonomy came a new governance structure and a new Board of Trustees was created, ably led by Koh Boon Hwee (he had been the Chairman of the earlier NTU University Council). He shared the same vision as the new leadership and he has continued to oversee and support the remarkable journey on which NTU embarked. This was also the opportunity for Guaning to bring Haresh fully on board. In 2006, Haresh became a member of the new Board, but, more importantly, in 2005 he became Guaning's Senior Academic Adviser and led the design of process of change and academic restructuring, modelled on American best practice led by the creator of Silicon Valley, Stanford University.

At that time, the university was, very much, based on disciplinary "silos" with very little interaction between schools, all of which were led by Deans. These had multiplied since the original NTU with its founding disciplines of engineering, business, communications (media) and education. It also meant that the President had a large number of people reporting directly to him with no lateral structure or links. This was the starting point. Therefore, the first task was that of academic restructuring, turning NTU into a modern multi-disciplinary college-based system with the introduction of an academic senate. Using the American model, the principal need was to have a provost to guide and develop the academic affairs of the university. Working through Acting Provost Er Meng Hwa and commuting between San Francisco and Singapore every two weeks, Haresh became, de facto, the Provost in all but name, and together with Guaning, set about this major restructuring. Therefore, when Bertil came on board in 2007, as the first Provost, the time was right for a remarkable advance. The academic structure had been changed to a typical "North American" academic structure; there was an autonomous and supportive Board, and the government had just approved a new five-year plan for research and innovation with a huge new investment of public funds into the universities. The overall scene had been set and the environment was there. What were now needed were academic leadership and vision, and a change agent (Bertil) to take NTU to the highest academic level. The self-assembly brought together three people — the "Troika" — with the same aim, but from very different cultures and backgrounds, and it is this combination of different but synergistic mindsets that was the crucially important catalyst for what was to occur. All three were committed to the mantra that "change means change".

What follows is a detailed account of how this was achieved in terms of the reform of education and research, the application of international best practice, how outside factors impinged on NTU and how NTU became a more comprehensive university of a special kind with an unusual blend and combination of disciplines. In fact, the success of NTU and its remarkable rise in the following decade has to be measured in comparison to when NTU started out. And it is a truly amazing story.

Chapter 2

From Third World to First — Singapore's Higher Education and Research

The research institutes and public universities in Singapore are an integral product of policy decisions made by the government. Therefore, it is important to understand the Troika's exploits in the historical context of Singapore's development as described in the book *From Third World to First: The Singapore Story: 1965–2000*. The book is Volume Two of the memoirs of Lee Kuan Yew, the founding Prime Minister of Singapore. This book helps one to understand Singapore's history since 1965 and provides the historical and political context in which the Troika operated. It also documents the remarkable change that has affected the city-state which started out, at independence, with a gross domestic product (GDP) of US$500 per capita, to join the first world with, today, US$64,500 per capita.

Singapore was originally known as Temasek ("sea-town") in the annals of the Malays, who were early inhabitants of the Malayan Archipelago. Singapore (Singapura, "Lion City") was granted to the British by the Sultan of Johor and was established as a trading port by Sir Stamford Raffles, of the British East India Company, in 1819. The Chinese population grew rapidly as those from southern China saw it as a place of opportunity. Singapore was a British colony and the headquarters of the Straits Settlements comprising Penang and Malacca/Melaka (both in Malaysia today) besides Singapore. Eventually, all three merged with the Malay States to form the Malaysian Federation in 1963, based on an idea of Sir Cecil Clementi, the former Governor of Singapore. Two years later, when relations between the Malaysian leader Tunku Abdul Rahman and Lee Kuan Yew had deteriorated to a point of no return, the city state was asked to leave the Federation to become the independent Republic of Singapore.

Thus, Singapore came into being in 1965 because of the irreconcilable differences between the Malay-dominated Malaysian Federation and the economically dominant Singapore with an ethnic Chinese majority.

In the past, the city-states of Italy, for example, always controlled an adjoining region to supply all their needs. Unlike them, the modern state of Singapore is unique and an anomaly in being a successful modern, advanced economy city-state without a geographical hinterland, which reflects the rather unusual and unique circumstances of its becoming an independent state. People do not realise that at independence in 1965, Singapore was just another third world city with its share of squalor and slums, and, at that time, poorer than Manila or Colombo.

On becoming a separate independent state, three observations stood out as Singapore contemplated the way ahead. This was the post-World War II period when many colonies were agitating for independence, not the least Singapore and Malaya. The communist threat, as perceived by the West, meant that Singapore could not realistically stand on the side of the People's Republic of China if it wanted to develop its economy. The suspicion of the Chinese minorities in Southeast Asian countries (especially in Indonesia), typically economically dominant, implied that Singapore could not rely on the region to be its hinterland and that it had to take great care not to become seen as an extension of China in the eyes of its neighbours. Finally, the way the ruling People's Action Party (PAP) had come to power in Singapore, with the first general election and self-government in 1959, tapped precisely the left-wing Chinese radical movement among the workers and students. Reliance on this base for growth would immediately raise problems with the UK and with neighbouring countries alike, generating the spectre and associated problems of an international perception of Singapore as a leftist radical Chinese base in Southeast Asia. Lee Kuan Yew faced a terrible dilemma: how could he sustain his political base while avoiding this likely path to ruin?

If the founding generation, led by Lee Kuan Yew, saw a clear solution ahead in tackling these apparently intractable problems, they did not write it down. As expected, when the PAP government faced up to its initial challenges and adopted a pragmatic economic policy, it led to a falling out within the PAP between the left-wing led by Lim Chin Siong and the right-wing led by Lee Kuan Yew. The left split off in 1961 to form a new political party named *Barisan Socialis*, Malay for Socialist Front. The defection of many PAP assemblymen to *Barisan* nearly brought down the PAP government through a no-confidence motion. At that time, students and graduates from the Chinese-based Nanyang University (*Nantah*), NTU's precursor with left-leaning ideas, stood on the *Barisan* side against the government. This did not exactly endear them or their university to the PAP government. The history of Nantah is dealt with in detail in the following chapter.

Britain, the colonial power responsible for security; the Federation of Malaya, the prospective merger partner with a vested interest in the security of Singapore; and the PAP government took action in "Operation Cold Store" in 1962 against an alleged communist conspiracy to destabilise Singapore and Malaya. It dealt a fatal blow to *Barisan*, removing their most charismatic leaders from political contention. In 1968, *Barisan* essentially performed the ultimate act of self-destruction by walking out of Parliament in favour of armed struggle, thus ceasing to be a political force. To this day, there are conspiracy theories that the PAP had engineered this by infiltrating *Barisan*. Whatever the real story, this act cleared the deck for the PAP to single-mindedly pursue its new economic direction, courting multinational corporations (MNCs) to set up low-cost manufacturing in Singapore to export to the world. This was an unconventional innovation at a time when conventional theories of development called for protected markets and import substitution. Since then, this model has been adopted by many others, most notably by Deng Xiaoping during China's reform and opening-up from 1978 onward (actually, this followed his visit to Singapore in that same year). This policy positioned Singapore to become the key production partner of MNCs, then in a post-war ascendancy, pursuing world markets. Singapore had found its new hinterland — the entire world.

While all this was happening on the economic front in the late 1960s and 1970s, the PAP government relentlessly transformed the education system to meet the nation's economic needs. The education system had been divided into two main streams, Chinese and English, equal but separate. During this time and over a period of 10 years or so, it became a system dominated by English, but with the twist that mother tongue study was made compulsory. Lee Kuan Yew rated this decision as the most difficult he had to make, no doubt because of the political backlash. He had to do this, even against the advice of his closest allies, if he was to be successful in taking Singapore forward as part of the international economic system. Inevitably, this decision led to the decline and demise of Nanyang University (see the chapter on the early history of the university), then at the apex of Chinese-based education. In 1980, Nanyang University was merged with the University of Singapore to form the English language-based NUS.

At the same time, the government was not standing still. Enhancements to the Singapore higher education system continued to be studied and introduced at a rapid rate throughout the 1970s, 1980s and early 1990s. In the bibliography, there is a list of studies and reports commissioned or written by MOE, starting in 1998, to develop a university sector to support the overall economic strategy. From this list, it was quite clear that a transformation to a world-class university ecosystem was being sought, at least since 1997, with the formation of an International Academic Advisory Panel (IAAP) and with the ambitious terms of reference, "to advise the Singapore government on how NUS and [Nanyang Technological University (NTU)] can be developed into world-class centres of excellence in research and scholarship."

A quick glance at this list of studies conducted to guide the future development of Singapore's state-funded universities will convince readers that the sustainable development of these universities towards a world-class stature was an objective actively pursued by the Singapore government. With the help of external experts, the solution converged in two milestone events that MOE, NUS and NTU as well as the Prime Minister's Office (PMO) spent much of 2005 preparing to implement from 2006 onward. These were the autonomous university governance framework and the complementary establishment of the NRF.

First of all, the NRF is based on a unique funding model in that its budget is drawn from investment returns of government reserves and is not subject to the vagaries of the normal national budget. Second, it provides an integrated and balanced portfolio of basic and applied research, university and institute research, company research and development (R&D) and manpower development that can be put together in a holistic manner. In addition, it relies on scientific and technical advice from an advisory board consisting of some of the most authoritative personalities in research from outside Singapore providing insightful comments and advising on the award of grants.

To bring the story up to date, the government, now under the leadership of Lee Kuan Yew's son, Lee Hsien Loong, has set Singapore on course as one of the world's leading knowledge-based and balanced economies. Starting in 2006, just as NTU embarked on its upward trajectory, and with Guaning at the helm, the government dramatically increased its funding for research, particularly focusing on the universities. With continuing increased investment in research with each new five-year plan, this has seen Singapore take its place in the front rank of "research" countries and is seen now as one of the go-to places for young researchers alongside the rest of the developed world in Europe, North America and Australia. It now has a gross domestic expenditure on research and development (GERD) of around 2.5% — the benchmark for an advanced nation. Now, Singapore may be counted as one of the so-called "small and smart" group of nations, namely the Nordic nations, Switzerland and Israel.

We have seen the path Singapore took to escape from the harsh realities of a desperate economic situation at independence. In parallel with economic development, the PAP government developed the education sector in synchronicity with the economy. Since the strategy was to develop and increase the "value-add" in Singapore ever since the wake-up call of the 1985/1986 recession, the attention of the Economic Development Board (EDB) was very much on having the educational outcomes at the right level for the companies being wooed to come to Singapore. This also meant that education was not just the portfolio of MOE but had to be seen as a key competitive advantage of Singapore and the concern of all ministries. It has often been said that the Minister for Education "behind the veil" was really the Prime Minister, Lee Kuan Yew. The focal point of education development over the years spanned the entire spectrum from secondary school to polytechnics to practice-orientated engineers all the way to the top tier of academic research and a truly international cast of the best researchers in the world.

The progression of Singapore from being in the "Third World" at independence to its leading position in the "First World" is covered in the second volume of Lee Kuan Yew's memoirs. Clearly, to enter the First World, higher education, science and technology, and research and development play crucial roles. We begin with higher education in colonial Singapore, move on to key political developments impacting the economy, restructuring of education, science and technology plans and end with developments in NTU. The reader would be well advised to refer to this timeline as he reads our book to clarify the sequence of events as well as cause and effect.

Chapter 3

Nanyang Technological University — Its Early History and Evolution

The previous chapter set out the route taken by Singapore from Third World to First. This chapter provides, in more detail, the history of Nanyang Technological University (NTU) and its predecessor on the same site, the Nanyang University (known as *Nantah*). The story of NTU's rapid rise to excellence has to start somewhere and, in NTU's case, the distant roots of the story begin even before Singapore became an independent country in 1965.

Nanyang University — *"Nantah"*

Nan (南, meaning south) and Yang (洋, meaning ocean) are two Chinese characters often joined together as 南洋 meaning the Southern Ocean (known internationally as the South China Sea). Nanyang is a very common name in Singapore for two reasons. One, Singapore is majority ethnic Chinese who brought their language, culture and traditions with them. Two, Singapore, indeed the whole of Southeast Asia, lies on the shores of the "Southern Ocean" and was explored and known by Chinese seafarers and fishermen. As more and more Chinese migrants settled in these regions, schools, clan associations and other Chinese organisations took on this name and it became a synonym for the Chinese Southeast Asian diaspora.

The British had established the Straits Settlements and Federated Malay States Government Medical School in 1905, renamed King

Edward VII College of Medicine in 1912. Raffles College, a higher education institution teaching arts and sciences, was established in 1928. In 1949, these institutions were merged to become the University of Malaya, renamed University of Singapore in 1962, and finally merged with Nanyang University to become the National University of Singapore in 1980. As Lee Kuan Yew said in his memoir, "It was our good fortune that, under the British, Singapore had been a regional centre for education...."

The Chinese community in Singapore, in its Chinese tradition, saw education as a priority and set up many schools teaching in Chinese, forming the dominant Chinese stream. Traditionally, they returned to China for university studies. In 1949, when the Chinese Communist Party won the civil war and declared the People's Republic of China, the route to China for a university education was cut as the British would not let a student back into Singapore and Malaya after graduating from a mainland China university. This was a crisis for the Chinese community. This obstacle had not only cut off the Chinese universities from the students but also cut off the flow of Chinese-speaking teachers to Nanyang.

One prominent philanthropist with a passion for education was Tan Kah Kee (陈嘉庚), a leader in the Fujian clan and a prominent rubber trader, who had founded many schools, including Hwa Chong Institution, formerly the Chinese High School in Singapore, and Xiamen University in China, and voiced the desire of the Chinese ("Nanyang") diaspora in Southeast Asia to have a centre of learning operating in their own language and meeting the needs of their children, while retaining and fostering their culture.

Gradually, the privately funded education system in Chinese grew into a mainstream educational opportunity, but the system lacked a university. In 1951, Tan Lark Sye (陈六使) kicked off the fund-raising by pledging a donation of five million Straits dollars, a vast fortune in those days. The pent-up desire of the Chinese to establish a university for their children, reinforced by a tradition of veneration for scholarship, created an eruption of donations region-wide. It resulted in the establishment of the Nanyang University (colloquially known as "*Nantah*" — combining a short form of Nanyang, and the Chinese word for university, daxue 大学). *Nantah* began classes on 15 March 1956 with the first intake graduating in 1960.

Encouraged by Tan Kah Kee, the Fujian Clan Association (Hokkien Huay Kuan 福建会馆 — the clan association of people whose ancestry defines them as ethnic Chinese from the Fujian province, of which he was Chairman) donated 523 acres (210 ha) in what was then a remote part of Singapore island, among the orchards and rubber plantations of Jurong, to become the university campus.

What was special was that the university (a private institution) was established by public demand and public contributions from the entire Chinese community across several countries in the Nanyang region, from the richest rubber tycoon to the poorest trishaw rider. Due to the cold war that put China and Britain, the colonial ruler, in opposing camps, the university faced adversity from day one, as it was not supported by the government of the day. In fact, it had to be registered as a company as it was not recognised by the colonial government. This triggered a spirit of steadfastness in the face of adversity, now known as the *"Nantah* Spirit", among Singapore's pioneer generation — a spirit and memory that remains strong to this day among the oldest alumni from this period. Nanyang University was built on a landscape of rolling hills, and the campus took on the original name of the plantation that stood on the land, Yunnan Garden (云南园). The Yunnan Garden campus remains the main campus of NTU today.

Commemorating this historic event, NTU renamed a road "Tan Lark Sye Walk" and the School of Humanities Building as the "Hokkien Huay Kuan Building" in 2019.

This sprawling site, with its imposing entrance arch, became the home of *Nantah*. Legacies of the original university still remain on the NTU campus. The most prominent is the iconic administration building, now the Chinese Heritage Centre, watching over a Chinese garden of beauty and meditation (recently enlarged and renewed into a spectacular green space with waterfalls and exotic plants). The replica of the entrance arch, to many the symbol of the *Nantah* spirit, stands at the foot of the garden and was unveiled by George Yeo, the then Minister for Information and the Arts. The original arch is still owned and maintained by NTU as a national monument, but now stands forlornly at Jurong Street 92 next to a cluster of houses and behind a modern sports complex, separated from the campus by the busy Pan-Island Expressway.

Nantah, as a Chinese-medium institution, struggled to survive in an increasingly English-dominated environment at a time of Singapore's rapid development and nation-building (the 1970s and 1980s) as a multi-ethnic and multicultural society, and its emergence to become a much-admired part of the economically advanced world. English was the dominant language of administration and international business, with the role of Chinese education rapidly shrinking. Enrolment was falling and its graduates were less well paid than those coming from the English-medium University of Singapore. *Nantah* also had difficulties hiring good faculty, with the consequent concern about the quality of its education. In 1979, Prime Minister Lee Kuan Yew commissioned a study by Lord Frederick Dainton, FRS, Vice-Chancellor of Nottingham University and Chair of the UK University Grants Committee, to look into the future of university education in Singapore. The Dainton Report stated that "the arguments for maintaining two universities … are extremely weak whilst those in favour of a single, strong university at Kent Ridge are compelling and I recommend accordingly". Thus, Dainton proposed to merge *Nantah* with the University of Singapore to become the National University of Singapore (NUS). So ended the 25 years of *Nantah*'s existence, a legend of self-reliance and celebrated in the Chinese community for the *Nantah* spirit.

The closure of *Nantah* was a very traumatic event for the Nanyang Chinese community in Singapore and Southeast Asia. To assuage this pain, Lee Kuan Yew promised to replace the old university with a new, different and better one within a decade, to site it on the old *Nantah* campus and to continue to include "Nanyang" in its title. Thus was born Nanyang Technological Institute, an engineering school that, later, formed the core of modern NTU. We believe the founders would have been proud to have NTU today, a top global university, as successor to *Nantah* as Lee Kuan Yew had promised.

Most *Nantah* alumni saw this as a tragic outcome and destruction of the *alma mater* that they held dear. Subsequent events demonstrated considerable misgivings and concerns at the political costs on the part of the government. There were numerous attempts to mitigate the negative impact of the demise of *Nantah*. In 1995, the 40th anniversary celebrations of *Nantah's* creation were held on the NTU campus. The *Nantah* alumni rolls were transferred to NTU. The establishment of the Centre for Chinese Language and Culture at NTU and the establishment of the Chinese Heritage Centre were announced, the latter located in the former administration building of *Nantah* and supported by an endowment funded by prominent Nanyang Chinese. All this action somewhat helped to pacify the Singapore-based *Nantah* alumni, but failed to satisfy the more vocal alumni further afield in such places as Malaysia and Canada. The global *Nantah* alumni continued to organise reunions at which sentiments against the Singapore government were sometimes expressed.

Although traumatic, this *Nantah* chapter was perhaps an inevitable part and necessary sacrifice of Singapore's nation-building, given the need for a neutral common language for the multiracial society in Singapore as well as the economic strategy that was adopted for survival. The entrepreneurial spirit of the *Nantah* graduates, necessitated by the adverse circumstances they faced, was part of the vaunted *Nantah* spirit that Guaning, as the newly inaugurated NTU President, had hoped to tap onto in developing NTU's entrepreneurial ecosystem to contribute to the national economy.

Nanyang Technological Institute

Singapore had prospered in the 1970s and 1980s on an economic model as the production base for multinational companies. A severe recession in 1985 rammed home the point that Singapore had to increase its "value-add" to its economic production. To do so required an army of engineers. Even before the recession, the government realised the need to produce a substantial cadre of trained and skilled engineers to drive the country's industrialisation and economic progress. In 1981, the government decided to establish an undergraduate engineering school on the old *Nantah* campus to produce the large numbers of practice-orientated engineers needed. This was the Nanyang Technological Institute (NTI), teaching practice-orientated engineering and giving degrees from NUS, which was the body responsible for ensuring NTI had reached the required academic standards. Thus, NTI became the direct precursor of NTU. Professor Cham Tao Soon (Dean of Engineering at NUS) was appointed to lead this development. His memoir about the establishment of NTI and its evolution to become NTU was published in 2014.

A modern campus and buildings were needed, and, in 1981, the Singapore government engaged a renowned Japanese architect, Kenzō Tange, to create a modern campus on the challenging hills and valleys of the old *Nantah* site in Jurong. Tange's concept, consisting of two white concrete spines with spurs to each side, remains the academic core of modern NTU.

A decade later, by 1991, NTI had grown to a student body of more than 6,000, consisting of engineering (with a core set of engineering disciplines — civil and structural, electrical and electronic, and mechanical and production engineering), a school of accountancy (later to become the Nanyang Business School), and a school of communication and information (and media) (now the Wee Kim Wee School of Communication and Information named after a former President of Singapore). It had become a substantial educational hub on the island and was recognised as an excellent engineering teaching institution. In fact, in 1985, only four years after opening its doors, the Commonwealth Engineering Council recognised NTI as one of the best engineering teaching institutions in the world.

Then, in 1989, Lord Dainton was again asked to lead a further comprehensive inquiry into higher education in Singapore, and his later vision was to create two large and competing universities, offering a wide choice to Singaporean citizens wanting higher education. In his report, he said, "By 2000, Singapore should aim to have two strong university-level institutions, one at Kent Ridge and the other at Jurong, with many subjects being offered at both campuses. This would introduce a healthy element of friendly competition for students, for current and capital resources and for research grants ... and links to industry and commerce." At the same time, Dainton, committed to the Humboldtian concept of the intimate link between research and education, had insisted that both universities had to have substantial research activity and had commented on the low level of research at NTI. The Singapore government accepted his recommendations, although, initially, the promotion of research at NTU was neglected.

Nanyang Technological University

In 1950, during Britain's colonial rule, a Teachers' Training College (TTC) was established to provide trained teachers for Singapore's school system in addition to the provision being made by the School of Education at the University of Malaya (the forerunner of the University of Singapore). This dual provision continued until 1973 when the TTC and the University of Singapore established the Institute of Education (IE). In 1984, a College of Physical Education (CPE) was formed by IE to train specialist teachers in physical education. In 1991, IE and CPE were merged to form the National Institute of Education (NIE) and in the same year, the government decided to link the new NIE to NTI to form NTU. Thus, NTU was established as a degree-awarding institution in 1991, at which point the formal history of NTU begins, 26 years after Singaporean independence. This made NTU one of the world's youngest universities. The only overt link with the old *Nantah* was that it occupied the same campus and retained the name "Nanyang". Other than that, this was a completely new and different institution. Emotionally, however, it depended very much on how NTU would treat the *Nantah* alumni, either embracing them with open arms or looking at them with the suspicion of being communist sympathizers. Of course, it did the former and now the alumni rolls of *Nantah* graduates are with NTU.

NTU — The Early Days

On 1 July 1991, NTU was formed and NTU's history began with the inauguration of the new university by the then Prime Minister Goh Chok Tong. The first President of NTU was Professor Cham Tao Soon, the President of NTI and a key figure in the establishment and growth of NTI that had culminated in the institution gaining full university status with degree-awarding powers.

As was the case for the following 14 years, NTU, like its sister NUS, was administered as a statutory board (a government agency governed by a law or statute passed by Parliament) under MOE. It was governed by the MOE-appointed University Council and remained operationally very much under the wing of the Ministry. The MOE appointed the Chairman and Council members who were responsible to the MOE for governance of the university in accordance with the policy and budget directions of the Ministry. Under the circumstances, it was inevitable that such a body would be generally risk averse. Guaning became a member of the NTU

Council in 1996. His recollection is that while there was good discussion at Council meetings, decisions tended to be taken directly between the NTU President and MOE. While global in outlook, the two main universities continued to focus on their role in producing graduates for the Singapore economy and tended not to venture into areas not directed by the Ministry. In particular, they did not take up global academic challenges in leading-edge research.

However, the ever-innovating minister in charge of the universities, Dr. Tony Tan Keng Yam, then Deputy Prime Minister, had another innovation planned to stir up competition. That was the "new kid on the block", Singapore Management University (SMU), established in 2000 under an entirely different governance framework. This framework had SMU set up as a company limited by guarantee, in other words a private company that is non-profit, with a board appointed by the Ministry and chaired by Ho Kwon Ping (何光平), a hospitality industry entrepreneur. SMU also had a link to the University of Pennsylvania Wharton School of Business in the form of a cooperation agreement. The first president of SMU was in fact the Deputy Dean of the Wharton School, Professor Janice Bellace. This new model of university governance proved successful in the "small" experiment of SMU and subsequently applied to great effect in the two flagship universities, NUS and NTU.

Two of the authors (Guaning and Haresh) started their association with the fledgling NTU in the 1990s. Later, as Rector of Linköping University in Sweden, Bertil visited NTU in 2002 to explore the possibility of developing a Swedish–Singaporean student exchange. So, each of the three Troika members had close encounters with NTU before they became formally involved with the university.

Many of the details of the discussions leading up to the creation of the university and its development during the following decade (the 1990s) into a mainstream primarily teaching institution are set out in *The Making of NTU: My Story* by the first President, Professor Cham Tao Soon. He was responsible for the creation of the campus with its excellent infrastructure on which we have been able to build and progress. In Guaning's view, the most valuable legacy left by Tao Soon was the strong financial position of the university, upon which the Troika was able to build on.

As an institution, NTU then began to develop into a broader-based university, especially during the first five years of this century.

Originally, NTU had started out with three "traditional" engineering disciplines — civil and structural, electrical and electronic (EEE), and mechanical and production engineering. As engineering continued to expand and develop, these schools evolved with civil and structural engineering becoming civil and environmental engineering (CEE) and mechanical and production engineering expanding to become mechanical and aerospace engineering (MAE), reflecting both disciplinary evolution and a changing demand for graduates with different backgrounds. NTU was the only university in Singapore boasting of an aerospace programme which especially attracted male students.

At its start in 1981, NTI had 582 students that increased to 6,832 some 10 years later when NTU was formed. Graduate students did not make their appearance at NTI until 1986 when the first PhD and Master programmes were started. A new School of Applied Science was created in 1988 with materials engineering and computer engineering branches. For quite a while, they were considered poor cousins of the "proper" engineering schools, partly because of weak leadership. After some years of growth, both became engineering schools in their own right in the year 2000.

NTU — A Fresh Start

Guaning was appointed NTU President on 1 January 2003. One of the first meetings he attended was the Fourth International Academic Advisory Panel (IAAP) meeting, at which a paper from the Ministry proposed to increase the government-subsidised university places from 20% to 25% of the birth cohort. This was to be achieved largely by a major expansion of NTU by 6,300 undergraduate students, with the creation of three new schools: the School of Physical Sciences, the School of Humanities and Social Sciences, and the School of Art, Design and Media (ADM). These plans were laid out in the IAAP recommendations adopted by the Ministry. The then second Minister for Education, Ng Eng Hen, accepted the IAAP recommendations, including this expansion plan. Guaning saw this as an opportunity to build a more comprehensive university and focused on this task in the period 2003–2005.

The School of Humanities and Social Sciences (SHSS) was established in 2004, to be followed, in 2005, by the new School of Physical and Mathematical Sciences (SPMS), and the School of Art, Design and Media (ADM). During this time, the College of Engineering had developed into new areas, establishing a new School of Chemical and Biomedical Engineering (SCBE), also in 2005.

Around the turn of the millennium, with an increasing need to train doctors, Singapore started to plan the expansion of its medical training. There was discussion about how to meet this rising demand, and NTU proposed that it should host a new medical school. Following an international review, this was rejected as it was considered that the university did not have the scientific base on which such a medical school could be founded. In the aftermath of the review, it was recommended that NTU should start to develop such a background expertise with the establishment of a School of Biological Sciences (SBS) with a strong emphasis on biomedical studies (2002).

The following timeline chronicles the development and growth of NTU:

1991   NTU established, merging NTI and NIE

   NTU schools: Civil and Structural Engineering (CSE later CEE — Civil and Environmental Engineering), Electrical and Electronic Engineering (EEE), Mechanical and Aerospace Engineering (MAE), Applied Science (later becoming Computer Sciences and Engineering (SCSE), and Material Sciences and Engineering (MSE)), Accountancy and Business (later becoming the Nanyang Business School (NBS)), Communication Studies (becoming the Wee Kim Wee School of Communication and Information (WKWSCI)) and NIE

1995   Institute of Defence and Strategic Studies (IDSS), becoming the S. Rajaratnam School of International Studies (RSIS) in 2007
2002   School of Biological Sciences (SBS)
2004   School of Humanities and Social Sciences (SHSS)
2005   School of Physical and Mathematical Sciences (SPMS)
2006   School of Art, Design and Media (ADM)
2013   Lee Kong Chian School of Medicine

2015   Asian School of Environment (ASE)
2017   SHSS splits into School of Humanities (SH) and School of Social Sciences (SSS)

When Guaning became the President of NTU, his overwhelming initial impression was how top-down the university was. This deference for authority was not healthy for a university, especially with Guaning's new ambitions for the institution.

Despite the success story of the early days in establishing NTU as a degree-awarding university, and its earlier reputation as a good engineering teaching establishment, the perception of NTU among Singaporeans (especially parents) was that it was definitely the second best choice if one failed to gain admission to NUS. Now, with both universities equally highly ranked, students and their parents look deeper into the strengths of each institution and their chosen discipline before selecting one or the other university. However, there is still an element of "snobbery" in Singaporean society, so many parents prefer (if they can afford it and especially the elite) to send their children to prestigious universities in the US (e.g. Harvard, Massachusetts Institute of Technology (MIT), and Stanford), the UK (Oxford, Cambridge and Imperial College London) and elsewhere before "going local".

With its concentration on teaching, NTU lacked a research tradition with faculty being somewhat discouraged from pursuing their research interests (unlike at NUS). By the turn of the millennium, NTU was falling behind as its educational programmes had not kept pace with modern developments and its administration reflected its top-down earlier beginnings. In fact, until well into the next decade, administration saw itself as "controlling" rather than supporting and facilitating. It also lacked the formal academic structures for faculty participation such as a Senate and Academic Council. These failings only served to accentuate this perception of NTU among faculty members as not keeping up with the times. It also lacked a modern international outlook, as Haresh describes in his tale, illustrated through the recounting of his experiences in the mid to late 1990s. Particularly telling were his remarks about the lack of understanding of entrepreneurship among the faculty, despite the efforts of Cham Tao Soon and his senior colleagues to create technopreneurship courses and install a good infrastructure.

Another challenge arose with the founding, in 2000, of SMU. It was first conceived three years earlier to be different from both NUS and NTU, and modelled on American best practice (the Wharton Business School, University of Pennsylvania). As Dr. Tony Tan said, "From its conception, SMU was designed to provide a different model of university education here in Singapore. We wanted to start with a clean slate instead of just adding another public university in the mould of the existing ones. From this starting point emerged a confluence of factors that make SMU special." Rapidly, SMU developed a trendy image ("cool") for its students, in contrast to which NTU appeared dull and staid. As is described in later chapters, during the Troika period, NTU had overcome this image to become the exciting and stimulating institution that it is today.

Guaning, as the incoming second President of NTU in 2003, recognised the scale of this challenge. Competition had arrived and it was crucial to establish a forward-looking and exciting image, as envisaged in his inaugural address in March 2003. Because the top-down culture and civil-service-like mentality was so entrenched with two decades of practice, any change had to be engineered in a manner encompassing the whole university, which required simultaneous action on multiple fronts to be taken to engage the faculty. But universities are complex and unwieldy organisations, so changing direction has to overcome considerable inertia. The faculty had become used to being directed "from above", and those who are keen to change often had ulterior motives related to power grabs and jockeying for position.

Being parachuted in from outside, Guaning needed time to assemble an executive team ready to push for change. Even though he put together a team based on existing leadership motivated for change, those with motivation for change often did not have the skill set to support the action being taken. So, Guaning focused on the three new schools where there was at least no existing baggage, on infrastructure development where there was significant budget and reserves and urgent action on reforming the curriculum to make NTU programmes more attractive for students. Guaning was not only faced with instituting change but also in dealing with a new opportunity for all three universities with the coming of autonomy in 2006 as well as dealing with the outcome of the Quality Assurance Framework for Universities (QAFU) exercise in 2005.

Things came to a head in 2003 when Guaning set out a series of fundamental changes that would be necessary to take NTU to its next stage of development.

The government had directed a review of university governance in 2005 and the report had recommended setting up NUS and NTU as companies limited by guarantee, similar to the model established for SMU since the year 2000. So, Guaning was not only faced with instituting far-reaching changes within NTU but also with having to prepare and deal with a new challenge and opportunity with the coming of autonomy in 2006.

University Autonomy

As mentioned earlier, NUS and NTU were structured as statutory boards, a form of government agency, administered by MOE, through its governing Council. But, rather like French and German universities, with staff being seen as government employees, this structure tends to inhibit change and innovation. The one advantage with this system was that directions, once set, can be realised rather expeditiously. Both Lim Pin, who headed NUS for 19 years, and Cham Tao Soon, who had led NTI and NTU for an impressive 22 years, were trusted people who could be relied upon to deliver what the government wanted.

As Singapore's economy matured, the requirement of teaching-only universities faded, while the importance of creativity and innovation grew. The first step undertaken by Dr. Tony Tan was to bring in MIT (as a best-practice engineering university) to advise him. An MIT faculty team was engaged to review NUS and NTU engineering in 1997. They found NUS having the lion's share of top students from Singapore schools and increasing its emphasis on research. In the case of NTU, it was seen as an excellent teaching university with lower student quality. "We see their educational program as being rather narrowly technologically focused and their management being strongly top-down directed." This was also Guaning's observation upon taking over as President.

The ocean tanker analogy applied very much to the implementation of the MIT recommendations. They were still in progress when Guaning came to NTU. However recommendation no. 11, "establishing an elite world class endeavour involving NUS and NTU with close collaboration with an existing world leading technological institution" was implemented in the form of the Singapore–MIT Alliance (SMA), a post-graduate degree and research collaboration programme funded by Singapore. For NUS and NTU, the most important outcome of SMA was the confidence generated that Singapore's best could match some of the best in the world, encouraging our ambition in recruitment.

As an interesting aside, NTU's fourth President is Subra Suresh, who was one of the MIT review team members who had served, *inter alia,* as MIT Dean of Engineering; Director, National Science Foundation; and President, Carnegie-Mellon University. NTU has progressed so much that he, as a highly distinguished academic leader, had no hesitation accepting the appointment. If someone had suggested in 1997 that one of the MIT team members would become the President of NTU, there would have been plenty of sniggering in private. If someone else had predicted that NTU would catch up with NUS as a research-intensive university and run ahead of NUS in at least one world ranking, he would have been laughed out of court.

Then, in 2004, Dr. Tony Tan and the then Minister for Education Tharman Shanmugaratnam (who later became Deputy Prime Minister and then Senior Minister) set up the Steering Committee to Review University Autonomy, Governance and Funding (UAGF Committee) chaired by Lim Chuan Poh, the then MOE Permanent Secretary. The committee included the presidents of the three universities NUS, NTU and SMU, as well as senior officials of the Ministry of Finance, MOE and a director of a national research institute. The committee organised a visit to the US to look into the finer details of the experience of three universities: MIT, completely private; University of Virginia, public in name but with only 8% of revenue from the state budget; and University of Michigan, one of the best public universities in the world.

Essentially, the conclusion was that while the top private universities in the US are the world's leading institutions, it would be impossible to create such an institution in Singapore with public funds. Singapore settled on a hybrid framework called "Autonomous University" to create a contractual relationship between the government and the university that provides the safety of continued public funding, retaining the national roles undertaken by publicly funded universities. A crucial feature was the transformation of the universities into "not-for-profit" companies. Guaning already had some experience with such a structure, having corporatised the defence science organisation as a not-for-profit company, the Defence Science Organisation (DSO) National Laboratories. The company framework provided considerable leeway for the management as long as fiduciary responsibilities were properly discharged. In contrast, as a government agency, the university would be subject to very detailed government regulations, especially in procurement that often hinders innovation and research.

In 2005, the committee presented its findings in a report entitled "Autonomous Universities, Towards Peaks of Excellence". The committee recommended applying the company limited by guarantee model of governance of SMU to NUS and NTU, with associated funding and contractual agreements as a new autonomous university governance framework. With the recognition by Singaporean political leaders, especially Dr. Tony Tan, that to compete with the best universities in the world and to pursue the ambition to be a leading knowledge-based economy, inhibitions to change needed to be removed. The Corporatisation Bills of NUS and NTU were then presented to Parliament. The universities worked closely with the Ministry on the necessary legislation that was enacted in March 2006. At the same time, the committee had recommended the creation of a Foundation for Research Excellence. This had been developed at the request of Dr. Tony Tan, who was reorganising the overall research organisation in Singapore after the completion of the first three five-year plans for research. This resulted in the creation of the NRF.

Thus, NUS and NTU officially became autonomous universities and Lim Chuan Poh (later Chairman of the Agency for Science, Technology and Research (A*STAR) and now leading Singapore's new Food Agency) led the implementation of this policy. NTU, under Guaning's leadership, welcomed this model as it was similar to the autonomy models he had established in 1997 for DSO. Only NUS had some reservations because of worries about possible budget cuts.

Anticipating the granting of autonomy, Guaning was lining up candidates for the new Board of Trustees. The Board included four new members, established by Guaning as a Board of Advisors that included two prominent alumni from the *Nantah* days, a well-known property developer and philanthropist, and Haresh Shah, whom Guaning had met on his sabbatical in the US and could provide input based on his experience as a leading faculty member at Stanford University (see Chapter 5).

With a new proactive Board of Trustees chaired by Koh Boon Hwee, who had previously served as NTU Council Chairman, Guaning began to make use of the opportunities this Autonomous University Framework presented. As the academic governance model was being set up, guided by the successful example of Stanford, an increasingly important order of business was to reform and renew the faculty, for which a highly qualified academic leader was being sought as Provost.

Without waiting for such a person to appear, Professor Er Meng Hwa, one of the research-active faculty, former Dean of Engineering, was appointed as Acting Provost, while an international search was started, with the search committee chaired by Haresh. As luck would have it, such a person literally fell into their "lap" when Bertil Andersson came to Singapore as a member of the Scientific Advisory Board of the newly created NRF (see Bertil's tale in Chapter 6). There was no time to lose as the three Troika members got together in February 2007 to plot the course for NTU — "the super-tanker". Their objectives were to drastically boost research, modernise teaching and internationalise the whole university. The objective was parity with NUS in reputation, resources and achievements, somewhat similar to the vision of the second Dainton Report.

NTU today is an institution ranked well within the top 15 universities in the QS World University Rankings and recognised as the top in Asia. Now, NTU and NUS both compete and collaborate in the way envisaged by Dainton in his second report. This is something of which students, parents, all its alumni (now close to a quarter of a million) — whether they date from *Nantah*, the NTI period, the first decade of NTU or from now — together with Singapore, as a whole, can be justifiably proud.

A Visit From the Minister Mentor Lee Kuan Yew

The Principal Private Secretary of the then Minister Mentor Lee Kuan Yew (who had stepped down as Prime Minister becoming, in turn, Senior

Minister and then Minister Mentor, with a seat in the Cabinet), Lee Seow Hiang (now Changi Airport Group Chief Executive Officer (CEO)), called Guaning one day in late 2006 and indicated that Lee Kuan Yew wanted to visit NTU. He had not visited for a number of years and specifically asked for a visit in the daytime. Guaning was happy to have the opportunity to present to him the progress that had been made in NTU, especially since the Autonomous University Framework was something that Lee Kuan Yew had strongly influenced. He had been very much a top-down authority who frowned upon universities deviating from straightforward discharge of their economic functions and undertaking activities that he considered irrelevant. Dr. Tony Tan's particular advantage was that he was trusted by Lee Kuan Yew. In our opinion, no one else could have convinced Lee Kuan Yew to give the universities autonomy, as they were often seen by him as troublemakers.

The timing of the visit was clearly so that he could see at firsthand what NTU intended to do with the new autonomous framework. Guaning took the opportunity to introduce Bertil who happened to be in Singapore. The visit went very well and university autonomy received the clear thumbs up from Minster Mentor as did this Swedish guy — Bertil!

Lee Kuan Yew was to repeat his visit to address students and staff in 2008.

Chapter 4

A Farewell to Arms — Guaning's Tale

My ancestors came from the Kingdom of Xu (徐国) in what is now Shandong province. Apparently, the Xu Kingdom was strong enough to worry the Zhou Dynasty at one time, but, over the centuries, it weakened until it was conquered by the Kingdom of Wu (吴国) and the descendants with the Xu surname scattered. Xuzhou (徐州) in present-day Jiangsu province was a major centre. My branch of the family subsequently moved south to Jiangxi province and then my ancestor joined the revolt and military campaigns that overthrew the Mongolian Yuan Dynasty to establish the Ming Dynasty. He eventually settled in Dehua county of Fujian province after retirement from officialdom in Quanzhou City. I am their 19th generation descendant. Examining the clan chronicles on the occasion of my father's 88th birthday, I saw some prominent scholars, officials and military officers among them. My story in Nanyang originated with a scholar who was my grandfather and a soldier, a local warlord who was nominally the county magistrate and commanded a regiment of troops. My career started with a scholarship followed by defence research, in a faint echo of my grandfather and his warlord kin.

The 1920s was a period of turmoil in China. The revolutionary government in Guangzhou had no control over numerous warlords throughout the country, each with their own armies holding suzerainty over local areas. My hometown Dehua county was no exception. A military officer in my clan, who became the local warlord, wanted my grandfather to join his army as one of the rare scholars in the county. To get away from this unwanted attention, my grandfather proposed to raise funds in the

Nanyang region for the local school. His first foray yielded good results, so he went on a second fund-raising trip, but did not return. Instead, he set up a private school in the state of Johor in present-day Malaysia.

This story was related to me by my father and uncles and may have become embellished in the mists of time. The story came full circle in 2006 when I received a request from the Xu clan in my hometown to do two pieces of calligraphy, as a prominent son of the clan. These calligraphic works were to adorn the halls in an ancestral temple to be rebuilt, called the Hall of the Red Stone (红石堂), which, in turn, was sited within a hillside fortress called Fortress Within the Cave (洞内寨). In 2009, when I visited the reconstructed fortress and ancestral temple on the hillside, I discovered, on the wall, an account of the career of the warlord in question. It turned out that in the many battles he fought, he was extremely lucky to escape harm. Legend has it that he was hit, once, by a bullet, but the bullet hit the ammunition case that he was carrying and so he escaped injury. There was also a legend that the Hall of the Red Stone was the temple protecting him; therefore, his enemies burned down the original version of the hall. This had the desired effect as he was subsequently killed in a munity by his own soldiers. This ancestral temple remained in its ruined state until the recent reconstruction that resulted in the request for my calligraphy.

It was fortuitous that my grandfather escaped the warlord by migration to the Nanyang region for, if he had been forced to join the army of the warlord, he may very well have been killed. I would not have been born and there would not have been a Troika!

My grandfather and grandmother raised a large family in Johor with seven sons and three daughters. At that time, education in Johor was poor, so the eldest son, my eldest uncle, went back to China to our hometown to study. My father, who was the third son, tagged along. He therefore had all his education in China, culminating in a degree in electrical engineering from Xiamen University and a job in Taiwan's electric company. My mother was a student at the same high school in Fuzhou and graduated in physics from the same university. After graduation in 1948, they got married in Taiwan. I was their firstborn in Taiwan in 1950. My brother was also born in Taiwan in 1951.

My parents brought the family back to Malaysia in 1953 when they were recruited as teachers for Chung Hwa High School, a Chinese school in the town of Muar, Johor. After three years, they became teachers at the Chinese High School (Hwa Chong Institution today) in Singapore and the family has been in Singapore since 1956. I first went to school in Johor and later in Singapore at Nanyang Primary School. After the Primary School Leaving Examination, I entered Catholic High School, a Chinese school known for being apolitical in an era when the leading Chinese-medium schools were mired in political movements. Catholic High was also known for its bilingual emphasis with English, Mathematics and Physics taught by Indian teachers using English textbooks. After sitting for my School Certificate (Chinese) Examinations, I transferred to the English stream.

I was first assigned to Tanjong Katong Technical Secondary School even though I applied to Raffles Institution. Mr. Koh Beng Thiam, who was the Head of Chemistry, interceded to the Principal on my behalf, and as I was the top student in the Chinese stream, he was kind enough to give me a place. I did not disappoint him, coming in first overall in the science stream as well as in all my mathematics and science subjects. In 1967, I was awarded the President's and Colombo Plan Scholarships to study electrical engineering in Canada.

The electrical engineering programme at the University of Alberta offered three options: engineering, business and research. I took the research option with a heavy emphasis on advanced mathematics and physics. Participating in professional activities through the Institute of Electrical and Electronic Engineers (IEEE), I was elected project chairman of the University of Alberta Student Chapter and led the team competing for the Vincent Bendix Award with our proposal to build a collision avoidance radar. All this naturally drove me to apply for graduate school.

I was admitted to the California Institute of Technology (Caltech) with a full fellowship and was fortunate to be allowed to defer returning to Singapore to pursue a Master's degree. It was natural at Caltech to want to go on to a doctorate. Being admitted to PhD candidacy with Professor Amnon Yariv as my advisor, I began to apply for permission from Singapore to continue towards a PhD. Professor Yariv helped me present the value to Singapore of advanced technology, such as integrated optics, which I intended to pursue, starting with building a laser in the summer of 1972. Had I continued upon this path, I might have got involved in Professor Yariv's subsequent optical start-up, a "unicorn" that was sold to Lucent Technologies for US$2 billion. Alas, that was not to be.

I doubt, at that time, that anyone in Singapore was aware of the importance of optical communications in the future development of telecommunications in order to appreciate integrated optics. Not surprisingly, I was not granted deferment. There was an option of paying up the bond, but coupled with my national service liability, this would have made my position in Singapore untenable, so I returned to Singapore in the fall of 1972.

While waiting for the conscription notice, I received a telephone call from my friend Chan Chee Hon, a fellow scholar from the University of British Columbia (UBC), asking if I would be interested in a research and development position in the Ministry of Defence (MINDEF). This inflexion point saw me joining the embryonic defence research team of MINDEF and determined the direction of my career for the next 30 years.

The Vietnam War had brought to the fore the value of electronic warfare in sustaining air superiority. I only learned years later that the secret project to develop electronic warfare capability that I had joined was code named Project Magpie and conceptualised by three of my friends, all of them engineering scholars in Canada.

A unit called Electronics Testing Centre was being set up under the Security and Intelligence Division. With only a "skeleton" staff, this was the humble beginning of Defence Science Organisation (DSO) National Laboratories, the defence research establishment of Singapore with thousands of engineers today, later to become DSO. I was to spend 25 years in DSO, beginning with work on electronic warfare. In my early years at DSO, I spent three months working on a system integration project in Israel. Although electronic countermeasure techniques were too sensitive for other countries to share with us, the experience gave me confidence in building major systems. Subsequently, I was in Switzerland for a course on cryptosystems. This helped me start developing capabilities in communications security. By the time DSO was formed in 1977, I was head of the Electronics Systems Department with primary responsibility for electronic warfare and communications.

We had the brightest scholars in the outfit, but despite our utmost efforts, we did not make much headway in building electronic systems. I soon realised shortcomings in our developmental approach. We were developing systems based on existing systems that others had implemented. No matter how well we did, we were simply good followers and always steps behind the state of the art. This was not what we set out to achieve in defence research. By 1980, I had become Deputy Head of DSO. Still determined to complete my doctorate, I had a second go at a doctorate at Stanford University in 1980.

At Stanford, I joined the research group of Thomas Kailath and Martin Morf in the Information Systems Laboratory. Martin Morf had received a grant entitled "Distributed Sensor Network" from the US Defense Advanced Research Projects Agency (DARPA) with the intention of tapping the Advanced Research Projects Agency Network (ARPANET) technology to achieve intelligent battlefield situation awareness. My thesis research developed a theoretical framework for wide-band emitter location. Related algorithms are still in use today.

In 1983, I returned to DSO to become Deputy Director (Electronic Systems) in DSO and Deputy Director (Radar and Command and Control Systems) in Defence Materiel Organisation (DMO), where I acquired valuable project management and defence systems acquisition experience. This culminated in my appointment as Director, DSO in December 1986.

By this time, I had accumulated considerable experience in research and development as well as in the issues involved in putting scientific achievements into application, something quite unique in Singapore. When the Vietnam War triggered Project Magpie in 1970, Singapore was in the low-cost labour stage of economic development with Singapore industry basically absent from research and development. The university did not require faculty to do research. There was the Singapore Institute for Standards and Industrial Research, but it was mainly concerned with standards and service to industry. DSO was in a unique situation of needing to create technology from scratch. This was made doubly hard by the prevailing security shroud that covered the "black art" of electronic warfare, later on to include guided weapons and command, control and communications and information systems that I was tasked to create. Over the years, my colleagues and I had developed the courage to take on open problems with no assurance of success, along with the inevitable failures. This attitude endowed us with courage to venture into the unknown, an attitude that was to serve me well in the NTU era, especially the development of the Troika and the ambitious journey that the three of us undertook.

My directorship of DSO was capped by one final act of organisational innovation — the reorganisation of DSO as a not-for-profit company in 1997, when it was renamed DSO National Laboratories, and I became the first Chief Executive Officer. Less than a year later, I was appointed to a bigger job, the Deputy Secretary (Technology) responsible for all acquisition and procurement, research and technology, construction and information technology functions in MINDEF. I also began to work on a bigger reorganisation — the integration of six technology-related organisations into a seamless whole as an autonomous government agency established under a law passed by Parliament, in other words, a statutory board. This was a common organisational structure among specialised government agencies. The challenge lay in integration and in gaining the confidence of the armed forces.

The resulting Defence Science and Technology Agency (DSTA) was inaugurated in April 2000, with me as its founding Chief Executive. Although DSTA was not incorporated as a company, one key feature that I fought for was the status of a self-financing statutory board that has most of the flexibility of a company except that the employees remain government officers. This status as a government agency was essential in undertaking the considerable procurement activities of the agency. In fact, our performance was critical to MINDEF as we were spending most of the capital budget on behalf of the armed forces. The most important agenda in this merger was to consolidate the trust of the Singapore Armed Forces that DSTA would always look after their interests. This required not only a dedicated top leadership but also the tight integration of the six civilian organisations and the assumption of the professional leadership of the maintenance and logistics departments of the army, navy and air force.

In the early years of my presidency at NTU, I attempted to use some of the methods that I had developed in DSTA. Unfortunately, I found academics too smart to be as idealistic as my colleagues in DSTA. The nature of their work makes their prime motivation their own careers. I had to take a different approach.

Innovation was a crucial element in which DSTA had to shine and succeed. Through my friendship with the leaders of the Research and Development, Test and Evaluation functions in the US Department of Defense, I became impressed with how well they tapped on innovations coming out of their civilian economy through DARPA and the Central Intelligence Agency's (CIA) In-Q-Tel venture fund. I then became involved in the promotion of research and development in Singapore's civilian economy through my membership of two sub-committees of the Economic Review Committee set up by the government in 1987 and chaired by the then Minister for Trade and Industry (now Prime Minister) Lee Hsien Loong. I was a founding board member of the National Science and Technology Board (NSTB), which became A*STAR. I was also Deputy Chairman in 1998–1999 when it was promoting technological start-ups. These two factors made me particularly interested in the start-up ecosystem in the US. When DSTA was well on track in 2002, I was offered an opportunity to attend the Advanced Management Programme at Harvard Business School, but, instead, decided to take a three-month sabbatical in Silicon Valley on a DSTA Fellowship to study the US entrepreneurship ecosystem. Thus, it was in Palo Alto, California that I received the fateful telephone call from Koh Boon Hwee, Chairman of the then Council of NTU, informing me of my selection as the next president of NTU.

Singapore is a small place. While in DSO, I was encouraged to do part-time teaching at the University of Singapore's Engineering Faculty so that we could headhunt the best students. Subsequently, I was appointed to the Council of NTU in 1996. Technological leaders in Singapore were a relatively small group. Most of us knew each other. Professor Cham invited me to NTU on a number of occasions including as a Convocation Speaker. As Director of DSO, I was a major employer of engineers who graduated from NUS and NTU, and I remember being interviewed by the press on the difference between NUS and NTU engineering graduates.

I told them that NUS engineers were stronger theoretically, but tended to be somewhat scruffy and unkempt, whereas NTU engineers were quick to get down to the nuts and bolts and were immediately useful. They were also better prepared for the interviews. NTU tends to turn out very employable engineers who were quick to become productive.

As one of the members of the small group of technology leaders in Singapore, I was often roped into national technology issues. When NSTB was set up in 1991, I became a founding Board Member and later in 1998–1999 Deputy Chairman. I left the Board in 2001 when it was reorganised and renamed A*STAR. My service on the Board was fulfilling, but sometimes frustrating. I learned, firsthand, the difficulties of pushing a research initiative. For example, the Institute of Molecular and Cell Biology (IMCB) was set up in 1988 by former Deputy Prime Minister Goh Keng Swee and achieved international recognition under Chris Tan with support and guidance from Nobel laureate Sydney Brenner. IMCB was put under NSTB where the mantra was "industry relevance". Unfortunately, Singapore's economic strategy was very much based on foreign technology, methods of production and markets. When the emphasis shifted to high technology, we did not sufficiently encourage our own innovation. As a result of this preference for technology not invented here, the opposite of the normal behaviour, IMCB had a hard time in NSTB despite its significant achievements on the world stage, until Philip Yeo came to their rescue in 2000.

One interesting connection between me and Bertil was that, during my time in Defence, I visited Sweden many times to meet the FOA (Sweden's defence research establishment, now renamed FOI). During these visits, I also went to Linköping to the FOA that was actually located at the Linkoping University campus, only a couple of hundred metres from the Rector's Office. This was the mirror image of Bertil coming to NTU prior to the Troika period, foretelling our future partnership. Although we never actually met in the 1990s, I did visit much later in 2008 for the Troika meeting in Sigtuna, when Bertil showed me around Linköping University and his "farm retreat" nearby.

I was appointed as the second President NTU on 1 January 2003. My predecessor, Cham Tao Soon, had by then chalked up 22 years as President of NTU and its predecessor, Nanyang Technological Institute (NTI). The government needed a new man at the helm of NTU to take on its transformation. By then, I think I had acquired a reputation as a change agent who restructured and guided DSO into becoming an internationally respected defence research partner, followed by corporatisation for greater autonomy. I had also been responsible for the integration of the acquisition, project management and technology development functions under a single autonomous agency, DSTA. Both reorganisations were done during the tenure of Dr. Tony Tan Keng Yam, who was then Deputy Prime Minister and Minister for Defence. Dr. Tan was also the Minister in charge of universities and he was to play an indispensable role in NTU's ascent.

NTU had set up a three-man presidential search committee, chaired by Koh Boon Hwee, the then Chairman of its Governing Council. Early in 2002, President Cham Tao Soon called me to seek my consent to be a candidate in the NTU presidential search process, and I readily agreed. When my selection as President was announced, it was revealed that 150 candidates had been evaluated, among whom five finalists were identified. I was one of the five and had a half-day interview in Singapore before I went to the US on the DSTA Fellowship hosted by Stanford University.

I left for Stanford in April 2002 to spend three months exploring the US high-tech start-up ecosystem. The two indicators of the possibility that I may be appointed President of NTU were my appointment to the NTU Council and my inclusion in the Fourth Leadership in Administration Programme (LAP4) training programme that had the reputation of preparing people for appointment as ministry permanent secretaries (university presidents are considered equivalent to permanent secretaries). The programme participants also included Tan Chorh Chuan, who became NUS President in 2008, serving for the next 10 years.

I had my inauguration ceremony on 28 March 2003. In my inauguration address, I set out my vision and guiding philosophy as President and emphasised the need for reform and the intimate association of research and teaching if NTU was to scale the heights of academia. Later, at our first Troika meeting, I elaborated on my directions which my other two partners thought were very essential. Our Troika adventure was clearly influenced by the vision enunciated in my Presidential inaugural speech when my NTU adventure began!

Chapter 5

An "Earth-Shaking" Trajectory from California to Singapore — Haresh's Tale

Why would a highly esteemed and renowned academic from one of the top universities in the world, at the heart and soul of Silicon Valley, come to the then relatively unknown academic "backwaters" of Singapore and Nanyang Technological University (NTU) in the 1990s?

It is important to get an understanding of my academic trajectory from early childhood to why and how I ended up as one of the three "movers and shakers" whose transformation of NTU is the subject of history. In my mind, it was by happenchance that such an unlikely set of circumstances would occur to bring everyone together as members of the NTU Troika from their very different backgrounds.

I was born in 1937 in a small town named Godhra in the state of Gujarat in western India. My family comes from the trading community of Gujaratis. Both my parents had only received high school education. I was the youngest child of six children — four daughters and two sons. My father had moved from there to Poona/Pune, a city located southwest of Bombay (now Mumbai), in 1925. This was during the British Raj and Poona was the seat of the summer state capital due to its more temperate climate. My father worked for a British lady, Ms. Emelie Windrow, who had a garment business named Emelie Stores. As Poona was the headquarters of the Military Southern Command of British India, there were many families of British officers based in Poona, which sustained the Windrow business. After Indian independence in 1947, Emelie Windrow decided to move back to England and my father was able to buy the business from her, renaming it as just Emelie.

My parents educated all their six children well. The daughters were all college graduates — with the two youngest having Master's degrees. My brother received his Bachelor's degree in Science from the University of Poona and his Master's degree in Civil Engineering from the University of Arkansas in the US.

I was a very good student throughout my academic career, always graduating in the top 1% of my classes. I received my Bachelor's degree in Civil Engineering from the College of Engineering in Poona (which is one of India's oldest higher educational institutions based on colleges originally established in the 19th century — the "Oxford of the East"). After graduation, because of these excellent grades, I applied to Stanford University in California. Admitted to Stanford in 1959 in the Department of Civil Engineering, I completed a Master's in Civil Engineering (Structural Engineering) in 1960, ending up with a doctorate in Civil Engineering in 1963.

I then embarked on my academic teaching and research career at the University of Pennsylvania in Philadelphia in 1962. After six years of a very satisfying and successful career at Penn, I returned to Stanford as an Associate Professor of Civil and Environmental Engineering in 1968.

After this defining moment, I continued my academic journey, rising to the rank of full Professor with tenure at the very young age of 34. My main research was in the field of earthquake engineering, an appropriate topic for California, focusing on developing a better understanding of seismic risk, loss estimation technologies for future seismic events and trying to understand how to quantify risk of rare events. In 1976, I established the first Earthquake Engineering Research Center (John A. Blume Earthquake Engineering Center) as one of its founding Directors. The Center had been named in honour of one of the most famous earthquake engineers of the 20th century and a Stanford alumnus.

In 1986, while serving as the Director of the Blume Center, I was appointed Chair of the Department of Civil and Environmental Engineering.

During my tenure as Chair, from 1986 to 1996, the Civil and Environmental Engineering programme was recognised as one of the three best programmes in its field in the world.

During this period, I became entitled to sabbatical leave, which I eventually took in 1992, in order to write papers, conduct research and, in general, to re-energise my work in the field of risk analysis and risk management. Having chosen to come to Southeast Asia to study earthquake risk in Indonesia (especially in Sumatra), I was not too keen about staying in Indonesia and so I contacted Professor T. C. Pan (TC) at NTU, whom I had known in the past, to ask whether TC could host me and provide an office and other support facilities. TC and NTU were kind enough to extend an invitation to come to NTU and Singapore and I arrived at the university in January 1993 after spending the first three months of my sabbatical at the University of Tokyo.

It was at that time that I first met many of the senior academics in the university, with whom I would later interact, not knowing that this was to be in the not too distant future.

I found NTU to be a somewhat strange and inward-looking place, although having a superb campus and great buildings. I quickly realised that research was not really encouraged and the manner of working seemed a long way from what I had been used to at Stanford and in the US. Even though NTU was hosting me, and, after all, I had *chosen it*, there seemed to be no real recognition that it was not every day that a senior US academic would come to NTU and this represented an opportunity to engage with one of the world's top universities.

My wife and I were given an apartment at Nanyang Lodge, which later became the international building and is now the university's health centre. It was an excellent location for access to transport, my office, and eating places. My first surprise was when I found out that there was no phone in the apartment except an intercom between it and other units in the lodge and to campus security. There was no way to contact outside parties, including my family in the US or my office at Stanford. When I requested a phone line (which I offered to pay for), the response was that, according to some mysterious "regulation", it was not possible to have a landline in the apartment. This was in the "Stone Age" era before mobile phones and smartphones.

Another surprise was that the office was not available for use in the evening or at night. Being a night owl, this was most inconvenient as I was used to American working habits, where the offices and labs were available for work 24/7. It is hard to believe that if I wanted to make a copy of a document (even a single page), I had to go through an NTU faculty host and pay cash per page for that privilege.

A particular example of this inward-looking and rather bureaucratic institution was when I received an important telephone call from my company (Risk Management Solutions that I had established as a spinoff company some little time before) regarding a key acquisition, which clearly needed my approval before it could proceed. This was a critical matter. One of the campus security guards arrived at Nanyang Lodge one evening to say that he had received a call from the US and that the caller would phone back shortly. On asking for this to be transferred to my apartment when the second call came in, I was told that this was impossible — this was an international call which could only be taken in the main building. Despite my protests and knowing the importance of the call, I had to go to the security guard's office. Although the call was generated and paid for in the US, the guard nevertheless attended closely and noted down the length of the call for the university's records. Obviously, in NTU, receiving such a call must have been strange and out of the ordinary and not something that one would expect in a university!

For me, it demonstrated how insular and inward-looking NTU was at that time, despite its protestations that it was an international institution. More recently, I learned that, even as late as 2007, international telephone calls were viewed as something that had to be strictly controlled by the administration of the university.

The culture of research was almost nonexistent and most faculty seemed to spend all their time grading assignments and exams. There was no time for any research. It was general knowledge amongst faculty that "you do research on your own time" and not on university time. To a person like me, coming from Stanford University, this was quite surprising, shocking and strange. I am a firm believer in the Humboldtian principle that to bring new knowledge, innovation and state-of-the-art progress in your classroom and to your students is essential and a faculty member in a university must be a part of the community of researchers creating new knowledge. Anyway, as I was interested in pursuing earthquake risk research for Southeast Asia (Indonesia in particular), I had no particular desire, at that time, to get involved in trying to change the teaching/research culture of NTU.

During the early 1990s, there was a great trend towards entrepreneurship among students. In Silicon Valley, young students from Stanford and University of California, Berkeley were creating many great companies and the migration of bright young entrepreneurs from Asia, Europe and the Americas was thriving. The question occurred to me that how was it that these bright, ambitious and entrepreneurial young people coming from Asia (India, China, Singapore, etc.) and doing so well in Silicon Valley were not doing the same in their countries of origin. In the mid-1990s, China and India were not in the same place as they are today. Therefore, my hypothesis was that if we could create a similar environment and culture and give encouragement and resources to students in Singapore, we should see the same outcome as in and around Stanford University. To test this hypothesis, the Shah Family Fund offered to reward NTU students who were considered by their faculty and departments to demonstrate innovative and entrepreneurial characteristics. A committee was set up by the School of Civil Engineering to select one male and one female student from the graduating class for leadership and entrepreneurship traits and award them each a S$5,000 prize.

The first batch of winners was announced and the prizes were distributed. My wife and I returned from California to attend the award ceremony. During that trip, I asked the Selection Committee about the criteria they had used for selecting the winners. To my surprise, the Committee Chair explained that the selected candidates had the best academic grades among the graduates. It was intriguing that the Committee saw a perfect correlation between academic grades and entrepreneurship. The first year, I accepted this explanation and told them that the Shah Family Fund would continue to offer the award for the next two years and set up an endowment for future awards. The second year, once again to my great discomfort, the selection committee selected the two winners who happened to have the best grades. Same for the third year. Then, I realised that the faculty themselves did not understand what entrepreneurship meant and that to them, good grades equated with leadership as well as future entrepreneurial success. Needless to say, the Shah Family Fund discontinued the award and I decided that what was necessary was to focus on changing the attitudes of the faculty. This story underlines the state of the NTU faculty mindset and what they thought was leadership, innovation and entrepreneurship.

After spending six months at NTU in 1993, I returned to California to continue as Chair at Stanford. Between 1986 and 1996, besides providing leadership to the Civil and Environmental Engineering programme, I also founded a company to provide risk assessment and management services to insurance companies in the US, especially for low-probability and high-consequence catastrophes such as earthquakes. Between 1995 and 1998, the company was growing very fast and I needed to pay more attention to its growth. As a result, I decided to take early retirement from Stanford University becoming Professor Emeritus. The company (Risk Management Solutions, Inc. or RMS for short) has now grown from an initial two employees to few thousand employees located in 11 global offices around the world. I sold my majority stake in the company at the end of 1998, although I retained a family connection through my son, Hemant Shah, who became the Chief Executive Officer (CEO) of the company (since retired from this post).

My next contact with Singapore was rather serendipitous. Stanford University hosts the Hoover Institution, with which George Schultz, the former US Secretary of State under the first President George Bush, was associated. He had invited Lee Kuan Yew to be a member of its International Advisory Panel. Naturally, as a senior politician, he was unable to attend most meetings and was deputised by Mr. S. R. Nathan, the then Singapore Ambassador in Washington D.C. I was a nominated member of the group representing engineering at Stanford. S. R. Nathan and I not only became acquainted but also became very good friends. Years later, when I started coming to Singapore regularly in relation to my role in NTU, I renewed contact with S. R. Nathan who, by that time, had become the President of Singapore. We used to meet frequently and this close contact and friendship was to stand myself and NTU in good stead in the future. Former President Nathan (the sixth President of Singapore) died in 2016.

Around 2002, I decided that, having some more time at my disposal, I should "give back" to the society my 35 years of experience of "growing" companies and universities.

Just about at that time, Professor Su Guaning, the newly appointed President of NTU, was at Stanford University on a short sabbatical to prepare himself for the challenges of President's position at NTU. Professor T. C. Pan, who had been at NTU since 1985, and whom I had known since my sabbatical in 1993, suggested that Su Guaning should make contact with me.

One of the things that I most appreciated about Guaning was that, after it had been announced that Guaning would succeed Professor Cham Tao Soon as NTU's second President, he invested three months of his time on a sabbatical to visit Stanford to learn about how US institutions operate and conduct their governance, to learn from their experiences as well as to study Silicon Valley and its relation to Stanford and other universities.

The first meeting between myself and Guaning was for lunch at the Stanford Faculty Club. Here, we discussed Guaning's plans and aspirations for NTU. Guaning wanted to create a powerhouse of teaching, research, entrepreneurship, thriving campus life and an environment for students and faculty of excellence. He told me about his background prior to the offer to become President of NTU.

This approach was an important signal. Here was a man prepared to listen and learn and who realised that he had not had direct experience of some of the complexities of academic management, having spent his life in defence research, first as an active researcher and later as a key research manager, director and someone close to government.

From our discussions, it was also clear that he had ambitions for NTU, which he would later deliver on — to start the process to change NTU into a leading research-intensive university and a beacon institution in Southeast Asia.

Guaning persuaded me that he needed someone close to him with the academic weight to help see through the reforms that they could develop together and he invited me to consider such a role at NTU in transforming the university. Impressed with Guaning's passion, plans and his humility, I accepted and so became part of the transformation of NTU into a world-class university.

The following year, Guaning took up his post. In the beginning, I kept in touch with Guaning on my trips to India whenever I made a stopover in Singapore. He kept me informed of developments. I really got involved during the QAFU exercise 2005 when Guaning and I met to discuss the outcome of the exercise (for more on QAFU and governance, see Chapter 8).

Having had experience with the old NTU and understanding where the academic members of QAFU were coming from, I was not surprised at the criticism implied in the recommendations, except that it was a little unfair to the new administration which had barely time to bed itself in. However, the observations and recommendations were spot on and Guaning was already working on some of them.

I told Guaning he would be overwhelmed if he did not have external help of an external quality reference and I offered to help him with the comprehensive reforms needed, tapping on my Stanford experience. He immediately accepted my offer and arranged to make me his Senior Academic Adviser, which was subsequently extended to the end of March 2007, just before Bertil arrived. With the incorporation of NTU as an autonomous body, I was then appointed to the Board of Trustees, and thus started my decade-long formal and close association with NTU.

Through this, I came to know Koh Boon Hwee, one of the industrial leaders of Singapore, who had previously chaired the University Council and subsequently became the Chairman of the Board of Trustees of NTU. Koh Boon Hwee has continued to lead the Board with distinction and a passion to see NTU advance and has provided the space in which, first, Guaning and myself, and, later, the Troika with Bertil Andersson, could operate freely. Koh Boon Hwee also ensured that the Board supported all the proposed changes that subsequently emerged. Once on the Board, as one of the few truly academic members, I was designated as the Chair of the Board's Academic Affairs Committee and, therefore, had a key position from which to take things forward.

With autonomy, Guaning now had the freedom to act and consulted me about the direction that NTU had to take and sought my help in doing so.

Guaning made his intentions clear and public in his inauguration address when he spoke about moving NTU forward with his new research vision. This was an important break from the past when, as noted above, research had been rather undervalued at NTU. But, the key message that no one should forget was that Guaning had set NTU on a new course and I felt that this was an important opportunity to help him at the helm of this "big idea".

First of all, I realised that we were dealing with academics and academic prima donnas who would not accept direction from someone who was not himself a seasoned academic. The President would be telling them what to do in their academic life, their teaching and their research. I believed that Guaning needed to have academic title and rank and I was able to steer the process of getting Guaning to have a full tenured professorial title.

Now we were in business!

First, we had to clear up the messy structures that we had inherited. One could not expect to bring in a top-notch academic as Provost and then expect him or her to spend their energies on changing a deficient structure. This person would need to be charged with taking the university forward into a very new environment.

Beyond this, there were at least three major challenges to be addressed.

The academic structure was all wrong, research quality was poor, NTU was uncompetitive and the pedagogy needed to be reformed. The last task would have to wait until several years later. Reforming the structure was urgent. But, first of all, we felt that we needed ministerial approval, even if the university was now autonomous; so, I arranged to meet the then Minister for Education, Tharman Shanmugaratnam, who was convinced by what I had to say and basically said "let's fix it".

In fact, after my first sorties into Singapore, I had been nominated by S. R. Nathan to be a member of a group developing policies to help the poorer Tamil community that had become somewhat of an underclass in Singapore. Minister Tharman was a member of this working group, so that was how he and I got to know each other — yet another valuable contact for the future.

Of course, there were two aspects to the reform of NTU. The management structure was a nightmare. Each school was headed by a Dean, reporting directly to the President, which meant that at least 10 voices, sometimes discordant, were competing to get his ear. Then there were the three Deputy Presidents and a phalanx of Vice Presidents, not only academic but also the heads of service departments (who had a Vice President designation) reporting directly to the President. Altogether 28 direct reports. It was most definitely a less than sub-optimal structure.

Leading professors and the Deans were quite happy with this arrangement, especially sheltering within their silos. As long as they had resources to continue and not reach across the walls with which they had surrounded themselves, they were quite content. Interdisciplinarity was unknown and something of a dirty word. How was this to be broken down? How was this to be achieved?

I admit that my principal academic experience was at Stanford University and so I fell back on this template. If I am to be criticised, perhaps I tried too hard to create a "tropical Stanford", but I would say that this model, which was part of academic orthodoxy, has generally served us well as a foundation on which to build.

Therefore, first, we had to group schools together on a "superdisciplinary" basis and for these to be headed by Deans. The title had to be reserved not just for a "head of department" but for someone capable of academic strategic leadership. With Guaning, together, we determined that we could group the schools into four cross-disciplinary colleges with each being headed by Deans reporting directly to the President. At a stroke, we could reduce the academic reporting number to a third of what it had been!

This meant asking the current Deans for their resignation so they could be redesignated as Chairs. Some were very reluctant and I was given the authority to fire them, if necessary, which, in some circumstances, I had to threaten to do. Even several years later, at least one Chair insisted that within the school he was to be addressed as "Dean" even though the term was now reserved for the heads of colleges!

We could still have appointments such as a Vice President (Research), and we did, but the service departments would not be Vice Presidents but Heads. Some of course would continue to report to the President. At least we now had a manageable management structure and a coherent academic structure.

However, I was unwilling and it was not sustainable to continue in this rather strange position as "unofficial Provost" and so, in 2005, we set about a recruitment process to find someone who would share our vision and bring their skills to bear on taking NTU forward. The timing was opportune because the Singapore government had set its sights on becoming one of the world's leading knowledge-based economies and through the five-year research and development (R&D) plan had increased spending on this area by nearly two and a half times, much of which was to be dedicated to university-led research through the newly created NRF. This was the brainchild of Dr. Tony Tan, who became the Chairman of the Foundation. NTU had to position itself to take advantage of this funding regime and could not leave the field empty for NUS to garner all the spoils on its own.

NRF had created a Scientific Advisory Board (SAB), one of whose members was Bertil Andersson, at that time the Chief Executive of the European Science Foundation (ESF) based in Strasbourg, France.

Although we had instituted a search to fill the new Provost position, we were not wholly satisfied with what we had and wanted to broaden the search when we became aware of Bertil. He was not one of the names initially being considered, but the information that we had gathered indicated that he was someone who was ideally suited to this role and so we set about persuading him and the Board. We succeeded and the rest is history!

Chapter 6

From the Arctic to the Equator: A Viking's Journey — Bertil's Tale

It was during my high school days that I first became aware of the place called Singapore. I remember that, in 1965, back in the small industrial town of Finspång, our teacher told us that a new country had been born, led by someone called Lee Kuan Yew. Little was I to imagine that, in March 2015, I would have the honour, as President of NTU, to lead thousands of students, faculty and staff in a memorial tribute to Lee Kuan Yew, the "father of the nation" of Singapore. It was a very moving experience for me, especially looking back to when, as a teenager, I first heard of the arrival of this new country and its leader on the international stage. Again, I never expected to spend 11 years of my professional life in a leadership position at a university in Singapore, first as Provost and then as President.

Born in 1948, to a rather "blue-collar" (working class) family, I grew up on a small family farm close to the industrial town of Finspång in Sweden, some 200 kilometres southwest of Stockholm. The farm has been in the family since 1831 and so its occupation of this land is almost contemporaneous with the whole history of modern Singapore. I was the first member of my family to go to university, although I am very proud of my roots. The Swedish government provided free higher education to everyone who qualified and was admitted to a university and this was the only way in which my family and I could have afforded such an endeavour. There was pressure from my family to follow in my father's footsteps as a factory worker, but it was my grandmother who encouraged me to take the opportunity which I had gained through my natural abilities and it was she who convinced my parents that I should start out along this academic path which has taken me to the Nobel Committee and to many of the world's elite universities and finally to NTU in Singapore.

I had other aspirations as well, including that of skilled cross-country (Nordic) skiing and other sporting interests. As a member of the "Beatles generation", I was also very much into pop music and during my national military service in Sweden, I ended up in the same barracks as a member of what became the famous ABBA group — Bjorn Ulvaeus.

My scientific career started out in Umeå University, in the far north of Sweden (Sweden's "Siberia"!), where I completed my BSc and Master's degrees in chemistry and biology, finishing in 1972. There, I commenced my doctoral studies, eventually moving, with my supervisor (the late Professor Per-Åke Albertsson) when he moved to a new appointment in the very south of Sweden, at Lund University. It was at this time that I developed my interest and enthusiasm in understanding the key molecular-scale processes of photosynthesis in plants. So began my love for biochemistry and the realisation that if we could understand the processes by which the Sun's energy could be converted and stored — a system that all plants have perfected and which has created the Earth as we know it — then we could have the secret for unlimited renewable energy for mankind. So, early in my career, I realised that one needed to be a specialist in one's field, but be able to understand the power of inter-disciplinary research and the need to collaborate with specialists in other disciplines.

I had started my studies in the far north of Sweden where winters are long, dark and cold. Perhaps not the ideal place for photosynthesis! Upon completing my doctorate at Lund in 1978, I chose to undertake a European Molecular Biology Organisation (EMBO) post-doctoral fellowship that took me to the other side of the world: the Australian National University (ANU) and the Commonwealth Scientific and Industrial Research Organisation (CSIRO) in Canberra. At that time, these were two of the then world-leading centres for plant sciences. In Canberra, I worked with Professor Jan Anderson. She was not only my mentor but also a highly respected colleague. It was a very successful period in my scientific life where I developed a new understanding of how the photosynthetic apparatus was constructed. After a two-year spell in Australia, where my eldest daughter (Matilda) was born, although offered a post to stay in Australia, I chose to return to Sweden, becoming a young academic in Lund University, thus furthering both my research and my academic career. It was while going to Australia in 1979 that I first touched down in Singapore — my next crucial visit would not be until 2001.

Having been an active researcher (a typical "lab rat" in my terms) in biochemistry trying to unravel the fundamentals of nature's power-conversion system (photosynthesis), my next move was into academic administration. It was both gratifying and surprising when in 1986 I moved to the prestigious Stockholm University as one of its youngest Professors in charge of the very large Department of Biochemistry as well as being Dean of the Faculty of Chemistry. This was my first taste of academic leadership and management and something with which I would be increasingly involved in as my career progressed. Yet, at the same time, I managed to continue to lead a big and active world-leading research group. With both research and administration, this was probably one of the busiest and most productive periods in my life. At this time, I was honoured to become involved in the activities of the Nobel Foundation, first as a member and later Chairman of the Chemistry Committee choosing Nobel laureates. Later, I became a member of the Board of the Nobel Foundation. Not only was this both an interesting and demanding activity in the public spotlight but it also provided me with my very extensive network of high-level scientific connections from around the world. It was, in my opinion, the "Piccadilly Circus" of the scientific world. In addition, I became involved as a member of the Swedish Research Council (Vetenskapsrådet), gaining experience in research funding management.

I guess that I must have shown promise at university management because 12 years later, I was appointed by the Swedish government to become the Rector of Linköping University, a relatively new (founded in 1975) and technologically-based institution some two hours' train journey southwest of Stockholm. It was once said that this university was "the youngest among the oldest and oldest among the new universities" in Sweden. In fact, after my military service in 1968, I had taken an academic course in statistics at Linköping, so, in some ways, it was a case of a homecoming as it was also close to my birthplace and the family farm.

I approached this role with a commitment to the Humboldtian philosophy of the intimate link between research and teaching. Coming from a scientific disciplinary background, I quickly came to appreciate and was convinced by the inter- and multidisciplinarity of Linköping. Here, having known a lot about a little, I started to learn a little about a lot and was able to expand my horizon in understanding the force of interdisciplinarity. Linköping had been structured on a thematic rather than traditional disciplinary departments and this forced people to think in new ways and from new perspectives. Looking to broaden academic collaboration as Rector, I soon became convinced that the 21st century was going to be Asia's century, and so it was important for both myself and the institution to create good links with leading universities in that part of the world. Therefore, at the turn of the century, with colleagues, I decided to embark on exploratory tours of East and Southeast Asia, ending up in Singapore and visiting, among others, NTU. Su Guaning, while he was at DSO, had passed through Linköping to visit its Swedish equivalent located there during this period, but his and my paths did not cross at that time.

In August 2001, I was graciously received by Professor Cham Tao Soon (NTU's founding President) and signed a general cooperation agreement. I was impressed by the campus, but noted that research was not, at that time, at the forefront of the university's endeavours. Nevertheless, I noticed that things were moving in research and I met Professor James Tam, a high level researcher then at Vanderbilt University in the US, who had just been appointed as the founding head of the newly created School of Biological Sciences (SBS). At that time, it never crossed my mind or was it in my life plan that, only a decade later, I would be occupying Professor Cham's place as the NTU President.

A year after my Asian tour, I was offered the post of Rector at the much larger and prominent Stockholm University. This was very tempting, but, just at that time, I was approached by a number of key people in Sweden to see if I would be interested in the post of Chief Executive of ESF in Strasbourg in France. This put me in a dilemma — should I stay in Sweden and take a safe but prestigious appointment there and remain very much a Swedish academic or take up the challenge at the age of 55 in embarking on a new direction and commence building an international management career? The day before the government's cabinet meeting to confirm my appointment as Rector at Stockholm University, I was summoned to meet the Minister for Education who told me that "with your experience and energy we need you more in Europe", but the final decision was mine. This was very gratifying, but it was a difficult choice and, ultimately, I bowed to this pressure and embarked on this new international career direction. Being a believer in the necessity and benefits of collaborative research and keen to play my part in European research, its stimulation and integration, I took up my appointment as the ESF Chief Executive and moved to Strasbourg at the end of 2003. This was an opportunity to expand my horizons yet again and develop myself as an academic leader on the international stage.

This was just at the time when the European research community was campaigning to try to establish a European Research Council (ERC) funded through the European Union (EU) Framework Programme. Therefore, I threw myself into this ultimately successful campaign. I also developed the implementation of a scheme to support bright young researchers in that difficult "transition to independence" period. This became the European Young Investigators Awards (EURYI) scheme, the precursor and template for the now much-admired and prestigious European Research Council Young Investigator Grants scheme. It also became the template for both the prestigious NRF Fellowship scheme and NTU's own Nanyang Assistant Professorships (NAPs), which I championed. However, although leading the ESF was rewarding and progress was made on many fronts, it was nevertheless frustrating, especially to struggle against the nationalism and self-interest of the ESF member organisations (mainly national research funding agencies) in trying to get coordinated action underway. They often came to the ESF meetings full of Euro-enthusiasm, but within hours of returning to their own organisation, their nationalism and protection of their own organisation kicked in. That may have a bearing on the more nationalistic tendencies that have reappeared some 10 years later in Europe. It was during this time at the ESF that I met Tony Mayer (working at ESF and the European Cooperation in Science and Technology (COST)) with whom I worked closely both in Strasbourg and, later, in Singapore.

In 2005, I was asked to join the Science Advisory Board of the recently created NRF in Singapore. Dr. Tony Tan had inspired the establishment of the NRF that he chaired. He also chaired the Advisory Board. He had been an influential member of the Singapore government, was later to become the President of Singapore, and the Chancellor of NTU when he and I once again interacted. As a member of this Board, I argued from my experience of the ESF that Singapore should initiate a similar scheme as that of EURYI and I am pleased to say that I was successful. NRF created its Fellows Scheme which was added into its portfolio of research funding programmes and has attracted top young scientists to Singapore.

So, what has this to do with NTU?

As part of the NRF Advisory Board's activities in spring 2006, it was scheduled to visit both NUS and NTU. By then, Guaning had succeeded Cham Tao Soon as President. I was impressed by the new developments at NTU and by its new emphasis on research compared to my previous visit. The evidence for this was that, during the NRF visit, and in contrast to NUS, NTU had "showcased" its research students to meet the visiting committee. This was refreshingly different from only meeting managerial professors and was indicative of a significant change of attitude.

During this visit, there was a dinner hosted by NTU for the Advisory Board. This, I was later to realise, was a critical moment in my journey to NTU. I was at a table with someone called Anthony Teo (the NTU University Secretary) and we enjoyed an interesting conversation. I was to learn later that Anthony had followed up our conversation by speaking to the Chairman of the NTU Board of Trustees, Koh Boon Hwee, who had, in turn, spoken to the Chair of the Search Committee for a Provost of NTU (Haresh Shah) that I should be approached about this post. I was aware of the search for a Provost as, in late 2005, I had been approached by a head-hunting company charged with looking for a Provost for NTU, which I had ignored at the time. I was then contacted by Haresh, who visited me in Strasbourg, to persuade me to allow my name to be shortlisted for the post. This was gratifying as such recognition is always pleasant to receive, and so I forwarded my CV as I had already seen the potential of NTU. Seeing was believing!

One month later, during a stopover in Zurich on a trip to Israel, Guaning proposed to meet me in Geneva, which we subsequently did. There we talked about the possibility of my going to Singapore. This was to be the first of what would be many tête-à-têtes and inspiring meetings. It was followed, soon after, by a Skype interview with Haresh and his Search Committee, which included T. C. Pan and Jennie Chua, one of the prominent female business leaders in Singapore. What concerned me most, at the time, was that having been a University Rector and then Chief Executive of an important European organisation, should I now become "number two" in Singapore? I joked that maybe if I came to NTU, I should not be number two, but number one and a half!

Later, I again expressed my hesitations to Haresh and he then explained that both he and Guaning had agreed that not only was I to be the Chief Academic Officer of the university, but that I would be in charge of the budget and with an important role in strategy development. In other words, I was really going to be number one and a half!

The meetings with Haresh and Guaning confirmed what our working relationship would be and I learned of their ambitions to transform NTU into a research-intensive university working on the world stage. This was to be the major challenge for the university leadership and did I want to be part of it? The ambition of Haresh and Guaning to start on this journey was one the most important reasons behind my decision to accept the offer and begin one of the most exciting and rewarding periods in my career. Another was the conversation that I had with the then Minister for Education Tharman Shanmugaratnam. He endorsed the ambitions of Haresh and Guaning and this was also confirmed when meeting Lim Chuan Poh, who was just stepping down as Permanent Secretary at the Ministry of Education to take up the chairmanship of A*STAR. In fact, I had just touched down at Changi Airport and rushed to Lim Chuan Poh's farewell party! It was on this visit that I had the first of many positive meetings with the Chairman of the Board of Trustees, Koh Boon Hwee.

And so, a short while later, I was offered the post.

Little was I to realise at the time of my first visit that only a few years later I would be back and working for NTU and living on its beautiful tropical campus with my wife, Susana, who became a professor in the School of Biological Sciences, following on from her earlier career working at the Hebrew University and then at *w national de la recherche scientifique* (CNRS, the French National Centre for Scientific Research) in France. Thus, I was able to escape from some of the frustrations of trying to advance research in Europe and become part of the Asian, and particularly Singaporean, advance to the forefront of research and academia. I became part of the Asian environment where they really "walk the talk".

Once ensconced at NTU, my early days convinced me of the importance of the task ahead in shaking up some of the complacent attitudes that had built up, especially with regard to research. At the same time, I had to come to terms with, to me, new cultural attitudes. For example, one of my first general meetings was with the faculty of the College of Engineering to discuss putting proposals together in response to an opportunity that had arisen to collaborate with ETH Zürich. I started off by saying a few words in *Schweizerdeutsch* (Swiss German) and then making a joke. Most present sat with mouths open at this "creature from another world" and not knowing whether they should laugh or not!

On another occasion, Guaning and I met with the senior administrative staff. After Guaning had introduced me, I talked about our ambitions and concluded by inviting comments and questions. There was silence. In order to break the silence and encourage some discussion, Guaning made a comment to which I replied that I disagreed with him. Turning to the audience, I saw a look of horror on everyone's face as I had dared to disagree in public with the President — this was unheard of!

I also embarked on visits to all the schools, in what became known as my "royal tour". The aim was to set out our vision and invite a genuine exchange of views with faculty. On one occasion, I was greeted with silence as the Chair made it plain that contributions from faculty were not acceptable and only he should respond to me. I have to say that, coming from Sweden and being used to open dialogue, this made me mad. I had to tell him to be quiet as I wanted to listen to what the faculty really had to say, critical or supportive.

Certainly, there was a big contrast between being Rector of Linköping University where students addressed me as "Bertil" and NTU where students, even if they dared to respond, would say "Sir"!

Recapping somewhat, when my move from the ESF to NTU became public knowledge, I was interviewed by reporters from *Nature* and *Science* magazines. I said that in Europe we talked too much, while in Singapore they acted. I have to say that after many years in Singapore and NTU, this joke has turned into a rewarding reality and I experienced the speed of change for which Singapore has become legendary. This book reflects that speed and its impacts within just one single organisation — NTU.

Here, I must acknowledge that I also benefitted from and enjoyed, the interactions that I have had with the many Singaporean thought leaders both in the Board, MOE, A*STAR and in politics, and, of course, with Haresh Shah and Su Guaning. This has been a big factor in turning an initial four-year contract into more than a decade in the exciting country of Singapore and the dynamic NTU.

During my time in Singapore, I was extremely gratified that my contribution was recognised in a number of ways. I was particularly honoured to be the first European in 10 years to receive the Meritorious Service Medal (a most prestigious Singaporean award) from the Singapore government for my contributions to NTU and to the nation. I also received the Singapore President's Science and Technology Medal for "a lifetime achievement in science and research that has advanced society". Even more, I became a national (not a foreign) Fellow of the Singapore National Academy of Science for my contributions to science development in Singapore.

Now, I have become a member of the NRF Board and its Science Advisory Board, so, in one way, things have come full circle for me.

In the end, I stayed at NTU for 11 years, living on its beautiful tropical campus and making my contribution to the advancement of this unique country. It has been much more than a job and something that I would not have missed for worlds.

Stage II

Plotting the Route

Chapter 7
Troika: The Council of Three

Troika, *n.*

Notes: **1(a)** a Russian vehicle with a team of three horses abreast; **1(b)** this team; **2** a group of three people, esp. as an administrative council. [Russian, from *troe* "set of three".]
Source: Taken from the Collins English Dictionary.

For the three of us, the Troika shall always be, in alphabetical order, Bertil Andersson, Haresh Shah and Su Guaning. The music we played was the sweet sounds of universities — teaching, research and service. The vehicle that we were pulling in tandem was Nanyang Technological University Singapore (NTU). We started off on three independent trajectories in which NTU played a very minor role. However, as a new millennium opened up before us, changes started to happen, which are described in our three tales.

Guaning was announced as President (Designate) in 2002, while on a DSTA Fellowship visiting Stanford, where he met Haresh. From 2003 to

2005, Guaning began to change NTU into its modern and research-intensive mode using internal human resources. By 2005, when it was clear that Guaning considered that he needed external assistance, he turned to Haresh who was invited to be Senior Academic Advisor to Guaning and, some months later, he became a member of the Board of Trustees. A Provost search began that we tell of elsewhere. That paved the way for Bertil to enter as the new Provost — the Chief Academic Officer. On 23 February 2007, the three of us met in Haresh's seaside home in Aptos, California, as the three principal drivers of NTU's future and this marked the birth of the Troika (the term was originally suggested by Bertil). This was not the first time that we had met, but this meeting marked a "turning point" in our relationship and desire to set NTU off in a new and exciting direction. Thus, the Troika consisted of the three key people in the NTU management structure, namely, the President, the Provost and the Chairman of the Academic Affairs Committee of the Board of Trustees of NTU.

Guaning and Haresh were already part of the NTU structure, but, at that time, Bertil, although he had been appointed and had accepted the position of Provost, was still the Chief Executive of ESF. Haresh's position was unusual in that he sat on both sides of the fence, i.e. management and governance. In the former capacity, he was a Senior Academic Adviser to the President and in the latter, he was a member of the Board of Trustees and chaired its Academic Affairs Committee. Yet, most of the Board did not see this as a conflict of interest, despite minor criticism from some members — rather it was considered to be a strength.

Bertil arrived in Singapore to formally join NTU as its first Provost as from 1 April 2007. Before Bertil's appointment to this "new" position, NTU did not have any "Chief Academic Officer". Therefore, for the NTU Board, for the President and for the Provost, it was a new experience. The three of us had to embark on a learning curve as well as to develop strategies which were aligned, and to which we could speak with one voice to the Board. This was not due to any conflict with the Board, but due to the desire to demonstrate to the Board a well-thought-out way forward, which we believed was necessary for the university to progress. It was also a structure that would interact with all levels in the university — management, faculty and administration.

With Bertil on board, the three of us felt that we needed to discuss matters in private and away from the inevitable distractions of everyday life at NTU. There was a desperate need for change and we were ambitious for our institution. However carefully one plans one's day, there will always be interruptions, telephone calls or people who insist on being seen. So, one of first decisions was that we would met over weekends at a variety of locations well away from the hustle and bustle of NTU and Singapore. This would then become the crucial forum for us to freely float ideas, analyse, criticise and improve them and then see how they could be realised. It was entirely unofficial and we did not feel the need to inform or ask the Board of Trustees for permission, although it was fully aware of the Troika. It became a key and yet informal management tool from which the university leadership could influence the Board and the rest of the university management.

The function of the Troika, as agreed by its members, was to promote an agenda for change, as set out below. In addition, it was necessary to plan on how best to overcome the inevitable resistance that was expected in changing a conservative and complex organisation institution such as a university:

1. Critically analyse the status of NTU in terms of its faculty, students, teaching, research, academic and administrative organisation, resources, infrastructure, processes for appointments, reappointments, promotions and tenure.
2. Understand the competitive environment of the existing universities at the local, Asian and global level and learn from that assessment what makes a good university better and what are the key drivers that make a great university.
3. Create a bond and a working relationship between the three members of the Troika. This was important to understand the diversity of background and experience of the three members. That way, one could extract the best of their talents towards developing strategies which were realistic, implementable at NTU and, given the constraints, could achieve the goal of being one of the leading universities in Asia and the world.

4. One of the most important analyses that was made early on was to come up with a set of actions that were needed to kick-start the process of leading NTU to become a major centre for research, teaching and learning, based upon best practice. From this list, prioritised strategic (and tactical) targets were identified for implementation. It was clearly understood that such a list would evolve with time and would vary with the progress made by the university.
5. The role of the administration had to change. At the time of the Troika's inception, despite the best efforts of Guaning to reform it, the university administration and its leadership saw themselves in a controlling rather than a support function. This had to change.
6. To review and check strategic milestones by having two-day Troika retreats every six months or so. At the end of each Troika retreat, a set of strategies and goals were mapped out that the Provost and the President, after discussion, together with the Board of Trustees, would initiate and implement. Each meeting would start with a review of progress (or lack of) of the strategies that had been agreed upon at the previous meeting and what changes, if any, were needed to be introduced to reach the stated objectives and goals. A hard and honest look at the resources needed and the political, social and economic constraints was conducted, and in depth, to make sure that the road to excellence was properly charted. Of course, the financial situation was good and this helped to "oil the wheels of change".
7. The process that was developed was "tweaked" at each meeting to overcome constraints and difficulties. It was important for the three Troika members to make sure that they openly and honestly criticised each other's suggestions and, at the end of such discussions, pursue what had been agreed with passion, vigour and focus.

In the end, the Troika finished up with a list of interesting places where its meetings could be held in seclusion and where the three members were able to debate with each other in a much more relaxed atmosphere. That is not to say that we always agreed with each other. Indeed, life and these meetings would have been boring had this been the case. But, we did accept the concept of "collective responsibility". In other words, once a decision on a course of action had been taken, the members stuck to it however much this may not have been to everyone's total liking. Thus, the

Troika was able to present a united front and consensus view to the Board and to our colleagues at NTU.

What follows is a more detailed description of the Troika meetings as seen through the eyes of the participants and taken from Troika meeting records and notes, as well as in their own words and from their recollections.

Our first meeting was held in Haresh's house at Aptos, California, in connection with a study trip to Stanford University. This is a small town near Santa Cruz on Monterey Bay. Naturally, as befits an earthquake engineer and the founder of a risk management company, Haresh had taken the precaution to build this house a little way inland and a 100m above the sea so that it would be reasonably tsunami proof! The meeting was held on 23–24 February 2007. As previously indicated, Bertil had yet to take his formal position as the Provost and, hence, this meeting can be considered as our first planning meeting — Troika '0'.

It was also influential in another way in that Haresh drove Bertil and Guaning to Aptos in a hybrid car. This so impressed Bertil that, on his arrival in Singapore, he bought the same model and even with the same colour!

The first coming together of the Troika was probably one of the most important meetings for the whole collaboration and where perhaps our most far-reaching and fundamental strategic decisions were taken. We agreed that we had to address faculty assessment and renewal as the highest priority action to be taken. This is discussed in greater detail in the later chapter on recruitment, but we cannot overemphasise the importance of the decisions taken at this time. We agreed on a way forward and the necessity of taking advantage of the window of opportunity provided by the change in tenure rules in Singapore. Get this right and the rest would follow! We all agreed that the key would be to adopt the highest level of international best practice and scrutiny of our faculty. We knew that this could create the space for new recruitment and put this whole process at the heart of the NTU reform.

How this would be done, in practical terms, was left to Bertil to take forward. It was definitely a case of people, people and people!

We itemised all the important challenges that needed attention and made a long list of strategic issues that would need to be discussed during future meetings. It was also the occasion at which we started to debate how best to introduce the concept of an Academic Council and Senate.

During the 2007 to 2011 period, we met a further seven times. Frequently, this was in combination with study visits to nearby interesting academic institutions that enabled us to compare and contrast what we were doing with others. It was also useful in providing a benchmarking for our progress:

0. *Aptos, California — the big "kick-off", March 2007.*
1. *Rigi Kulm near Zürich, Switzerland. 12–14 August 2007. This enabled us to visit ETH and meet with key personalities, who would be later linked to NTU.*
2. *Goa, India. 17–20 January 2008, with side trip to Pune (the "Oxford" of India).*
3. *Sigtuna (near Stockholm), Sweden. 29 June–1 July 2008. We were able to look at how the Royal Swedish Academy of Sciences and the Nobel Committee functioned.*
4. *Wuxi, China. 9–12 March 2009, where we looked at local enterprises and entrepreneurship, as well as met with local authorities and visited a research centre.*
5. *Healdsburg, California (California's Wine Country). 1–4 November 2009.*
6. *Strasbourg, France. 23–25 June 2010. This was at ESF and enabled Bertil to demonstrate the value of coordination and collaboration in the international conduct of research.*
7. *Bali, Indonesia. 22–24 March 2011. This represented the transition period when Bertil was appointed President to succeed Guaning and Professor Freddy Boey (now Deputy President (Innovation and Enterprise) at NUS) became the new Provost in succession to Bertil.*

The second meeting was at Rigi Kulm. This Alpine resort is at the heart of Switzerland in the Schwyzer Alps close to Luzern and so provided an entirely new setting. It was here, in a very beautiful and isolated spot, that the second major decision was taken when we discussed the problems that had been identified in terms of the challenges associated with undergraduate educational programmes. These were indeed very full and intensive programmes, but the discussion centred on whether they were up to date and fit for the current world.

Rigi Kulm was one of the most memorable meetings of the entire series. By the time that meeting was held, Bertil was already at NTU as its Provost and was hard at work on various issues that had been discussed at the Aptos meeting. Besides, after four months, he was already developing his own priorities and plans that needed to be implemented to improve the academic landscape at NTU.

This was the meeting where there was considerable bonding and agreement among the three of us on the development of strategic and tactical plans. Perhaps this was aided by having an unexpected dinner in an almost deserted and surrealistic neighbouring hotel while the music of Édith Piaf provided the background. After this, we could all say, individually, "Je ne regrette rien"!

It was also significant as it was during this meeting that Bertil received an SMS message inviting him to join the MOE Committee on the Expansion of the University System in Singapore (CEUS) that would lead, in the end, to the creation of the medical school. This was a crucial moment both for Bertil and for NTU. It was also at Rigi Kulm that another very important decision was made which was to initiate a Blue Ribbon Commission under Haresh's direction to review undergraduate education, something that had already been agreed upon as a key part of NTU's reform process.

Looking back, these first two Troika meetings were probably the most significant, as we faced the two key problems to be addressed in taking NTU forward — ensuring that our faculty were of top quality in research and teaching on one hand and, on the other hand, that our students were properly educated for the modern world with NTU providing them with the best opportunities and time of their lives.

What is most remarkable about these meetings and the close working partnership among the three Troika members was the level of frank, honest discussions and the commitment to follow through with the implementation of all decisions that we agreed upon. Each meeting, as a result, brought us closer to where the NTU academic world needed to be. By this date, many of the items discussed during the first two meetings were in place, albeit with much more nuanced evolution and improvements.

As Bertil would often remark, he was a "builder/contractor", building on what the architects (Troika members) had designed and planned. It was a transition from talking to doing.

One particular structure that was put in place from June 2007 was the Provosts and Deans Group (PDG) comprising Bertil, as Provost, the Senior Associate Provost (Er Meng Hwa) and the Deans of the four colleges (Arts, Humanities and Social Sciences: Lawrence Wong; Business: Hong Hai; Engineering: T. C. Pan; and Science: Lee Soo Ying). This not only provided a discussion forum but also implicated this important management level in the strategic directions emanating from the Troika and the Board of Trustees. By the time of the Rigi Kulm, the PDG had held a retreat at Bintan, Indonesia, at which the practical details of the faculty appointment, promotion and tenure system and the review of faculty following changes to the tenure system had been agreed upon unanimously by all the PDG participants. This represented a dramatic "sea change" to what had gone before. Naturally, the PDG's membership changed with time as people changed position. Other members were added including the new Associate Provost for Graduate Education & Special Projects Professor Lam Khin Yong and the Director of the National Institute of Education (NIE) Professor Lee Sing Kong. The PDG system worked well in creating a consensus approach, although there were a couple of exceptions when individuals unsuccessfully attempted to take their own independent lines.

The style and mode of the Troika meetings having been set, we continued, from the two meetings described above to the last meeting in Bali held in March 2011. By then, NTU had reached a level of excellence and global ranking that we aspired to but could not imagine when we first met in Aptos way back in early 2007.

Having met in Europe and North America, it was now time to return to Asia and so our third get-together was in Goa, not too far from Haresh's origins in Pune. This meeting was held at a time when Bertil was already working hard and implementing ideas and programmes that were discussed and agreed upon at the first two meetings. Challenges and hurdles faced were being overcome and the task of taking NTU towards its stated goals was well under way. Therefore, this meeting in Goa was to review our status, articulate new thrusts and accelerate our implementation strategies. By that time, we could sense the support of the Board of Trustees, that we already had, but also that from faculty and students was extremely encouraging. We could see and feel the "changes in the air" all over the NTU landscape.

The focus of the Goa meeting was to evaluate the then existing academic governance structure develop a more inclusive and robust governance as well as academic structure and develop plans and a timeline for their implementation. It was at this meeting that a new governance structure, based very much on that of Stanford University, was proposed and adopted. This was because of Haresh's Stanford experience that had convinced him that it was a sound model to follow. A similar structure for NTU was developed, discussed and agreed upon in considerable detail. This was later sent to the Board of Trustees for its approval, which it received. This academic governance structure made it possible for the President and the Provost to implement various thrusts in consultation with the faculty and other stakeholders. Now, the Troika felt that it had the tools and the means to improve the functioning of the university with a proper reporting structure plus checks and balances. Another important outcome from Goa was to decide on the new academic advisory structure and it was here that Haresh presented his plans for a system, modelled closely on that of Stanford.

However, despite all the progress that was being made, there was one "fly in the ointment" when the problem of the new Dean of the Business School and his unwillingness to conform to the implementation of the university's policies that had led to disputes with the Provost first surfaced in the Troika. However, even before one year of having the full President and Provost team in place, we were starting to see changes and NTU was slowly improving.

After Aptos, Rigi Kulm and Goa, it was back to Sweden for Bertil when we met in the old capital of Sweden, the delightful town of Sigtuna. By then, we were already familiar with each other's style, strengths and operational habits. It demonstrated how we had come together as a team focused on one thing — the reform of NTU and its drive towards the top. The three previous meetings had resulted in important decisions regarding NTU's academic governance structure, organisation chart, Appointment, Promotion and Tenure (APT) process and requirements and faculty hiring with strategic goals in mind.

The President and the Provost were already hard at work, implementing the decisions agreed upon in the previous three meetings and approved by the Board of Trustees. The engine of progress was really humming and a lot of positive energy and excitement among students, faculty and the community at large was visibly evident.

The main theme for discussions at Sigtuna was to first take stock of the progress of NTU towards the strategic goals and then to develop some new thrusts to strengthen and smoothen the processes. It was here that Bertil presented his vision of the disciplinary components and their interactions to promote interdisciplinarity through his so-called "planetarium" diagram. This was an attempt to show, diagrammatically, the structure of the university built around its core of engineering expertise (see page 129, Colour Plate 1, Figure 1). The Troika members were keen to promote inter- and multidisciplinary work based on the concept that all the NTU programmes had a synergistic and symbiotic relationship with each other with the core being Engineering, Science and Technology — this was the purpose of the diagram…

It was by now obvious that the momentum of growth and the march towards excellence was positive and on schedule. One of the issues that we had to keep in mind was in relation to a change of culture. It was much easier to develop policies, documents, reward structures, reorganisation charts and processes for granting appointments, promotions and tenure. However, it was much more difficult to change the culture of faculty, administration and academic leaders regarding what needed to be done to encourage the creation of a thriving, healthy and successful academic environment. The Sigtuna meeting convinced us that this change of culture would take time and would come about through role models. Hiring a few outstanding senior and many junior faculty from outside with the cultural affinity towards a passion for excellence and understanding the role of research, teaching and community involvement/participation would pay handsome dividends.

At that meeting, we decided to pay more attention to some of the tactical strategies through which "changes" could be introduced. These included a clear understanding of the role of President, Provost, Deans, Chairs and Heads of Departments and how to balance "top-down" versus "bottom-up". A reporting protocol was also established. A reward structure for faculty who were involved in research and who could solicit research funding through competitive proposal writing was established. We also decided that new and younger faculty members should be "shielded" from administrative duties and heavy teaching loads during the first few years until they had established their research programmes. We agreed to engage the Academic Council as well as the Academic Senate in soliciting their opinions and input to the President/Provost team. These actions were all part of our belief that to bring about cultural changes, more would have to be done through examples, role models and policies that rank and file of the university academic community could see and understand.

We accepted that a more structured engagement between the President/Provost and Deans was necessary. We also spent a lot of time discussing the importance of multi- and cross-disciplinary research as well as course offerings. We examined examples from great universities which had been successful in establishing multidisciplinary and interdisciplinary research centres. Bertil, with his expert knowledge of the Nobel system, presented statistics about the Nobel Prizes since 1985. This showed how multidisciplinary research teams had successfully produced Nobel laureates during this period. A strong case for a multidisciplinary Graduate School was agreed upon and we decided to press on with this particular initiative.

Another interesting topic, which we discussed at Sigtuna, was the management style. Historically, management in Asia, either in the private sector or in academic institutions, has been top-down. In many universities in the US, the academic management of bottom-up was the established practice. In Europe, it was somewhat a hybrid of the two. At NTU, until Guaning's presidency, the style was definitely top-down. Going forward at NTU, the question was: What was the efficacy of one or the other style? By understanding the arguments for top-down in the Asian context and bottom-up in the American context, it was obvious that neither would work with the cultural makeup of faculty at NTU. The best path to take was to solicit input from the wider academic community through vehicles such as the Academic Council, Senate and various fora of Deans and Chairs, filter those inputs with financial, academic and strategic priorities and implement the decisions as top-down. This style of academic management has been implemented since those early years and, to date, has served the growth of NTU well. It is best described, in Bertil's words, as "top-down but with big ears".

Finally, the Sigtuna meeting ended with a review of the significant achievements over the past year and a half since the Troika had been launched. It was generally agreed that the achievements were on target, but that we had to remain highly focused towards necessary changes and to make sure that as Troika members, we remained critical of our actions and that actions and results needed to be continuously monitored.

Then, it was back to Asia when we met at Wuxi（无锡）, an old yet modernising city in Jiangsu province close to Shanghai. This was two years after our first meeting and it was time to take stock of what had been achieved and identify what still needed to be done. It had also been almost two years since Bertil joined NTU. The Wuxi meeting discussions were mainly dominated by two items — the ways in which we should develop the overall university management structure plus a detailed report by Bertil, which articulated his two years of work at NTU, progress made, successes and concerns regarding future directions.

By the time of the Wuxi meeting, it was clear that the strategies we had put in place for implementation were clearly demonstrating that we were on the right track to achieve excellence. NTU was starting to rise in all the university ranking systems. The faculty, students and staff of the university, with the support of the Board of Trustees, were implementing the plans laid out by the President and the Provost which had been developed during the previous four meetings of the Troika. The faculty reviews (PT1 and PT2 as discussed in Chapter 14) had or were taking place and there was starting to be a new spirit among faculty. There were still some "pockets of resistance" to change in places as disparate as the business school, biological sciences and in communication and information (media), but these were being gradually overcome and faculty won around to acceptance.

The next meeting was held in November 2009 in Healdsburg in the wine country of California and was mainly devoted to reviewing the progress made at NTU since 2007 and to plan for the upcoming changes in the senior management of the university. Since Bertil's arrival and the first Aptos Troika meeting, three years had gone by. Issues such as the functioning of the Board and its close working relationship with the management of the university were discussed. It was observed that the progress was *good, but still needed improvements in terms of information flow and better social interaction with the Deans and Chairs. There was general satisfaction on how well the Board was working with the senior management. It was also clear that the processes implemented for Appointment, Promotion and Tenure (APT) were continuously improving our faculty in quality and functionality. However, it was felt that the change of culture to become a really research-intensive university with great teaching skills was not happening as rapidly as the processes that were being put in place. It was decided to give more attention to how such a cultural change could be brought about and instilled. Of course, new recruits were joining NTU without any previous "history" and so we recognised that the problem would eventually disappear over the medium term.*

Discussions were also centred on how to "codify" the gains made by NTU in terms of APT processes, the academic structure of the university and the functioning of the Senate and faculty renewal. It had been agreed that strategic plans were necessary to consolidate the changes and to constitute an instrument of change. Topics including Board involvement and support, academic leadership development and development of a supportive administration with a clear understanding of the role that it plays in enhancing the excellence of the academic environment were some of the major discussion topics at Healdsburg. At this meeting, Bertil introduced his ideas for the plan and we discussed this in some detail. The Troika's decision to advance the strategic plan was the most critical output from the meeting when it was recognised that one had to address both structural as well as cultural changes.

Universities are complex, thriving and living entities. To succeed and excel, the university must develop a strategic focus for support and growth of its faculty and its programmes. Developing a strategic plan to be initiated by Koh Boon Hwee and the NTU Board of Trustees was essential. After evaluating the strengths of our faculty, the interests of society to address important challenges and the availability of resources for research and teaching, the Troika decided to present to the Board five thrusts as part of strategic planning:

1. Sustainable Earth
2. New Media

3. Future Healthcare
4. New Silk Road
5. Innovation Asia

For each of these five thrusts, existing programmes and their leadership were identified. A plan for implementing university-wide, multidisciplinary programmes for these five thrusts was discussed and developed for further input and approval from faculty and the Board.

The final item for planning at this meeting was Haresh's wish to look at the future leadership makeup of the university. It was clear that the President, Provost and Chair of the Academic Affairs Committee would change within the next two to three years. There would be a new President, a new Provost and a new Chair of the Academic Affairs Committee of the Board, and the new personalities would need to decide on their own consultative structures and methods.

This topic occupied a substantial part of our discussions on the last day. It was decided that until such changes took place, the current Troika must keep its focus on innovations and implementation of strategic plans for excellence. The future Troika (if such a format were to be maintained by the future leadership) would need to develop its own plans and work with the chemistry, resources and support of the Board and MOE. It was felt that if the progress of the past few years had been both effective and impressive, then there would be no reason for the new team not to continue pursuing a road towards excellence laid out by the current team and to add their own strategic thoughts for growth of the university.

In June 2010, we met at one of Bertil's old "stomping grounds" in Strasbourg in Alsace, France. This enabled Bertil to show how coordination and collaboration in research had been a key to Europe's continuing research strength. In fact, Europe had needed to make a necessity out of the diversity within Europe and this had now become a source of strength.

We, the Troika, had been operating for three years as a coherent leadership team. We had come a long way and it was a time for reflection, to take stock and to plan how best to continue the momentum already developed. NTU, led by the Troika, had embarked on an unprecedented rate of progress in reform with a quantum leap in research intensity and with robust recruitment and promotion processes now firmly established.

We had instituted an intense scrutiny and review of our faculty, resulting in many hard decisions, but this had created the space needed for new senior and junior recruitments that were really beginning to pay off; against most expectations, we had gained two out of the five Research Centres of Excellence supported in Singapore, we now were competing against, and frequently out-competing, NUS in response to external grant calls; we had instituted new and productive collaborations with leading multinational technological companies; we were starting to attract more top students to our undergraduate programmes and this had resulted in a general raising of standards reflected in increasingly higher university rankings. It was agreed that the following five years would be critical in really embedding the long-term vision for the university as one of the top global universities.

Based on the above reflections and expectations, the whole meeting was devoted to self-analysis, peeking into the future and developing ideas and plans for the periods of 2011–2013 and beyond up to 2025. The gist was to always think big, tackle difficult issues first and always focus on taking the university to the next level of excellence. This seminal Troika meeting ended with a conviction that the university and its management were on the right track with the right vehicle and with the right navigators and drivers for continued improvement and the march towards excellence.

By the time of the meeting in Bali in March 2011, major changes had taken place. Bertil was becoming the new President with Professor Freddy Boey as the new Provost, although Guaning's term of office would not end until July of that year. However, this was to be the final Troika meeting in its original form where the three authors, as the Troika members, participated. The assumptions of the Troika in Strasbourg about the changes in senior management had not transpired as had been anticipated. Thus, it was thought appropriate to relook at what had been accomplished since the formation of the Troika and the strategic plans that were laid out in the first meeting in Aptos some four years earlier.

For this final meeting, we recapitulated our initial plans which we had formulated at the first Troika meeting in Aptos, February 2007. The aim was to arrive at a definitive analysis of where NTU now was relative to the plans that had been laid down then. We discussed and provided a plan to the new administration of what needed to be done to preserve the gains thus far achieved from 2003–2010 under Guaning's eight-year term as President. Thereafter, we concentrated on the plans from the new leadership team for the period up to 2015.

It was recognised that the work of the Troika was an ongoing project. As accomplishments were achieved, beyond 2015, new challenges and strategic goals would be developed by the incoming as well as future administrations. The path to excellence had been set and progress could be expected to continue at an accelerated pace to 2017 and beyond.

At Bali, we also focused on interdisciplinarity, a topic that we had started discussing in Strasbourg when consideration of the internal school structures had begun. All universities suffer from a "silo" mentality because everyone is educated on a disciplinary basis. Each of us came from different disciples — engineering in its two subdiscipline forms for Guaning and Haresh and biochemistry for Bertil. Everyone realises that it is at the interstices of disciplines that some of the most exciting and innovative discoveries take place or the place from which new disciplines and subdiscipline arise. Bertil, describing himself as a "simple biochemist", realises this more than most as biochemistry itself is a meld of two formal and distinct disciplines (the biosciences and chemistry). Now, within the life sciences generally, we see new disciplines arising such as bioinformatics. So, how were we to promote this more open mindset in NTU? We had started the process through new multidisciplinary research institutes, but was there something more fundamental preventing a new crosscutting approach? We focused our attention on the schools' structures. Within each school, we had divisions operating very much as small "empires" of their own. Having determined that this was the case, the next step was obvious, which was to abolish divisions and look at broader school structures. In keeping with our own mode of operating, having decided on this line, it was a case of putting it into operation. Here, we probably encountered the most opposition, but this was overcome and now, with our new structures in place, the recollection of what was past fades and the new reality is accepted.

We also felt that having completed these dramatic changes in the academic structure and ambiance of NTU, it was time to address the support and service components of the university that had not kept pace with the enormous and rapid changes which we had instituted. Therefore, the next stage was to look at and start a major reform of these services through an instrument, which eventually became known as "Administrative Excellence".

The Bali meeting was the termination of the original Troika concept. Bertil and his administration did continue that tradition for few more meetings, but they fall beyond the scope of this book.

Now, there is an accountability report to the Academic Council by the President, as a key part of the academic governance implemented by the Troika. Now, any young Assistant Professor has a right to speak and ask questions of the academic leadership.

During this later period from 2011 to 2017, NTU made further dramatic advances based on the structures and decisions of the Troika, eventually achieving the ranking of 11th in the world according to the QS World University Rankings, something that no one would have believed possible when the Troika first met in 2007.

In a retrospective look at the team created by Guaning in 2003 and reinforced by the arrival of Bertil in 2007, it is reasonable to question the role played by the Troika. The unique rate of growth of excellence and global recognition for NTU in a short span of nine years (between 2003 and 2011) was made possible by many timely and unique circumstances. By the time Bertil's administration took over from Guaning's administration, the pattern was set, cultural changes were afoot and the momentum for excellence was established. Bertil and his administration, from 2011 to 2018, accelerated NTU's brand with outstanding decisions on academic, research, physical facilities and administrative actions.

The Troika brought three most unlikely partners together to work with passion, ideas and single-mindedness. Guaning, a Chinese Singaporean educated in Canada and the United States and with a deep understanding of the sociocultural ethos of Singapore, started the ball rolling. He was joined by Haresh, an Indian with education in India and the United States, who brought with him an understanding of Asia and the drivers of excellence through his more than 35 years of association with Stanford University, one of the leading universities of the world. Finally, Bertil, a Swede (as he would say, "from the pine forest of Sweden") with his experience from the Nobel Prize Selection Committee, his knowledge and experience with ESF as the Chief Executive Officer (CEO) in Strasbourg and his unbounded passion as well as energy made up the third member of the group. Together, as members of the Troika, we created an environment of discovery, vision, risk-taking, and focus.

With the support and trust of the Board of Trustees and MOE, we aspired and succeeded to take NTU to a level that no one in Singapore (or even the three Troika members) believed possible. This is a wonderful example of synergistic effort. The sum of the three accomplished many times more than any single individual could have achieved or even postulated.

We sum up our achievements as follows: *By this time, we were several years down our chosen path and other changes were afoot. Nevertheless, the fundamental changes that had been wrought are very much the "children" of our Troika. To mix metaphors, we regarded ourselves as the "Three Musketeers" driving our vehicle, the "Troika", forward.*

Chapter 8

Academic Governance Evolution and Reform

At independence in 1965, Singapore had two universities: The government-funded University of Singapore (SU), teaching in English, and the privately funded Nanyang University (*Nantah*), teaching in Chinese. There was a complex set of political implications and cultural factors making the relationship between the universities and government quite complex.

With the PAP in power after independence, it was inevitable that Nanyang University had to be recognised as a significant part of the educational scene, especially since the Chinese community was the main support base of the party. The next move on the part of the government was to merge SU and *Nantah* into NUS, with the National University of Singapore Act in 1980 followed by the Nanyang Technological University Act of 1991 establishing NTU. Both universities had their own high-level Councils which were, formally, statutory boards of MOE, although with more autonomy than most statutory boards. There was a natural limitation as to how far either university could develop according to its own priorities and predilections. As with all statutory boards, the employees remained public servants subject to laws such as the Official Secrets Act as well as to periodic audits by the Auditor-General's Office. It was rare for a Board to act independently of the Ministry even though the Ministry tried not to micromanage the institution too much. Most of the time, the Council felt like a rubber stamp for decisions already taken by the President and the Ministry's Permanent Secretary.

Apart from private universities, and here one thinks, primarily, of the elite American universities (Ivy League and Stanford), the great bulk of the world's universities are funded from the public purse. However, there are some anomalies such as in the UK that has the strange position that although universities are essentially self-governing and classified as being in the private sector under Treasury rules, they are, nevertheless, substantially taxpayer funded. In Germany, university faculty are employed by the Länder (the regional governments) and are "civil servants". It is a similar case in France. So, almost everywhere, universities are seen as being part of the public realm, and however much one speaks of academic freedom, it is inevitably true, as the saying goes, that "he who pays the piper calls the tune". The same is equally the case in Singapore and other parts of Asia. However, as described below, the importance of autonomy was that it enabled the universities (even while remaining publicly funded) to chart their own course with less micromanagement by the Ministry.

University Autonomy in Singapore

In 1997, MOE set up an International Academic Advisory Panel "to advise on how NUS and NTU can be developed into world-class centres of excellence in research and scholarship".

Then, in 1998, it commissioned the US Massachusetts Institute of Technology (MIT) to carry out a strategic review of both NTU and NUS. The review team commented in its review report that "we see in NTU an outstanding engineering educational institution, focusing on *teaching*, with a strong '*hands-on*' emphasis, suitable to the *near term needs* of Singaporean industry. We see their *educational program as being rather narrowly technologically focused and their management being strongly top-down directed*...." "The undergraduate student body is drawn from the *top 25% of the Singaporean Grade I cohort*...." "We see an increasing awareness ... of the *importance of combining research with teaching*." Reading between the lines (the italic emphasis is ours), NTU was performing well in its initial role, assigned in 1982, as the Nanyang Technological Institute (NTI). But, at the turn of the millennium, it was time to change as Singapore moved to become a knowledge-based economy. The university faculty did not yet see the importance of the

Humboldtian ideal of combining teaching with research, and we were not competing for the best students of the university-going cohort. This is in contrast to its erstwhile rival NUS that took in the top 5% of the student cohort and had the advantage of being designated as the university to lead Singaporean research at the time when NTI was set up.

In April 2004, the Ministry set up a Steering Committee to Review University, Governance and Funding. The report recommending the Autonomous University framework was accepted in April 2005 and the corporatisation bills were passed by Parliament in February 2006. The importance of autonomy was that it enabled the universities (even though remaining publicly funded) to chart their own course so that peaks of excellence could emerge. It also allowed the universities to be better able to develop and compete in what was becoming an intensive global marketplace. The leadership of the universities (by this time there were three, with the Singapore Management University (SMU) joining NUS and NTU) were concerned about possible funding cuts. The then Permanent Secretary Lim Chuan Poh convinced them otherwise. In fact, funding was not cut but increased.

Autonomy was a significant development. For both NUS and NTU, this was an important time as both institutions had changed Presidents. At NUS, Shih Choon Fong had taken over in 2000 and for NTU, Guaning had taken over the presidency in 2003. Together with new Boards of Trustees to represent the government and public interest, Singapore's universities were able to design their own way forward. During the first few years of the new century, NUS developed rapidly from its already strong base into an internationally recognised global university, leaving NTU trailing in its wake. NTU had to focus on building three new schools and accommodating 6,300 more students.

The NTU Board

The NTU Board was made up of leading figures from Singaporean commerce, industry and society, as well as the Chairman of A*STAR. It has, over the years, included external high-level academics such as Haresh himself, Sir Keith O'Nions (former Director General of the UK Research Councils and former President and Rector of Imperial College London) and Professor Alexander (Sascha) Zehnder (former President of the

Board of ETH Zürich). New academic members included Sir Leszek Borysiewicz (former Chief Executive, UK Medical Research Council and former Vice-Chancellor, Cambridge University) and Professor Gene Block (Chancellor, University of California, Los Angeles). It is a multi-ethnic and multicultural body and includes NTU alumni, of whom Mr. Inderjit Singh (a successful entrepreneur and former Parliamentarian) has been a prominent member. It normally meets some five times per annum and breaks into committees to cover specific tasks including finance, remuneration, alumni and development, enterprise and audit and risk, and an Academic Affairs Committees. The Committee was chaired by an academic member of the Board and, for a long time from 2006 until 2016, this was Haresh. This committee is relatively uncommon, although it exists elsewhere, e.g. Technion (Israel Institute of Technology), within the top level of university governance. It approves new academic educational programmes, tenure recommendations and promotions to full professorships. The logic on having tenure approvals at the Board level is that tenure is a long-term commitment of employment and, therefore, is a substantial investment of public funds for which the Board is accountable to the government and, through it, to the Singapore taxpayers.

The President of the university is an *ex officio* member of the Board. The Chancellor (Ceremonial Head) of the university is the President of the Republic of Singapore, who has the same role with NUS, assisted by Pro-Chancellors from senior figures in Singapore society.

The NTU Board of Trustees Chairman

From its outset, the Board has been led by Koh Boon Hwee, who also chaired the NTU Council before autonomy. He is a very proactive, energetic and supportive chairman who brings his vast experience of industry and management to the Board. He is an engineer (alumnus of Imperial College London and Harvard Business School), became the Managing Director of Hewlett Packard Singapore and was former Chairman of Singapore Telecom, Singapore Airlines and DBS Bank, as well as being a member of the Board of Temasek Holdings. He also runs a private equity fund, Credence Partners. Not only that, but Koh Boon Hwee has shown his personal commitment to the university by way of the Koh Boon Hwee Scholars Awards. In terms of its official description, the awards are to "nurture, enhance and recognise teaching excellence and the impact that great teachers have on their students". NTU initiated the University Scholars Award with the graduating class of 2007. In 2010, the University Scholars Award was renamed the Koh Boon Hwee Scholars Award in recognition of Koh Boon Hwee's personal gift of S$2.5 million to the university. Together with the Singapore government's dollar-for-dollar matching, the gift established a US$5 million endowment fund to support the award. This award gives recognition to the influence of inspirational teaching, and the enduring bonds that are forged between teachers and students. It aims to establish long-lasting and fulfilling relationships between the university, the students and their teachers.

The Board has developed a proactive ("hands-on") role in the governance of NTU and this certainly keeps the President, Provost and senior staff on their toes! Its success is a reflection not only of its proactivity but the high ambition that it has and which it shares with the university leadership. Sir Keith O'Nions remarked that the Board was positive and engaged and contrasted with similar university boards elsewhere which took a more formal position. This is very much because of Koh Boon Hwee's committed and engaged chairmanship of the Board. His technological background, coupled with his vast experience in business and society, has been an important factor. This experience has led him to be a keen advocate for pushing the envelope of the increased use of information technology (IT) in NTU education and in administration. The 2010 quality assurance exercise commended the Board of Trustees for its active engagement in the governance of the university including in strategic planning where its ongoing support was seen to be a key factor for success.

Quality Assurance Framework for Universities (QAFU)

When initiating autonomy, the government wanted to be assured that the new structure was not only delivering what was envisaged for the benefit of Singapore but that the new Boards of Trustees and the university leaderships were developing strategic visions and plans for their implementation.

One never gets something for nothing in this world and the price of autonomy is accountability, which is the price most individuals and organisations would willingly pay in order to chart their own course into the future. Accountability is essential, especially when public taxpayers' money is involved.

Therefore, MOE, as part of the new autonomous system, instituted a quinquennial review system made up of eminent academic leaders from around the world meeting together with leading high-level personalities from the public and private sector in Singapore to assess a university's actions and progress and to make recommendations for improvements and future actions. This is QAFU — the Quality Assurance Framework for the Universities. To quote from the official description in the introduction to the initial QAFU 2005 report, this is "a holistic framework and development tool for institutional self-learning and quality enhancement in the universities as well as a vehicle to ensure institutional accountability in return for greater operational autonomy devolved to the universities". Cut away the jargon and it is what it sets out to be — an accountability mechanism that embraced visionary and strategic views and set a new baseline for the university. This is probably unique in its concept, for unlike, for example, the British Research Excellence Framework for universities, it is concerned with the holistic development of the university including both education and research and is not being driven solely by impact measures and key performance indicators. With its systematic approach, it is a necessary mechanism to deliver transparency and accountability to elected politicians and through them to the public at large.

QAFU operates on a five-year cycle and so, over the period covered by this book, NTU has experienced three such reviews starting in 2005 when NTU was still in the highly centralised Statutory Board System before autonomy. The later reviews in 2010 and in 2015 took place with autonomy firmly in place.

The exercise actually starts off some two years prior to the review as each university prepares a comprehensive self-assessment document, which is discussed and approved by the Board of Trustees. This is then forwarded to MOE and forms the basic paperwork for the External Review Panel (ERP). MOE convenes the Panel and arranges site visits to the university over a whole week. The ERP is made up of very senior figures from worldwide academia and the private sector. It truly is a review of university leadership by its peers. During its week of site visits, Panel members start by meeting the university leadership and then meet with faculty, students and administrative staff, and may visit laboratories or sit in on teaching. The Panel also meets with the Chairman of the Board of Trustees and other members so that it is receiving firsthand input from all levels. At the end of the visit, and after a private session, the Panel gives an oral report to the university leadership comprising the President, Provost and the Chairman of the Board of Trustees. This is followed, a little later, by a written report of the Panel on which the university comments, primarily to check matters of fact. After this, MOE makes its own assessment for the university to comment on and develop its responses and implementation. Then, this will be reviewed as part of the following cycle of self-assessment and further QAFU review.

One only has to look at some of the names of those who have been on these panels to realise how "weighty" they are. They include Professor Gerhard Casper, former President of Stanford University; the late Professor Gareth Roberts, Master of Wolfson College, Oxford University; Lord Ron Oxburgh, former Rector of Imperial College London and Chairman, Shell UK; Professor Henrik Toft Jensen, former Rector of Roskilde University, Denmark; Professor Ralph Eichler, former President of ETH Zürich, Switzerland; Professor Sir Steve Smith, Vice-Chancellor of Exeter University, UK; Sir John O'Reilly, former Director General of Knowledge and Innovation in the UK government and former Vice-Chancellor of Cranfield University, UK; and Professor Gene Block, Chancellor of the University of California, Los Angeles. This is an impressive roll call of the "great and the good" of international academia. They have been accompanied by local industrial leaders and heads of national agencies such as the Chief Executive Officer (CEO) of Singapore Press Holdings, the Chairman of the National Heritage Board, the CEO of Singapore Power and similar leading figures from the private sector. The first and second reviews were led by Ms. Jennifer Lee Gek Choo, from the Agency of Integrative Care, advocate for women, family and the elderly, and a member of the Singaporean Women's "Hall of Fame". That of 2015 was chaired by David Wong Cheong Fook, who also chairs the Board of Governors of Republic Polytechnic, and who has vast experience in industry and business. The female member of this QAFU was Dr. Josephine Kwa, Chair of Raffles Marina Holdings. The QAFU membership that this represents is a particular Singaporean phenomenon, a willingness to bring in outsiders to advise and help. This openness to external advice is an important factor in Singapore's overall success. In this regard, QAFU sets the standard of international best practice.

The rapid progress we recount in this book can be followed by the recommendations of the QAFU-ERP over this 10-year period. Of course, when the first QAFU review took place in 2005 with preparations starting in 2003, NTU had only just embarked on its remarkable journey and Guaning was on his own, surrounded by the "legacy" modus operandi, an ultra-centralised system with 28 direct reports to the President. Short of being in possession of a magic wand, he was in no position to change overnight to international best practice. Haresh offered to help after the 2005 QAFU exercise. Bertil, the last piece of the puzzle, joined in 2007. By 2009, with two years of hard work, the Troika had the thing well in hand, and by 2014, the abundant harvest of the reforms was there for all to see.

What Did the QAFU-ERP Have to Say in Its Recommendations?

The first review was quite severe in its critique of NTU, but recognised that the coming of autonomy provided just the right opportunity to chart a new course for the university. The review set out some urgent actions with high-priority recommendations. In this high-priority category, the QAFU-ERP asked NTU to urgently review and revise its vision and mission statement, to analyse where it saw itself in the academic world and to differentiate itself from others with a clear strategy, roadmap, targets and milestones. Faced with a planned increase in student numbers, the ERP was worried as to how NTU would cope without compromising quality.

One key and urgent recommendation, and one which Guaning and Haresh had already anticipated, was the appointment of a Provost.

Of course, a little more than one year later, this led to Bertil's appointment, as recounted in Bertil's tale and the start of the Troika partnership.

This review also pointed the way strongly towards more rigorous performance appraisals and it especially urged for the reform of the Promotion and Tenure (PT) system for faculty. It needed to be "rigorous, transparent and consistent". Elsewhere, we show how the system, reformed by Guaning and Haresh, executed by Bertil and the Deans, became a key moment in NTU's rapid advance. It also saw the restructuring of the schools as another key issue along with the promotion of interdisciplinarity and new systems of quality control through Visiting Committees of external experts. Along with these key recommendations was a phalanx of other recommendations covering better space planning and the establishment of an academic Senate structure. Unless the university was able to respond rapidly to the recommendations, QAFU-ERP expected that NTU would fall further behind its peers and the country's ambitions when NTU was created. It is worth remembering that NTU was not starting from scratch. Obviously, not all was wrong, as Bertil recounts when describing his visit to NTU from Linköping at the turn of the century; it had attracted good people from outside Singapore. The problem was that it had not built on its strengths and developed accordingly. The 2005 QAFU was also a significant learning experience for the Board. Koh Boon Hwee, who had been heavily involved in the old system, has always emphasised the importance of autonomy for the university and worked within the QAFU accountability procedures that were set in place.

There was a confluence of views between what QAFU was saying and the ideas of Guaning and Haresh. What was crystal clear was the desire of all concerned to see NTU progress. Support for reform at this high level, and endorsed by MOE, added weight to the idea that things had to change.

After Another Five Years, What Had the Next QAFU-ERP in 2010 Reported?

It saw that NTU had reacted with determination to all that had been recommended in 2005 and was now entering a new and critical phase as reforms were being consolidated and the baton of the presidency was being passed from Guaning to Bertil with Haresh still a major contributor to the university's development. Indeed, much had changed and Lord Ron Oxburgh, one of that year's QAFU-ERP members, said that he had not seen such a rapid advance in a university in his long experience. He also commented that this was a case of the heads of the troops actually leading and not following on behind!

This time, the ERP emphasis was less on major structural changes and strategic recommendations. Rather, in light of the huge progress that it recognised had been made in research and faculty assessment, APT, the review focused on teaching as the top priority with the need to develop methods for teacher assessment — not the easiest of tasks! It was considered that perhaps the pendulum had swung a little too much towards research. While the measures that had been introduced were correct, there was evidence that these had been overinterpreted within the schools to the detriment of high-quality teaching and the pendulum needed to be positioned with research and teaching being given equal weight. Linking this to the whole NTU brand was felt to be important. The review also turned its attention to the other part of the university — its administration — with the necessity of ensuring that it was both efficient and less bureaucratic with a real service orientation. Finally, the review looked at e-learning, teachers' language proficiency and the need for increased and transparent internal communication. Quite a big agenda, but not as fundamental as that of five years earlier.

In late 2007/2008, Guaning asked Haresh to chair a Blue Ribbon Commission on Undergraduate Education to conduct a "bottom-up review of NTU's undergraduate programmes". This was one of the 10 projects formulated at the first Troika meeting in Aptos, but deferred until the PT exercises were well under way. The outcome was the determination to radically change the programmes and reduce the excessive number of academic units required for graduation in favour of broader and more rounded education with the use of the latest in technology-enabled pedagogy. The full story of this and the other reforms is described in Chapter 13 on reforming education.

With the passing of yet another five years and NTU's spectacular advance in rankings, reputation, competitive research income, teaching and many other aspects of university life, how would this be regarded by the 2015 QAFU-ERP?

This time, there were no high-priority recommendations requiring urgent attention. Rather, the review was very impressed with all that had been achieved over the previous five years and found a pride and ownership of these achievements within the organisation. Recommendations addressed issues such as the increasing need for risk management, something which the whole global academic community has recognised; strengthening internal audit; increasing faculty engagement through the Academic Council and Senate; and other similar concerns such as improvements in research support, the use of equipment and a better calculation of overheads. Indeed, the QAFU-ERP was especially concerned about reputational risk, given NTU's rapid rise and worldwide visibility. This chimed in with our own observations and actions in developing good research practice, research integrity and ethics across the university. These are all necessary improvements, but at a different and more detailed level than those from early reviews and recommendations.

While QAFU has looked at the university as a whole, it was also necessary to dig deeper and review the different levels of the organisation. Therefore, NTU instituted mini QAFUs addressing matters at the level of the colleges. These Visiting Group reviews were constructive and positive, but were not at the intensity originally envisaged. For the future, a more intensive college-level review will be the way to go. We have already mentioned the Blue Ribbon Commission Review of Undergraduate Education after which we created another high-level review, led by Sascha Zehnder, using external expertise to look at all our graduate education programmes. Of course, the development of the reforms and the creation of strategic plans and our success have overtaken and covered much of the ground that needed to be examined.

Research Expansion

The third and last baseline from which we started the NTU story was what happened at the national level. In the chapter on history, one of the key dates is 2005 as this was when the fourth and most significant five-year plan for research was announced. This saw the expansion of the national research budget by just under two and half times to S$13.6 billion. While a considerable part of the increase was allocated to sustain and increase the activities of A*STAR, a large portion was devoted to university research, articulated by the creation of a new funding agency — the NRF. This was very much due to the influence of Dr. Tony Tan and his understanding that the country needed not only a thriving national research performing institution but also highly competitive research-intensive universities. The creation of NRF, which Dr. Tan chaired and which was located within the Prime Minister's Office, was the vehicle for this development. As recounted in Bertil's tale, he became a member of the NRF's first Scientific Advisory Board.

Two major initiatives were announced. The first was to establish Research Centres of Excellence (RCEs), co-funded with MOE, with substantial funding of S$150 million over 10 years. Elsewhere, we record that NTU was not properly prepared for the first competitive call in 2006 and it even failed to make the shortlist. However, in subsequent calls, NTU was to secure two of the five RCEs that were supported, in which it was able to initiate research in brand new areas both for NTU and for Singapore (earth sciences and biofilms).

Top International Institutions

The second major NRF initiative was the Campus for Research Excellence and Technological Enterprise (CREATE) programme. This was a somewhat unusual programme in that it aimed to recruit not just people but institutions that would work with the local universities, again in areas seen as significant for the long-term health of the Singaporean economy. In Chapter 16, the links between CREATE and NTU are discussed in more detail.

In summary, one can conclude that this *annus mirabilis* of 2005 created a new baseline. NTU had a new President, it had clear guidance as to what needed to be changed, it had a proactive Board of Trustees led by a visionary Chairman and it had the autonomy to change direction, all coupled with a new and huge investment in the university sector by the government. It was all set to go meet new challenges!

Chapter 9

Developing the Strategic Plan

As with many of the reforms that have taken place over the past 10 years or more, these can be traced to recommendations found in the 2005 QAFU report. In this instance, the review commented on the need for Nanyang Technological University (NTU) to develop a strategy by which the university community could use as a template or sounding board for new initiatives.

Nevertheless, even before then, Guaning, in anticipating autonomy and the Board of Trustees, had established a Board of Advisors as one of his first major decisions. By the end of 2005, the preparation to transform NUS and NTU into autonomous universities was reaching a climax as the legal, accounting and administrative frameworks were being put in place. Guaning was particularly concerned with the composition of the new Board of Trustees. If nothing was done, he considered that the existing Council would simply roll forward as the new Board of Trustees. However, there was a drastic difference between these two bodies. The Council was more like a guardian and monitor, whereas the Board of Trustees had total responsibility. By then, Guaning had lined up potential candidates to enter the Board of Trustees. Haresh would be the key academic resource, then there were two *Nantah* alumni lined up — prominent venture capitalist Tan Lip-Bu, Managing Partners, Walden Ventures, and the equally prominent high-technology corporate leader Lien Siaou-Sze, Senior Vice President Hewlett-Packard, responsible for the Asia-Pacific. A fourth member was Kwek Leng Joo, Managing Director of City Developments, a leading property developer and President of the Singapore Chinese

Chamber of Commerce and Industry. He had his finger on the pulse of the more traditional Chinese business community from whom NTU needed to derive external support including fundraising. The Council agreed to this creation of a Board of Advisors that set the scene for the Board of Trustees when it arrived. In a sense, this was the first attempt at strategising that was followed, in turn, by the Troika and the development of rolling five-year strategic plans.

By 2005, Guaning had a makeshift team in NTU fighting on many fronts against established practice. Adapting his experience at DSO and DSTA to build alignment and common cause, he used the same consultants as he had used before with "Culture Change" workshops. But he soon discovered the futility of such an exercise. There was very little alignment of thinking among even the academic leaders, and a tremendous gulf between the administrators and academics. In the Ministry of Defence, there was at least a common cause to safeguard the security of the nation. The NTU at that time seemed to have only departmental interests, apart from taking orders from above. It had become rather deeply embedded within a disciplinary "silo-mentality" that, subsequently, became very difficult to eradicate.

As long as NTU remained a part of MOE, it had to follow all the government rules and regulations. For specialised equipment, materials and chemicals, this could result in up to a year in lost time. Therefore, once autonomy was enacted and it was clear that there would be no diminution of budgets, everyone was looking forward to the corporatisation of NTU for autonomy and flexibility. In return, there were more onerous reporting requirements to MOE, the most important being the QAFU evaluation by an External Review Panel issued in the form of a Validation Report.

As referred to elsewhere, MOE had created an International Academic Advisory Panel (IAAP) to advise on the development of NUS and NTU into world-class institutions. By the time of its fourth meeting, a number of proposals had been formulated and accepted, and Guaning was faced with the challenge of establishing three new schools while putting up papers seeking the budget required to get the three schools going. For this fourth meeting, in 2003, the key paper discussed was entitled "Remaking Singapore — The Role of the University Sector". An overall objective was to raise the cohort participation rate in public universities from 21% to

25%. A multi-campus structure was proposed and endorsed for NUS to develop a second medical school (now the Duke–NUS collaboration and a graduate school for high-level research). NTU was to absorb the major part of the increased cohort by increasing the undergraduate enrolment by 6,300 students. NTU was to broaden its offerings by building three new schools in humanities and social sciences, physical sciences and design and media. The meeting endorsed the broad directions. Thus, the marching order was given to NTU and Guaning had a clear direction with delivery for the next few years. It was also an opportunity for the university to become more comprehensive.

The university apex structure at the time comprised three Deputy Presidents assisting the President in specific areas. Lim Mong King had the role of getting the projects done; Er Meng Hwa assisted in the delivery of curriculum reforms under the banner of the "New Undergraduate Experience" — an attempt at a holistic development incorporating the experience of communal living on campus, opportunities to study abroad as exchange students and flexibility to take general electives; and Cheong Hee Kiat assisted in infrastructure development although this was later devolved to Lim Mong King when Cheong left the university.

For the School of Humanities and Social Sciences, there were two ready-made departments that enabled the school to start up in the first semester of academic year 2003–2004. These was the Chinese division, tapping resources from the Centre for Chinese Language and Literature, and the Economics Division, transferred from the Nanyang Business School. This move was greeted with enthusiasm by the economists, as economics was not considered a core discipline for the business school. Guaning also recruited Tan Kong Yam, Chief Economist for the World Bank in China. His in-depth knowledge of China was second to none as he took the time and effort to visit every province and reached deep into the countryside.

The School of Physical and Mathematical Sciences, led by Lee Soo Ying whom Guaning recruited from NUS, recruited many new faculty, in particular eight faculty members from NUS which earned NTU a complaint from the then President of NUS, Shih Choon Fong. Building up chemistry was the result of the realisation by A*STAR that in its haste to invest in life sciences, it had neglected to invest in chemistry. California Institute of Technology (Caltech) President David Baltimore sent a team at A*STAR's request to review NUS and NTU. The Caltech team's recommendation was to start chemistry afresh at NTU as there was no past baggage to deal with. Chemistry has since proved to be one of the "star" attainments in research by NTU, across the university, in addition to this new school.

For the School of Art, Design and Media, a very new venture, NTU found it difficult to recruit a senior figure and eventually recruited Isaac Kerlow, a Vice President at Walt Disney. While he was highly accomplished, his style of management gave rise to problems later on.

Meanwhile, a budget was allocated for interim facilities for the schools to start operations while the permanent facilities were being built. The first building to be completed was the iconic School of Art, Design and Media, reflecting the valley and surrounding hills in which it sits, designed by the Singaporean architect, Timothy Seow. The second of the new school buildings to be completed was the School of Physical and Mathematical Sciences inspired by the design of the then new Chemistry building at Oxford University. The building for the School of Humanities and Social Sciences followed later on a sensitive site located next to the iconic Chinese Heritage Centre building.

Guaning inherited a generous legacy from the first President, Cham Tao Soon, upon which he could build. This legacy was the excellent infrastructure and solid finances. The budget was sufficient to build two important buildings: the Research Technoplaza and the Nanyang Executive Centre, its own campus hotel and high-level training centre, and there was still enough left to continue "Phase 3B" of campus development that was eventually to provide for a considerable expansion of residential space for students.

What could be surmised as regards the government's plans for NTU from the fourth IAAP meeting in 2003? Typically, the direction was shrouded in secrecy. There was little indication, and certainly no pronouncements as regards the role NTU was expected to play in higher education. A little bit of detective work gave us an inkling that NTU could have intended to fill a lower level of technology development close to industry and aimed at tapping, substantially, the polytechnic students pursuing a degree. But this was never stated formally. Much later, the intervention of the Troika ensured NTU developed to its full potential as the equivalent of NUS but with different strengths.

The 2003 plan for expansion of cohort participation was entitled "Restructuring the University Sector — More Opportunities, Better Quality".

The cohort participation rate was to be raised from 21% to 25%. NTU was to take most of the load. Students previously unable to access a subsidised university education could now do so. The 4% previously filtered out would naturally include a considerable proportion coming from the polytechnics. NTU was tasked to take most of them. At the same time, NUS was to set up a research-focused Buona Vista/Kent Ridge campus. It was clear that the differentiation between NUS and NTU, especially in research, was expected to continue, even though the second Dainton Report had suggested vigorous competition between two research-intensive universities, NUS and NTU.

Guaning was convinced, perhaps due to the subconscious influence from Stanford, that entrepreneurship and commercialisation constituted a natural part of a leading research-intensive university, and a university not engaged in leading-edge research will not provide sufficient numbers of leaders in technology management that were desperately needed in Singapore. His vision and strategy were clear from his inaugural address of March 2003.

Guaning was also convinced that the nation was better served if NUS and NTU engaged in friendly competition, both being research-intensive universities. One can quote so many examples around the world: Oxford and Cambridge, Harvard and Massachusetts Institute of Technology (MIT), Berkeley and Stanford, Imperial and University Colleges, London. This did not mean that NTU had to be the mirror image of NUS but equal in stature with different strategies and emphases.

From the outset, the Troika had to react to the external demands on NTU from the IAAP, from the 2005 QAFU report as well as from the expectations of the government and the public. Thus, in many respects, the Troika's agenda was already fixed. Initially, of course, the Troika had to address major issues of immediate concern such as how to develop a rigorous, transparent and fair Appointment, Promotion and Tenure (APT) scheme. Another major issue was to take steps to recruit senior research talents to "jump start" the move into a research-intensive mode as well as to compete for the new funding that was becoming available, especially with the creation of the NRF.

The First Strategic Plan (2010–2015)

All the issues, although requiring urgent action, had, in the long run, to fit into a coherent strategy which could be used to take the university to even higher levels. The demand for a strategy was agreed by Koh Boon Hwee and the Board, and its planning was started by Guaning in 2008, looking ahead towards the quinquennium 2010–2015. There were a number of iterations and substantial changes demanded by the Board of Trustees that had not been convinced by our initial version. Bertil was asked to substantially revise the approach and he prepared a draft that was discussed at the Healdsburg Troika meeting, after which the plan was accepted and the template for future activity was provided, as discussed elsewhere.

As described in the chapter about the Troika and its activities, the initial drive was discussed at its meetings and then developed within the higher echelons of the university. Obviously, a strategy has to address all aspects of the university's evolution and by the time the first strategic plan was formally adopted, NTU was already well on the path of reform. In particular, the review of undergraduate education was well underway and the APT process had completed its initial major activities and was settling into a steady state. The plan envisaged such developments continuing and accelerating.

As this was the first strategic plan that NTU had developed, the Board of Trustees had instructed the management that once the strategic plan had been accepted, then an implementation plan would be needed in order to start follow-up actions.

The process for developing the strategy was participative and iterative involving the university community including faculty, the Academic Council and the Senate, university management and the Board of Trustees. Although seemingly comprehensive in coverage, the consultation did not necessarily advance planning, probably because this was the first attempt at strategic planning and an added burden on faculty. As for the implementation, it was also the culmination of a detailed and intense process of internal deliberation over the preceding five months.

As there were no existing governance structures for the Five Peaks, President and Provost set up dedicated Implementation Committees to develop the detailed plans for the Five Peaks, with committee members drawn from the expertise within the Five Peak domains across the colleges and university research institutes.

The overall plan was built on the extensive changes, which had been accomplished over the previous few years. NTU now had to consolidate its gains and elevate its education and research fundamentals to an even higher plane. It was on this upward shift of the underlying landscape that the concept of the Peaks of Excellence for research would emerge, some based on existing excellence and others which would require deliberate nurturing. The Peaks of Excellence were envisaged as being the drivers to lead the charge in NTU's drive towards global excellence and recognition. They, together with education, the overall research effort, building on the basis of improved governance and a responsive and efficient administration, would lead the way towards global leadership. This is illustrated in Figure 2 designed by Jesvin Yeo from the School of Art, Design and Media, in Colour Plate 1 (see page 129).

The "Peaks of Excellence" Concept

The Five Peaks identified were Sustainable Earth, Future Healthcare, New Media, New Silk Road and Innovation Asia.

Sustainable Earth was chosen as it reflected a major global preoccupation with water and energy resources and natural catastrophes (driven by Haresh who specialised in this) with a rising demand for sustainable environmental solutions, especially with rapid urbanisation occurring worldwide. Added to this was the fact that it brought together many key activities within NTU. The university had already gained a research centre of excellence in the Earth Observatory of Singapore (EoS under Kerry Sieh) and was embarking on a second: the Singapore Centre for Environmental Life Sciences and Engineering (SCELSE led by Staffan Kjelleberg). NTU had taken a leading position in water technologies through the Nanyang Environment and Water Research Institute (NEWRI under the direction of Ng Wun Jern). In 2008, NTU had brought together all its energy-related research into the Energy Research Institute at NTU (ERIAN led by Subodh Mhaisalkar). Thus, not only had NTU gained considerable external research funding in the sustainability area but also by bringing these major initiatives and other related activities together under the Sustainable Peak "umbrella", there was huge potential for major new activities and coordination that would put NTU into a forefront position in the world. Thus, Sustainable Earth became the largest and most prominent of the Five Peaks of Excellence.

There was also major potential in *Future Healthcare*, with the need for affordable healthcare accentuated by an increasing age profile in many parts of the world, not least in Singapore. The prospect of achieving a new Medical School and the bringing together of research relevant to healthcare provided the motivation for this Peak.

Interactive and digital media innovations (*New Media*) had a continuing ability to radically transform human lives. Here, NTU occupied a strong position both through the relatively newly created School of Art, Design and Media and also through the recruitment, in 2007, of new senior people to NTU by Bertil to form the core of a new Institute for Media Innovation (IMI led by Nadia Thalmann).

At Guaning's initiative, the *New Silk Road* (basically the enhancement of NTU's activities and collaborations in China) theme's great promise lay in the growing flow of knowledge and ideas between Asia and the West, to which Singapore and NTU are intimately connected. This was supported by a new NTU office in China (an expensive initiative at the time).

Innovation Asia, based upon education and research, held the key to sustained productivity and economic growth. Innovation Asia represented more of a supporting activity ("Thrust") than a "Peak" but was nevertheless important to fulfil NTU's ambitions in this area and also reflected the government's preoccupation (in common with many administrations worldwide) to get more new research ideas into the marketplace.

Therefore, in reality, the strategy was made up, *de facto*, of three research Peaks with the other activities being more in the nature of supporting Thrusts.

The Five Peaks had direct national and global relevance and those of sustainability, healthcare and media were the same identified priorities within NRF's priority areas. Embracing all corners of the "Knowledge Triangle" representing the dynamic interactions between education, research and innovation, the Peaks held immense potential not just for research but also for education and innovation. Indeed, NTU was well positioned in these five areas and was deemed a world leader in the Sustainable Earth domain. This Peak was led by Alexander (Sasha)

Zehnder (former President of the ETH Board), one of the acknowledged world experts in water and soil science and a Board of Trustees member. Broad, inclusive and inter-disciplinary, the Five Peaks drew on the strengths of the university and built upon past and existing work of the colleges, schools and research centres. The Peaks provided useful platforms for interdisciplinary development and focal points for collaboration within the university. Interdisciplinary collaboration that has the potential to create new knowledge was integral to the development of the Five Peaks. Increasingly, scientific and technological breakthroughs reside in such interdisciplinary domains melded from traditional disciplines. Thus, the Five Peaks were designed to leverage on the multidisciplinary range of NTU and its core strengths in engineering. Interestingly, the Peak on Future Healthcare was conceived as an activity very much based on the new Medical School, which at that time was still only in its planning phase. However, the interface between engineering and medicine was seen as one of the most productive and promising areas with regards to a Future Healthcare Peak and it recognised and built upon NTU's strong engineering research base. The plan envisaged the coming together of the many small activities in engineering relating to healthcare to form the Nanyang Institute of Technology in Health and Medicine (NITHM), now the NTU Institute for Health Technologies (HealthTech NTU). The institute's role was to synergise research activities within the various colleges and play a leading role in multidisciplinary medical-related research and development activities as well as in education. A key focus of the institute was and is in biomedical devices and materials, areas of fundamental significance for Singapore's economy as identified by the National Economic Strategies Committee. The institute planned to collaborate with industrial partners and establish formal ties with renowned universities, hospitals and research institutes. Indeed, the institute had a tripartite mission of research, education and innovation.

As part of this push to both focus on research efforts and stimulate interdisciplinarity, the plan envisaged the establishment of a university-wide Interdisciplinary Graduate School with an initial thematic focus on three Peaks of Sustainable Earth, Future Healthcare and New Media. Interdisciplinary content was to be strengthened in undergraduate programmes, in line with the recommendations of the Blue Ribbon Commission. At the governance level, a matrix management structure was developed with colleges and schools as one dimension and the Five Peaks (with their constituent research institutes, centres and thematic graduate schools) as the other. Such a structure created porosity and pathways for cross-disciplinary collaboration and provided support pillars for enhanced stability in a complex, multidisciplinary academic environment. Within the matrix structure, a Governance Coordinating Committee, with a high-level Chair, was established for each of the Five Peaks to drive cohesion among the initiatives within each Peak. A key responsibility of the Committees was set as the provision of a detailed annual operational plan to secure the implementation of each Peak and to monitor its execution.

To take forward the plan's implementation, a Competitive Interdisciplinary Initiative Fund was created to support interdisciplinarity and the development of the Five Peaks. As the delivery of the Five Peaks was heavily reliant on talent, an additional measure to boost the recruitment of world-renowned academics to each Peak was introduced, besides employment by schools and research institutes via the normal recruitment route. This High Level Recruitment Fund (evolved from its "Big Elephant Fund" — see Chapter 14 on elephants and gazelles) was designed as a stimulus, funded centrally, to incentivise and support the recruitment of at least two such academics for each Peak. While prioritising resources to the Five Peaks, the university continued to develop the diverse range of activities in the NTU academic base as well as nurture emerging fields beyond the Five Peaks. At the same time, bottom-up "blue sky" research was encouraged to coexist with the more strategic and mission-orientated initiatives.

Elsewhere, we describe how NTU reformed its undergraduate educational programmes to form NTU Education and the plan laid down the framework for this development. It also foresaw the creation of the Renaissance Engineering Programme as a key contribution both to engineering education and to meet Singapore's needs for top talent to enter the engineering profession as leaders.

The plan envisaged a new push in innovation developments and, for the first time, addressed the need to develop academic leadership and to transform administration through an Administrative Excellence Initiative. Administration had seen itself very much in the "driving seat" in the university and it was not providing the right level of support to the *raison d'être* of the university, namely education and research.

Finally, the implementation of the plan was forecast to require an investment of S$1.3 billion, much of which was already in place, as approved by the Board of Trustees, from efficiency savings and by seeking external funding through grant agencies and elsewhere.

The Second Strategic Plan (2015–2020)

The first plan took NTU up to 2015, by which time Bertil was well into his term as President, after which a second strategy plan was required to guide NTU up to the end of the decade. This was at the time when the Singapore government itself was developing a strategic vision for the development of the nation. While NTU developed its second plan based on its needs and the progress already achieved, we were able to map the new priorities of the second plan onto the emerging national plan. Some related directly to such priorities while others spanned several of the societal needs envisaged by the government. This gave added confidence to the senior leadership of the university and to the Board of Trustees that the university was indeed developing along the right lines, achieving excellence in what it did and was being recognised as a new academic powerhouse.

In 2013, the process started to develop the second strategic plan for the university. While this was, in some ways, an easier task given that NTU had one plan "under its belt", this was not just a matter of rolling the 2015 plan forward. It had to be self-sustaining, although obviously taking into account what had gone before, especially the success of declaring peaks of excellence to drive interdisciplinary research forward. A very extensive process of consultation at all levels with repeated iteration laid the foundations of the strategy with the Board of Trustees consulted, finally approving this blueprint to take NTU forward.

The introduction to the NTU 2020 plan enumerated the progress that had been made over the previous five or so years. Of particular note were the changes that had been made in administrative support plus the new investment in the physical infrastructure of the campus. The introduction goes on to say, "Governance and administration have evolved to support developments in the academic sphere. Under administrative excellence, the administrative structure has been simplified, and common transactional services in finance, HR, procurement and IT centralised into a central shared services unit to achieve better service delivery and optimisation of resources, with savings reinvested in academic initiatives. In 2014, NTU achieved ISO 20000 (Service Management) certification, being among the first institutions of higher learning in Asia-Pacific to attain this widely recognised industry standard. In campus development, more than $1 billion worth of academic and other infrastructure was expected to have been completed between 2010 and 2015. Iconic buildings and modern facilities blend into the lush greenery and rich biodiversity of the campus."

The plan was to be a "balance between continuity and change, proven initiatives and new ambitions, riding on the momentum of growth built up in the last five years, and guided by its Vision and Mission, Identity Statement and Core Values. Education, Research and Innovation, which represent the three corners of the 'Knowledge Triangle', will be the key thrusts of NTU 2020 Strategy leading the charge towards 2020."

The plan envisaged the continuing development of NTU Education coupled with a culture of "responsiveness, relevance and rigour". It laid particular emphasis on the Teaching Excellence Academy to give teaching its due position in the university and to reward and encourage best practice. One area of NTU that had not been subject to extensive scrutiny, review and reform was that of postgraduate education and the plan identified this as a priority. It was only at the end of the period covered by this book that an exhaustive review was carried out, led by Sasha Zehnder who had inherited Haresh's role as the Chairman of the Board of Trustees Academic Affairs Committee.

This time, in research, the aim was to construct a complete and systematic structuring of NTU research, at the same time leaving space for individual-inspired initiatives with the provision of "white space". Therefore, beneath Peaks of Excellence, NTU now has "Strengths and Focus Clusters" and "Emerging and Aspirational Areas". Again, to quote from the plan, "The current research strategy focuses on the five Peaks of Excellence that bring together NTU's key strengths to address national and global issues. Providing an interdisciplinary platform for colleges, schools and research institutes to interact, the current Peaks have been instrumental in the rapid rise of NTU's research. In planning ahead to 2020, there needs to be a balance between continuity and renewal, given the dynamic and changing research environment.

The new research strategy envisages five pan-university **Peaks of Research Excellence: Sustainable Earth**, that constitutes the most prominent of the new Peaks; **Global Asia**; **Secure Community**; **Healthy Society**; and **Future Learning**. These represent NTU's established, mature, interdisciplinary and core research areas. The Peaks of Research Excellence are supplemented by a series of **Strengths and Focus Clusters** representing in-depth strength in disciplinary and established competencies especially within the colleges and schools. There is also a need to provide space for new frontiers of research and future ambitions in **Emerging and Aspirational Areas** plus provision of 'White Space' for the new investigator-led initiatives.

The new research strategy therefore comprises a three-tier structure:

- Peaks of Research Excellence;
- Strengths and Focus Clusters; and
- Emerging and Aspirational Areas."

How these relate to each other is illustrated in Figure 3 in Colour Plate 1 (see page 130).

The Peaks continued with Sustainable Earth as the largest and very significant research activity within the university. It built on the pan-university institutes of NEWRI and ERIAN joining with the RCEs, EOS and SCELSE, and incorporating the new Asian School of the Environment and the Complexity Institute. Overall, this was a very impressive combination that also included many other relevant projects, including those from the College of Humanities and Social Sciences.

Next was a new Peak, Global Asia (Understanding, Engagement, Growth), which was not merely rolling the New Silk Road Peak forward but was an *ab initio* development. It took advantage of Singapore's position at the heart of Asia and NTU's competitive advantage in areas, such as business studies, international policies and the arts. It was not to be an initiative just confined to China (although this included the innovation hub in Guangzhou that Bertil initiated and was brought to a successful conclusion by Lam Khin Yong) and had, at its core, the idea of building on Singapore's role as the meeting point between the East and the West. The Peak has three foci — Business Asia, Cultural Asia and Transformational Asia — and rests primarily on the strengths of the Nanyang Business

School; the College of Humanities, Arts and Social Sciences; the S. Rajaratnam School of International Studies; and a number of well-established research centres such as the Institute on Asian Consumer Insight.

Third was a new Peak addressing an emerging societal concern and one in which NTU has special strength. This was Secure Community (Preventing, Adapting, Resilience), which was a multidisciplinary Peak to address the preservation of societal security. This Peak brought together the unique expertise of the S. Rajaratnam School of International Studies in international relations, terrorism and health, food and energy security, the strengths of the Colleges of Engineering and Science in defence research including cybersecurity and the specialist expertise of a number of research centres including EOS in geohazards, the Institute of Catastrophic Risk Management in risk management and the Temasek Laboratory at NTU jointly established with MINDEF. Other parts of the university contributed to the Peak through their research into societies and financial institutions, and these include the College of Humanities, Arts and Social Sciences and the Nanyang Business School.

Fourth was Healthy Society (Healthy Living, Active Ageing), previously Future Healthcare, which was more of an ambition in 2010 but was now a reality with the establishment of the Lee Kong Chian School of Medicine (LKCMedicine). This Peak was aimed at addressing many of the developing health issues which Singapore was facing and, in particular, the problems associated with a rapidly ageing population — one of the most rapidly ageing population in the world. 2018 was the year in which those older than 65 matched those younger than 15 for the first time. With this new school, NTU really was able to move forward rapidly and intensively. Alongside the Medical School in this Peak were the world-leading genomics capability of SCELSE, the forefront work of the Nanyang Institute of Structural Biology and the School of Biological Sciences (together these formed a new and formidable cluster of research capabilities in life sciences — the Nanyang Integrated Medical Biological and Environmental Life Sciences (NIMBELS)). This represented a new interface between medicine and science and complemented NITHM that provided the interface between medicine and engineering.

Finally, and uniquely for a university, the last research Peak addressed philosophy and pedagogy of education. This Peak, Future Learning (Understanding, Learning, Teaching), was a new interdisciplinary Peak based on the forefront position of the National Institute of Education and a new interdisciplinary research initiative combining and interfacing neuroscience, pedagogy and psychology spearheaded by the Centre for Research and Development in Learning (CRADLE@NTU), and involving other schools and colleges including the School of Humanities and Social Sciences; School of Art, Design and Media; and the School of Computer Sciences and Engineering. While this Peak addressed pedagogical research, NTU was already well on the way to the practical implementation of many novel new approaches including technology-enhanced learning coupled with team-based tutorial style instruction, the so-called "flipped" classroom approach and was investing in new student learning centres, including the Hive, an iconic new building on campus. The identification of educational science and technology as a strategic base for a research peak was a unique NTU development.

After the Peaks came Strengths and Focus Clusters that had contributed to NTU's research progress and reflected the depth of NTU's research. They were areas of in-depth disciplinary expertise anchored in outstanding faculty, as demonstrated by the competitive external awards obtained and substantial publications and citations achieved. Many of the areas were also anchored in research centres. They were stand-alone areas although in many cases they also fed into the activities of the Peaks. These areas could develop into future Peaks of Research Excellence listed in Table 2.

Finally came Emerging and Aspirational Areas that represented new frontiers of research with the potential to transform the world and meet national and global needs. These were research topics that NTU had identified in order to build capacity, taking advantage of new research and national developments. NTU had already initiated and invested in several of these areas, such as Complexity Science, while others still needed to recruit and develop expertise. In addition, provision was made through a "White Space" for unexpected developments that were usually investigator-led.

The plan also laid great stress on continuing and further developing industrial collaboration with multinational corporations (MNCs), in

Table 1: Strengths and Focus Clusters	
Photonics (Light Technology)	Nanomedicine
Manufacturing and Remanufacturing	Synthetic Organic Chemistry
Aeronautics and Space	Genomics
Computational Science, Engineering and Data Analytics	Structural Biology
Applied Discrete Mathematics	Language and Cultural Diversity
Interactive Digital Media	

Table 2: Aspirational and Emerging Areas	
Complexity Science	Synthetic Biology and Biomimicry
Food Science and Technology	Man–Machine Interface
Plant Science	Digital Humanities and Social Data Analytics
Ecology	Urban Spaces
Phenomics	Quantum Physics and Quantum Information

which NTU has been phenomenally successful, and on innovation. Through the creation of NTuitive as a vehicle for innovation and technology transfer coupled with an incubator, NTU had caught up with best practice in this area. NTuitive did not just take ideas and developments from faculty but also encouraged worthwhile and innovative ideas from students, and others, which could be turned into new small enterprises. This was yet another strand to the NTU "bow" and bringing the university into line with best practice. Another area of emphasis in the plan was to strengthen the enabling activities by continuing the reform of governance and administration as well as faculty planning and development. Internationalisation was another strand addressed in the plan, as was, for the first time, community engagement in Singapore, generally, but more specifically with our neighbours in Jurong where we are situated in the west of the island of Singapore.

The second plan was both an evolution from the first plan together with the introduction of new concepts, and this is shown in Figure 4 in Colour Plate 1 (see page 130).

Thus, the second plan was fully comprehensive and ambitious and laid the basis for NTU's further and even more rapid rise to the frontline of the world's universities.

Chapter 10

The Chinese Connection

China claims an uninterrupted history of 5,000 years. Although the origins of the Chinese in the first two millennia are lost in the mists of time, it is apparent, from archaeological digs, that, in the geographical "heartland" of China today, a number of unrelated civilisations arose independently. Nevertheless, it is generally accepted that Chinese civilisation arose on the northern plains of China, on the banks of the two mightiest rivers, the Yellow River and the Yangtze River. After the largely legendary Xia Dynasty was the Shang Dynasty with its records carved on turtle shells and bones, then the Zhou Dynasty saw numerous feudal lords from which many of today's Chinese surnames originate, including that of Nanyang Technological University's (NTU) second President, Su Guaning.

Since the 1949 victory of the Chinese Communist Party in the Chinese Civil War, the country had been dominated by the rule of Mao Zedong (毛泽东) culminating in the Cultural Revolution that led to a state of near anarchy. Upon Mao's death, a power struggle led to Deng Xiaoping (邓小平) returning to the leadership overthrowing the "Gang of Four". Deng then embarked on the economic reforms that have led to the rise of China, making it the second largest economy in the world after the US. Deng Xiaoping, as the new Chinese patriarch, and soon after his rise to dominance, visited Singapore in 1978. Amazed by the progress of this once poor city-state, he was moved by Lee Kuan Yew's comment that if Singapore could do it with descendants of labourers, China could do better with the availability of descendants of scholars. Thus began the reforms in China that have driven the Chinese economy to the heights that we see today.

In 2003, when Guaning became NTU President, it was not yet apparent to most people what a behemoth China would become. At that time, NTU offered a Master's degree programme in Managerial Economics, taught in Chinese to senior officials from China. The programme had its origins with Deng's proclamation in 1992, on his southern tour to Shenzhen (深圳), for China to learn from Singapore. NTU responded by creating a short-term training programme, taught in Chinese, to convert senior Chinese officials, many of them Vice Mayors, to learn how to run their local economies in a market-driven mode. Because of the high positions of the students, the press had taken to dub the class the "Mayors Class" — a name that has stuck ever since. In 1998, the programme was expanded in time to one calendar year with the award of the Master's degree.

Then, following Guaning's inauguration and the ambitions for NTU that he set out at that time, he had to develop a strategy to compete with NUS. At that time, most NTU faculty had acquired a fatalistic view that we could never compete with NUS. China was one area in which NTU could do better, leveraging on the "Mayors Class" and invoking the old *Nantah* connection. Guaning recalls that the Education Counsellor of the Chinese Embassy contacted him requesting an improvement in the living conditions of the students in the "Mayors Class". They were not used to the heat and since there was no air conditioning, they had to go topless, which is rather undignified for senior officials. Knowing "loss of face" is very important in Chinese culture, Guaning instructed that the then vacant staff housing be converted for their use. Soon, other parts of the university were jumping on the Chinese bandwagon. In 2003, the Nanyang Business School initiated an Executives Master of Business Administration (EMBA) programme with Shanghai Jiao Tong University (上海交通大学), and, later that year, Guaning signed the agreement with his counterpart in Shanghai. With Guaning's encouragement to use the China connection as a sustainable advantage, NTU soon had six Master's programmes aimed at the Chinese market taught in Chinese (Managerial Economics, Public Administration, EMBA, Educational Administration, Technopreneurship and Innovation, and Finance). Short-term training programmes in various topics were also growing rapidly. For example, there were a series of Chinese banks sending their senior managers to NTU to learn global practices, starting with Minsheng Bank (民生银行), and eventually including the China Construction Bank (中国建设银行), one of the four largest banks in China. Guaning recalls the signing of an agreement with the China Construction Bank, at which virtually the entire provincial-level leadership of the Bank was present, showing how much they valued our programme.

Guaning was aware, even in 2003, that the senior Chinese officials who received our Master's degrees hardly ever came to the graduation ceremony due to their restrictions on overseas travel. Therefore, beginning in 2006, we held a special convocation ceremony in China that enabled the officials to attend the ceremony and bask in the recognition and adulation of their family and friends. Our first China Convocation was held in the Beidaihe district (北戴河区) in the resort city of Qinhuangdao (秦皇岛市), Hebei province (河北省), where the China leadership hold their summer retreats. Subsequent convocations were held in Dalian (大连) 2007, Chongqing (重庆) 2008, Xiamen (厦门) 2009, Guangzhou (广州) 2010, Harbin (哈尔滨) 2011 and Nanjing (南京) 2012. Since then, it has gone to Beijing (北京) 2014, Shanghai (上海) 2015, Qingdao (青岛) 2016, Xi'an (西安) 2017 and back to Beijing in 2018. These events bind our alumni and the university close together. The goodwill generated for Singapore is unimaginable. Even the temporary setback in Singapore–China relations triggered by the then Deputy Prime Minister Lee Hsien Loong's visit to Taiwan in 2004, that was exploited by the Taiwan independence movement, and the Chinese Communist Party's response not to allow senior Chinese officials to study for a degree overseas, was only a temporary setback.

There have been numerous requests from local governments in China, including one from Guangzhou (广州), for NTU to start an undergraduate degree programme in China. None succeeded. Generally, the Singapore MOE is not in favour of its universities creating overseas campuses, thereby diluting resources assigned to the university for national objectives. The closest it got was a generous package from the Tianjin (天津) local government authority to allocate land and construct all the buildings for NTU in that city. This was rejected by the Board of Trustees because

NTU was already getting very good Chinese students coming directly to Singapore. With the high fees required to sustain a flow of Chinese students to the branch campus, it would mean only rich people could afford it. If this was coupled with the inherent preferences of Chinese parents for top American universities, the intake of any NTU campus in China, necessarily, would be lower in quality.

In 2017, Bertil, working closely with Lam Khin Yong, succeeded in establishing a strong NTU research and innovation presence in Guangzhou, despite Bertil's lack of Chinese cultural and linguistic links. The Sino-Singapore International Joint Research Institute was set up in partnership with the Sino-Singapore Guangzhou Knowledge City (SSGKC) Administrative Committee, the SSGKC Investment and Development Co., Ltd. and South China University of Technology (SCUT). The joint institute focuses on research that translates to technological advances for Guangzhou City and Guangdong Province, especially the Guangzhou Development District, Luogang District, and the Sino-Singapore Guangzhou Knowledge City. Several research areas have been identified including next-generation electric vehicles and intelligent urban transportation systems, nutrition and food science, sustainable urban development, pollution control and environmental restoration, as well as biomedical materials and medical instruments.

The institute is based on significant funding of RMB (yuan) 200 million (about S$44 million) for the first five years of occupying up to 20,000 square metres at the Sino-Singapore Guangzhou Knowledge City. This success story was based on Bertil's negotiations with the Governor of the Guangdong Province (with 100 million inhabitants, this province has a bigger population than Germany!). Originally, there was a preliminary agreement between the parties, but the money was quite limited at around 30 million yuan (S$6 million). Stressing the need for realistic and substantial funding, Bertil was able to leverage considerably more direct financial support as described above. The overall agreement was eventually signed by Professor Lam Khin Yong (Vice President (Research)) in 2018 (witnessed by Singaporean Prime Minister Lee Hsien Loong) and Chinese President Xi Jinping. Not only is this a major success for NTU but it also underlines the need to have frank and open negotiations between the parties in creating a close and symbiotic relationship.

In the latter stage of his NTU presidency, Bertil received an honorary degree in China — an honour that very few Singaporeans (one of whom was Lee Kuan Yew) have received.

As mentioned earlier, NTU has now established substantial chapters of its alumni association throughout China. On the occasion of Bertil's farewell visit in Shanghai, over one thousand alumni were present. This demonstrates the energy and enthusiasm that NTU has been able to generate among its Chinese alumni.

Of course, in times of trouble, we cannot expect that our alumni would abandon their country and stand with Singapore. However, the fact that there are 20,000 Chinese holding important positions in government and industry, who spent months to a year in Singapore and learned firsthand what made Singapore tick, means that they would be able to interpret our actions in a rational, even benign way. Handled carefully, they are a tremendous resource for the university and for Singapore.

As a result of Guaning's initiation of the links with China and enthusiastic follow-up by Bertil, NTU has become one of the foremost, if not THE foremost, of the world's leading universities with the strongest connections to China, which adds to our global reputation.

Stage III

The Ascent

The following two chapters give the background as to how NTU, in less than 15 years, could develop from a teaching institution to a research-intensive university with the highest normalised citation impact in the whole of Asia, challenging several of the top-level US and European universities. This is a remarkably rapid development that probably has not happened before within academia, in relation to research.

Chapter 11

Restructuring the University

Haresh recounts that when he became the Senior Academic Adviser to the President in 2005, he was concerned to see the structure that Guaning had inherited. The early days of NTU were very much about laying the foundations of the new university, enlarging and developing it as a key part of the Singapore educational "ecosystem". Nevertheless, that did not mean that this structure was appropriate for the rapidly growing university, and with autonomy in place, NTU was able to chart its own course and reorganise to better able meet its new ambitions.

As Haresh says, *I became Guaning's "Senior Academic Advisor" in 2005, later becoming an academic member of the Board of Trustees. In 2005, I saw that, preceding Guaning's tenure, the university functioned totally top-down and almost all the decisions, actions, strategies and ideas came from the President's office with three Deputy Presidents helping the President. The university was a chaotic combination of individual kingdoms, silos and power bases. There were at least 66 individuals with a title of "Dean". These included Deans, Associate Deans, Assistant Deans and others. None of these people coordinated the programmes of individuals schools or departments or with each other. Once a student entered a department, he/she took almost all the courses in that department. As a result, there were many duplications of courses and offerings. All the 66 deans acted in parallel and independent of the central goals, visions and missions. Most of these academic administrators did not have a clear idea of what was the university's vision and mission. Frankly, it was an interesting mixture of individual personalities doing "their own thing".*

Therefore, Haresh and Guaning set about the task to "remake NTU". In consonance with the 2005 QAFU findings, their first conclusion was that the whole university needed a total "reorganisation" of the academic enterprise. To start, they needed to articulate what needed to be done and then to systematically set out to accomplish the resulting mission. Guaning appointed a high-level committee for this reorganisation effort with Haresh as the Chair. The mission was well defined, but how to go about making massive changes without a catastrophic fallout (politically and academically) was an incredible challenge. After considerable discussions and hand-holding, Haresh was able to convince the committee to develop a model in which there would be colleges, each headed by a Dean, with all the Deans reporting to a new position of Chief Academic Officer, in other words, a Provost.

The plan eventually agreed upon was to create four colleges: Engineering with six schools, Science with two schools, Humanities, Art, and Social Sciences with three schools, and Business, a single-school college. Thus, there would only be four Deans, with the S. Rajaratnam School of International Studies (RSIS) and National Institute of Education (NIE) as separate autonomous institutes, but still under the quality control of Provost and the President. Once this was agreed upon, the next stage was to implement the plan. The most challenging was redesignating the heads of schools as Chairs, not Deans. The path of least resistance was taken by transitioning from Dean to Chair when the Dean's term ends and another appointee takes over. However, this was not always possible, in which case the Dean's term would have to be shortened by order of the President. Amazingly, all went along with the plan and complied without any significant complaints even though one school head insisted that within his school, he should still be addressed as "Dean". Even before all these resignations had come in, Guaning and Haresh had worked out which four individuals would be appointed as interim Deans of the four colleges. Within each school, there were to be divisions — equivalent to departments in other universities. In NTU, the "department" designation applied to the administration sections such as finance or human resources. In 2011, and with the further move towards a more comprehensive university, NTU added another single school college — the Lee Kong Chian Medical School (that also has autonomous status).

The new designations for academic leaders, reporting to the Provost, were as follows:

1. Deans of Colleges.
2. Chairs of schools within colleges.
3. Head of Divisions (HODs) in each school (later, in 2011, these titles were abandoned in a move to further reduce the "silo" mentality). Not only were the posts of Division Heads abolished but so was the divisional structure within the schools. In some cases, this proved difficult, but, overall, we removed some three quarters of the divisional structure.

Deans reported to the Provost, Chairs reported to Deans and HODs reported to the Chairs. Without going into details, it is sufficient to note that this transition was accomplished not only from an organisation chart perspective (the theory) but also from an actual implementation perspective with names and individuals appointed to every position that was vacant. Once this was done, Guaning and Haresh went to the NTU Council (this was before autonomy and the Board of Trustees) and got its approval. The only thing missing at this point was an individual for the Provost position. Er Meng Hwa was appointed Acting Provost with Haresh advising him and working through him so much so that Haresh became de facto Provost when he was in Singapore. He tried to stay two weeks each month in Singapore, thus starting the longest commute to work anyone has ever heard of, until Bertil came in as Provost. So, at the end of 2005, the reorganisation of NTU's academic structure could be said to be "mission accomplished".

However, while this was all completed, Guaning and Haresh confessed to being worried and having sleepless nights over whether the old "kingdoms" would "go quietly" and yield to the proposed changes. It took lots of goading, talking and convincing before the old structure yielded and agreed to "try out" the new structure. Once in place, it gained its own momentum and there was no turning back!

After a rigorous international search process, which we describe in the authors' tales, Bertil was appointed as Provost in 2007. In the interim, before Bertil came on board, Er Meng Hwa ably filled in as Acting Provost. Initially, Bertil was supported by only one Senior Associate Provost — Er Meng Hwa (with later a second Associate Provost — Lam Khin Yong being appointed). This level of academic management needed to be further reinforced as the university began its rapid development after 2007. By the time Bertil took over from Guaning as President in 2011, it was clear that the Provost level was too "lean and mean". New posts were created as well expanding positions below the President at the Vice President level. One key appointment was that of Lam Khin Yong as Vice President (Research). Khin Yong had joined the Provost's team in late 2007 and had filled several high-level positions in the university since that time. NTU was taking on the structure of a major university which is found around the world, even though some designations may differ.

On Bertil's arrival in 2007, he created the Provosts and Deans Group (PDG) to be a key body in taking policy development and implementation forward. It also incorporated Deans into the decision-making process that was vital in the subsequent implementation of the Promotion and Tenure exercise. In this way, colleges, and schools, could not claim that they had no influence and that everything was top-down. The Deans (later including the NIE Director) were part of the decision-making and it provided a platform for greater rationalisation in policy making among the colleges. Thus, we were all working at the same level and "facing in the same direction". It also led to the encouragement of sharing of resources and interdisciplinary collaboration among schools.

The 2005 QAFU report expressed concern that NTU lacked a "normal" academic structure in which all tenured faculty would be able to express their opinions. In other words, "academic democracy".

As President Emeritus Gerhard Casper had suggested at QAFU, Guaning asked Haresh to come up with an academic governance system using the Stanford system as a template. This was the topic, as described elsewhere, of the Troika meeting at Goa in January 2008. While the overall concept had been agreed upon by the time Bertil arrived, it was not until the Goa meeting that some "flesh was put on the bones" of the initial concept.

The result was the creation of the Academic Council and the setting up of elected representatives of the Academic Council, to be called the Senate. This was not an easy task as one had to make sure that the strengths and voices of all the units within the university were represented in the Senate. The Council became the official faculty body and was chaired by the President. The formation of the Council has provided greater opportunities for the faculty to contribute to NTU's development. It has allowed the faculty to provide input on academic matters to the university leadership.

Of course, the Council itself with its large membership needs an executive body, and an elected Senate and Chair were created. The success of the system and the quality of the advice that it has provided to the university leadership has been variable, very much dependent on the attitude and energy of the Chair. Always, the danger is that it becomes seen as a place for grumbling and nothing else, something always present in such a large and complex organisation, rather than a more proactive body bringing forward ideas from the faculty for the further development of the university. One example of a positive approach was early on in the Senate's life when it debated the complex topic of teaching assessment and submitted a report with recommendations to the Provost. The quality of the discussions and the role of the Senate and Council are very much dependent on its elected leadership and, for the most part, those taking on these roles have been very proactive. It is noteworthy that the first Chair of the Senate (Kwok Kian Woon, now Associate Vice President (Wellbeing)), in an institution still dominated by engineering, was from the social sciences — maybe a first for a technology-dominated university.

So far, this chapter has dealt with academic restructuring and this is the "beating heart" of the university. However, it needs a skeletal structure to support the "fleshy" body of faculty and students. This is administration.

The problem that had developed within NTU, especially when it was part of MOE, was that the service departments were controlling rather than supporting. Naturally, NTU has to follow good practice for publicly funded bodies as set out by the government and in legislation. However, this has to be applied in such a way that while proper procedures are followed, the service departments are there to support the university body. There were cases where the human resources department would query the academic rationale in a recruitment decision rather than ensuring that correct procedures were followed in such a decision. In other words, rules and regulations were applied without sufficient thought and discrimination. Old civil service habits die hard and the area of procurement, and its slow pace, was always a bone of contention between the schools and the service departments. Furthermore, the administration had little knowledge or understanding about research as the university had been, for such a long time, a teaching institution. When new research initiatives were discussed, the administration people were uneasy asking about the procedures and seeing research merely as a cost. The Provost argued that one had to distinguish between a cost and an investment. Indeed, this is what happened in subsequent years as our seeding of top-level research brought in several multi-dollar grants providing money far above the original seed funding.

Therefore, very much encouraged by Koh Boon Hwee and the Board of Trustees, and following the educational reviews the stimulation of research and the development of strategic plans, it was decided to embark on a lengthy programme of administrative reforms. In particular, the university needed its administration to be more efficient, more supportive and with the objective of achieving administrative excellence alongside the drive for excellence in teaching and in research.

Over a period of three years, a root and branch review of all the support services was carried out, involving internal reviews coupled with external consultancy advice. This has resulted in a new streamlined structure dedicated to the support of education and research. It was a mammoth task, coming swiftly on the heels of all the other changes that had taken place, but was essential. A new Nanyang Shared Services (NSS) structure was created delivering financial, human resources, procurement, and transactional information technology (IT) services. Areas such as student services were also restructured and streamlined.

These essential support services are now headed by a Chief Operating Officer (redesignated by Bertil's successor as Vice President (Administration)), yet another essential development for a modern university, in place of service department heads all reporting individually to the Provost (after Bertil's arrival) and the President (from Guaning's appointment until the Provost position was filled). One word of caution is that one must be continually on guard in a university against the creeping takeover of activities by the administration, and the balance between academic and service functions needs constant resetting.

The university will continue to evolve and develop with new leadership and new structures, but what was put in place, with the Board of Trustees' support, has modernised the NTU structure, increased its efficiency and laid the basis for continuous evolution to meet new challenges.

Colour Plate 1

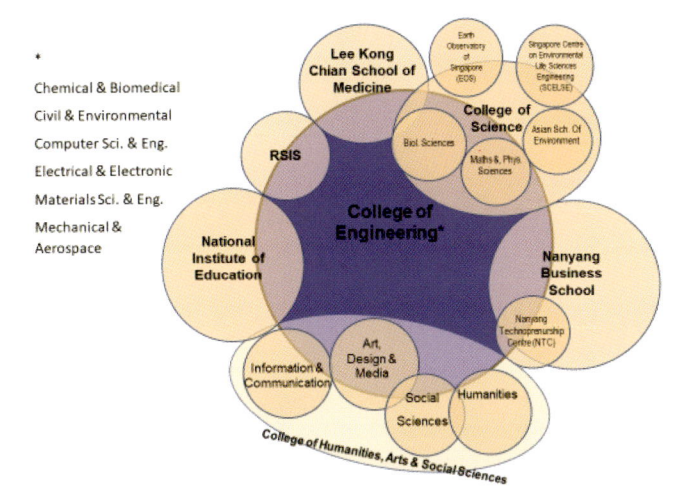

Figure 1: Bertil's 'Venn' diagram showing the interactions between the main units of NTU and the centrality of the College of Engineering (see page 74)

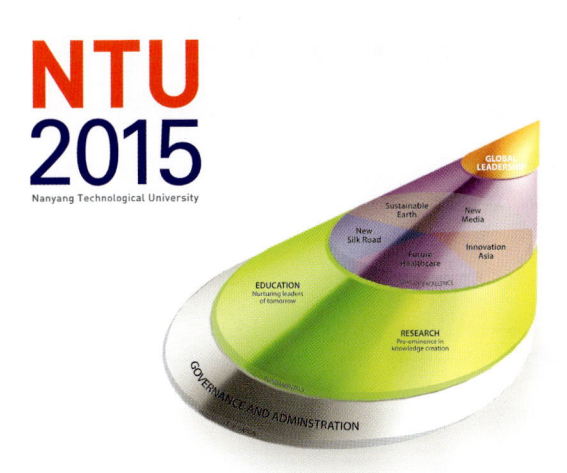

Figure 2: A representation of the First NTU Strategic Plan with its five peaks of excellence (*designed by: Assistant Professor Jesvin Yeo, School of Art, Design and Media*) (see page 101)

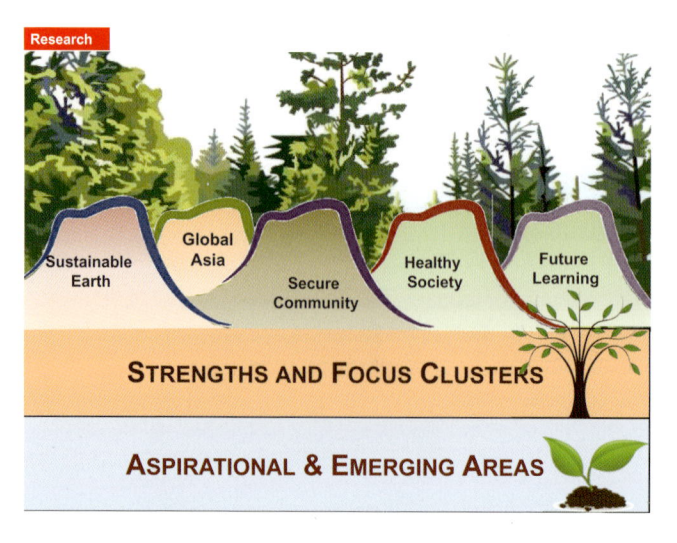

Figure 3: Illustration of the Second NTU Strategic Plan 2015–2020 (*courtesy of Professor Tim White*) (see page 107)

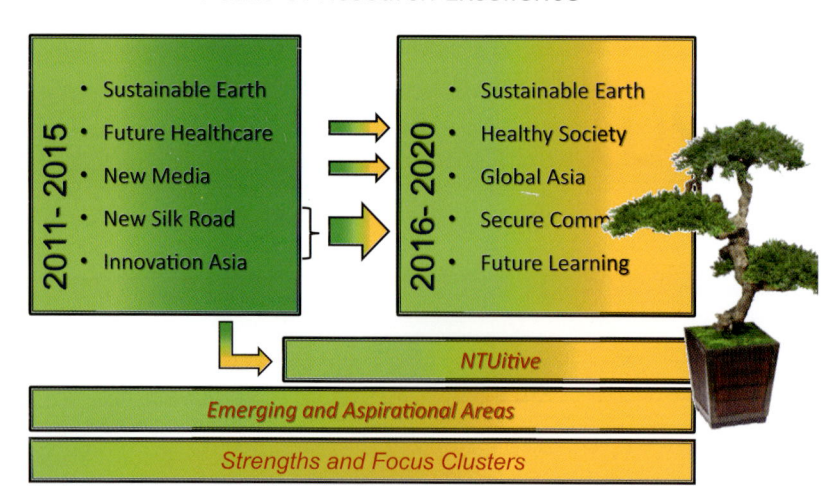

Figure 4: Evolution of the Second plan in comparison with the First Plan (*courtesy of Professor Tim White*) (see page 111)

Colour Plate 2

The Authors

Bertil Andersson

Haresh Shah

Su Guaning

Tony Mayer

The Troika in Session

First Troika Aptos, 25 February 2007

Troika Sigtuna, 30 June 2008, at the Royal Swedish Academy of Sciences

Colour Plate 3

Figures in NTU's Development
Chancellors of NTU

The late Sellapan Ramanathan (S. R. Nathan)
Former President of Singapore,
founding Director of IDSS now RSIS at
NTU Chancellor of NTU (1999–2011)
Source: Tabla © SPH Media Limited.
Reprinted with permission.

Dr. Tony Tan Keng Yam
Former President of Singapore
First Chairman of the National Research
Foundation (NRF) Chancellor of NTU
(2011–2017)

Chairmen of NTU Council and Board of Trustees

The late Michael Fam,
Founding Chairman,
NTU Council

Koh Boon Hwee
Chairman, NTU Council and
Board of Trustees

Professor Cham Tao Soon
First President of NTU (1991–2002)

Lim Chuan Poh
Former Perm. Sec., MOE and Chairman,
A*STAR

Colour Plate 4

NTU's Coat of Arms

Yunnan Garden Campus

The academic complex developed from the original Kenzō Tange concept

The Memorial Arch: Yunnan Garden

Chinese Heritage Centre
The former Administration Building of Nanyang University '*Nantah*'

Yunnan Garden

Colour Plate 5

Yunnan Garden Campus

Inside the North Spine

Students' Food Court

Older Students Residential Halls

New Halls of Residence

'Ski Slopes' of the Iconic School of Art, Design and Media and the Interior Court

Colour Plate 6

Yunnan Garden Campus

The Hive Learning Centre, Exterior and Interior Views
Designed by Thomas Heatherwick

The Arc – The Latest Learning Centre

The Wave Sports Complex
The largest wood framed building in Singapore

Colour Plate 7

LKC Medicine

The LKC Medicine Tower at the Novena Medical "City"

LKC Medicine at Novena

LKC Medicine — The Gallery & Annex at Novena

LKC Medicine Experimental Medicine Building at the Yunnan Garden

President of Singapore (Dr. Tony Tan) lays foundations of the Experimental Medicine Building (2015)

Colour Plate 8

Major Events at NTU

Lee Kuan Yew visits NTU, 2007 (seen here with Su Guaning (L) and BOT Chairman Koh Boon Hwee (R))

Prime Minister Lee Hsien Loong visits EOS, 2014

The late AP. J. Abdul Kalam, President of India, receives an Honorary Doctorate from President S. R. Nathan

Colour Plate 9

Bertil Andersson Arrives by Electric Scooter to Deliver the "State of the University" Report 2016

Final Convocation of the Troika Period Led by Dr. Tony Tam

Colour Plate 10

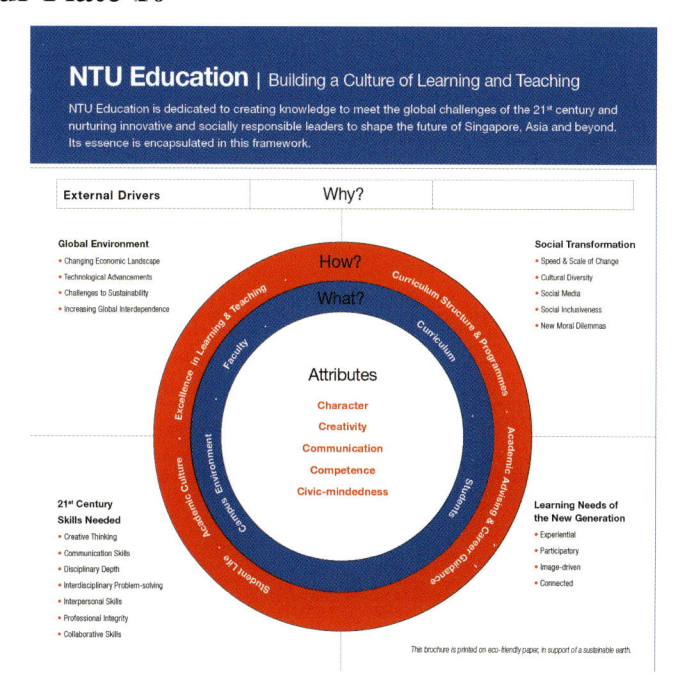

The NTU Education concept (see page 156)

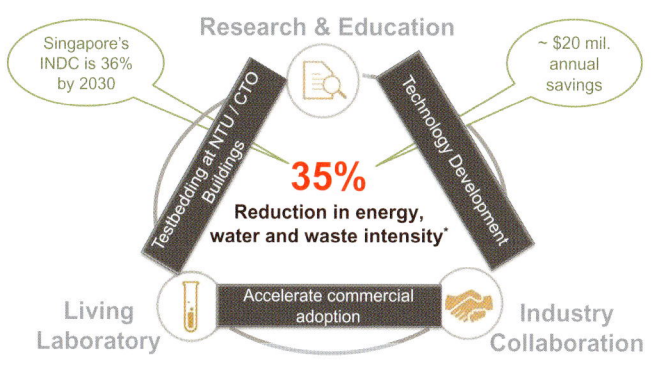

The EcoCampus concept

Colour Plate 11

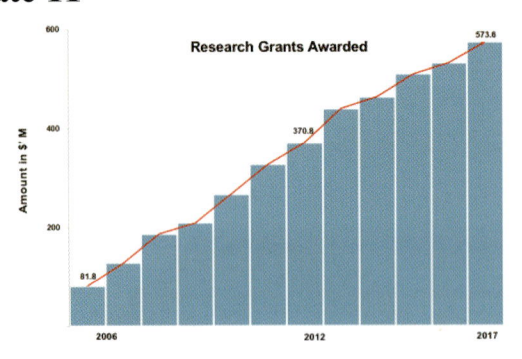

Growth of NTU competitive research income, showing how the Promotion and Tenure Review and the Recruitment Policy produced a dramatic effect increasing grant income tenfold.

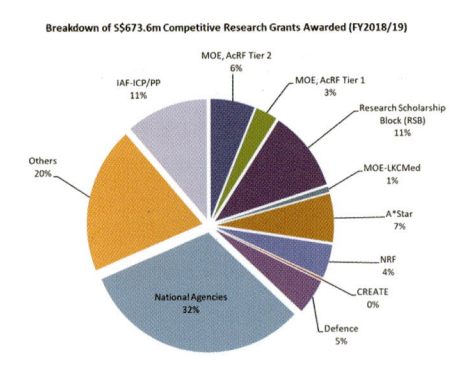

NTU's research income at the end of the Troika period.

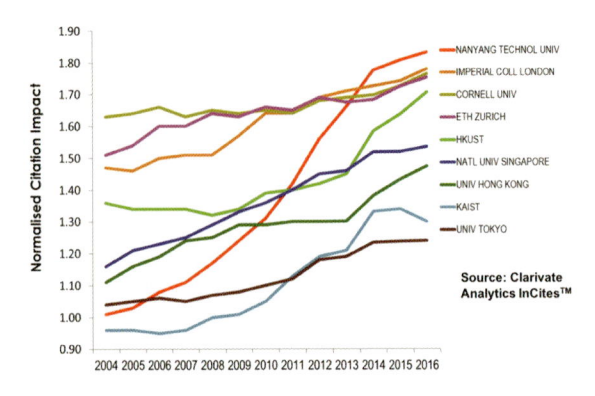

Change in normalised citations from 2004–2016 showing the dramatic rise of NTU. This is probably the most important indication of NTU's research success from 2003 until 2017 (see page 243).

Chapter 12

Finance and Budgetary Reform

Finance, as in all organisations, is the key to strategy implementation, spans all the activities of a university and is the essential "fuel" in the system.

As a public university, in common with all such universities, NTU relies on its basic grant from the taxpayer represented by MOE. Again, in common with systems elsewhere, the basic operating grant is based on and reflects student (undergraduate) numbers and provides for staff costs (faculty, administrative staff and other staff including security), the maintenance of the physical infrastructure and equipment, a component for research and similar basic expenses. On top of that, NTU receives additional MOE funding in respect of post-graduate research students and competes for external funding from both public and private sources and this provides its major research monies.

Thus, MOE funding comes, principally, in two tranches — the basic grant and post-graduate student support. Then, in terms of research, MOE has three distinct "tiers". Tier 1 is a grant to the universities to administer small individual grants (up to S$100,000 across the disciplinary spectrum) on a competitive basis (in accordance with MOE grant conditions). Tier 2 is a funding scheme up to S$500,000 operating within MOE and available, competitively, to all the universities. Finally, and only appearing in 2012, is the Tier 3 system of very major block grants that can be as high as S$25 million. Then, there is the very significant NRF funding system (with its support for a variety of special initiatives including, with MOE, the Research Centres of Excellence programme, Competitive Research

Projects, and, importantly, its Fellowship programme for outstanding young researchers). In addition, there are funds from other public agencies (including A*STAR and the Economic Development Board (EDB)), defence organisations, other public agencies and private sources, especially industrial collaborations. All these external-source funds add up to somewhat in excess of S$600,000 per annum in 2017 prices for NTU.

On his appointment as Provost, Bertil not only became the university's Chief Academic Officer but also took on the responsibility for the budget, as the key to the reform strategy that the Troika had instigated. In this capacity, and soon after joining NTU, Bertil met with Minister Tharman Shanmugaratnam. In that discussion, he was encouraged to plan based on concentrating on those areas in which NTU could excel. However, the Minister also said that within the basic grant there was a significant element for research support that could be considered as "Tier 0" and that this was important for NTU's research strategy. With this in mind, Bertil developed a new process for the disbursement of the budget across the university.

This now became a much more inclusive process than hitherto. All Deans and School Chairs, institute directors, as well as service department heads had to propose budgets and justify them before the Provost and his advisers. These sessions took a lot of time and went into considerable detail with all new initiatives having to be justified as part of the university's strategic vision to become a leading research-intensive institution. Nevertheless, the focus was not just on new initiatives but also required full justification for all the other elements of the proposed budget bid. In other words, it was no longer business as usual and money was not distributed automatically as had been the case in previous years.

Soon after arriving, Bertil discovered that there was a common tendency across almost all cost centres to significantly underspend. Given that this is taxpayers' money, such underspends could not be justified. In some cases, this could be due to delays in major capital provision, e.g. major equipment items could be delayed or there could be delays in faculty hiring. However, even considering such factors, large underspends seemed to be an NTU "tradition". Not only was this not justified in terms of either underspending or overestimating taxpayers' support but it also meant that the total underspends went into NTU reserves controlled by the Board of Trustees, which was always reluctant to release such funds, thereby "sterilising" these monies. Later, it has to be said, with a firm strategy for reform in place, the Troika was able to persuade the Board to release funds from the reserves for well-justified initiatives. The Chair, Koh Boon Hwee, was able to be persuaded to release such funds, even taking the lead himself, as is described in the chapter on the establishment of the Medical School.

In 2007, Bertil undertook a series of visits to each school (his so-called introductory "royal tour") and each consisted of an open session with the school faculty and leadership followed by a more restricted session with the school's leadership team. Such discussions included financial matters. This enabled the Provost to understand the issues facing the schools, plus their use of resources, and this became an important background to the budget discussion for the following financial year (2008/2009). It was very much about the university leadership having "Big Ears".

At the same time, Bertil had received a lengthy list of requests for equipment purchases in the 2007/2008 financial year. He asked the Senior Associate Provost, Er Meng Hwa, and his senior assistant, Tony Mayer, to review this list. They proposed various reductions, eliminating duplication, etc., but also reported to Bertil that these requests were rather indiscriminate and showed no strategic thinking.

Therefore, having tested the idea with the Provosts and Deans Group (PDG), Bertil's first budget included two important measures. The first was that there had to be a top slicing of the budget for central control by the Provost to enable him and the Troika to establish new strategic research initiatives and pump-prime them with such funds. The second was to retain part of the equipment funding at the centre to enable really significant and strategic infrastructure to be funded. The first of these was to establish a high-performance computing capability that could serve many users for advanced modelling and data processing (such as large volumes of genetic or seismic data). The second was to support the establishment of a structural biology facility to enable NTU to recruit top researchers in this field and to be able to compete at the world level.

This resulted in not only a new budget but also one that set out new strategic goals for the university. Returning to the "Tier 0" discussion with Minister Tharman, this inspired Bertil to create a "competition" between schools and institutes in terms of their thinking about and advancing new strategies for their areas of responsibility. Those with the best thought-out proposals, as well as being successful in gaining competitive external funding, would be "rewarded" with the others having to "make do" with a more basic budget settlement.

The process was repeated successfully each year and, now, it has become part of the standard operating procedure.

NTU was changing and the new way of allocating resources was one of the key measures taken that enabled this to happen.

Chapter 13

Reforming Education — Producing the Graduates of the Future

The Background Problem

Education is highly prized in Singapore and those involved in its provision are held in high esteem, from nursery assistants to university professors. Indeed, it honours teachers by providing high starting salaries for graduating teachers comparable to the salaries of young doctors and lawyers. This passion is reflected in budget priorities as Singapore devotes 20% of its annual national budget to education. It shows the seriousness with which Singaporean society considers education. Giving such a priority to education is something that other countries should emulate.

The public system is based on primary and secondary schools up to age 16/17 after which there are the Junior Colleges (JCs, equivalent to UK 6th Form Colleges and Lycées in France). Students sit for their Singapore-Cambridge General Certificate of Education Ordinary Level (GCE O-Level) exams at the end of their secondary schooling and then GCE Advanced Level (GCE A-Level) at the end of their JC period, prior to university admission. For the girls, this is at 18, while for the boys, their entry to university follows after their National Service, normally two years later. While the government has encouraged a more creative approach to school education, the system is still very much about "fact accumulation". Parents may also send their children to special classes to "top up" their schooling. Of course, this results in considerable pressure on the pupils on the one hand, but, on the other hand, it leads to the exceptional performance of Singaporean children in the Organisation for Economic Co-operation and Development (OECD) Programme for International Student Assessment (PISA) tests. These are standard tests for 15-year-olds in mathematics, science and reading, and, in 2015, Singapore ranked in first place in all three categories. Does this produce creative thinking and problem-solving as it promotes more of a "paper chase" for grades? The Ministry of Education, that has been encouraging a more creative approach, has recognised the problem, but Singaporean parents are very resistant to such changes. Thus, the intake to universities has been moulded by this "paper chase" attitude and overcoming it is a challenge. This is not a problem specific to NTU, but one which all Singapore's universities have to face. NTU and the other universities can only work with what the rest of the education system provides and, therefore, the university has to mentor its students in "learning to learn" and to encourage a different mindset from when they were at school. While the transition from school to university is a major one everywhere, it is a particular challenge for students in Singapore.

NTU is on the front line of teacher education and training as it hosts the National Institute of Education (NIE) as one of its autonomous institutes, ranked among the top 20 such institutes in the world. Not only does NIE supply graduate teachers for Singapore's schools but it is also involved in continuing education through the "top up" courses that school teachers have to undertake on a regular basis. NTU, in general, benefits from the transfer of the latest thinking and advances in pedagogy from NIE to NTU's own programme delivery.

Mostly, undergraduate education at NTU prior to 2007 was embedded in the philosophy of "producing" graduates for the industry and government to work on problems of immediate interest to the employers. With the globalisation of economies and technologies, this "legacy" philosophy had to be challenged and reviewed. The students graduating from NTU needed to look at the opportunities in Asia and the world, not only in Singapore. The mismatch between the profile of a graduate from NTU and that of a global graduate was becoming clear and more visible. The 21st century global opportunities for NTU graduates had to be aligned with the newly emerging demands of the marketplace and societies.

As one of the two major public universities in Singapore, NTU, from its inception, had always placed its education mission as its top priority over and above other activities, including research. As NTU, under Guaning, was now embarking on its new vision and mission to become a research-intensive university, this had to be based on the Humboldtian principle where teaching and research are interlinked and mutually reinforcing. This was something that the Troika considered was the necessary key to becoming a successful university fit for the 21st century. The public perception of a university professor in Singapore contrasts markedly with that from Europe. As Bertil tells it, *When a taxi driver asks me what I do and I reply that I am a university professor, in Singapore the follow up question is "what do you teach" whereas in Sweden the question is "what research do you do?"* Of course, as a true Humboldtian, the answer has to be that "I study a particular subject AND I teach in that subject as well".

Turning now to NTU's education, this had been the core activity in the early days of the university, to the neglect of research. Nevertheless, even here, although once recognised as a top engineering teaching university, mindsets had not changed nor had the way in which students were taught and NTU was falling behind best practice. Perhaps one of the most telling remarks came from a leading technology-based multinational company operating in Singapore. Its representative said that if one wanted more of a "technician", then an NTU graduate was ideal, because he/she had been stuffed with all sorts of technical knowledge, but if one wanted to recruit someone to solve problems or take on leadership roles, then one looked to places such as Imperial College London. In other words, we were filling our young people with lots of information, much of which could be found elsewhere, including on the Internet, but we were not educating them to apply their knowledge and become problem-solvers. Indeed many faculty members complained that if they challenged their students in class in this way, then, when it came to the faculty's annual appraisal, which heavily took into account student feedback, the result would be negative, as the students did not like to be taken out of their "comfort zone". Thus, there was no incentive to develop innovative and challenging teaching.

Moreover, was NTU falling behind in meeting the needs of industry and commerce?

Not only was the issue to create opportunities for NTU on the global scale but also to react to the changing opportunities in Singapore. Singapore, as a manufacturing hub of the 1980s and 1990s for many US and European companies, was changing and transitioning to an innovation centre. Industries and the Singapore government were demanding productivity gains through research and innovation in manufacturing and operations. The creation of A*STAR and the boost in research funding by the government was a result of this new environment. Certainly, NTU had to face the tendency towards "super" pragmatism of parents and students who see a university education as primarily the route to a good job in commerce, industry or public service. This contrasts with the students of Silicon Valley or Technion (Israel Institute of Technology) in Israel who see education as a route to create their own jobs! In fact, this lack of entrepreneurial spirit, on which Haresh comments in his tale, contrasts with Swedish students who have this entrepreneurial spirit as demonstrated by the student founders of Skype.

In 2003, there was already a desire within some NTU faculty to develop a more modern pedagogy and content. With the arrival of Guaning, he saw the need for change as urgent. The first step to be taken was an attempt to broaden the learning base through the New Undergraduate Experience (NUE). This was introduced with the aim to "foster artistic creativity, inventiveness, entrepreneurship and communication skills". While moving in the right direction, this new and commendable change added to the students' load without necessarily addressing some of the fundamental problems within NTU's educational programmes. Besides their major subject, students were given the opportunity to complete minors and electives as well as undertake an industrial attachment programme. While this looked to be an exciting programme change, the philosophy underpinning the core elements of the undergraduate programmes had not changed, neither had the workload for both faculty and students. Actually, it had increased and the underlying concept, which might have been described as "knowledge cramming", continued.

Having debated the problem in the early Troika meetings in 2007, and with the aim of totally reviewing undergraduate education and proposing a bold, realistic and implementable change for NTU undergraduates, Haresh agreed to take on the task of developing a proposal for the Board of Trustees to establish a Blue Ribbon Commission. This would study undergraduate education at NTU and elsewhere and recommend a new philosophical and pedagogical base for future programmes. The aim was to create more space for students to become independent learners, thinkers and researchers. It was also the aim, at the same time, to reduce the teaching workload of the faculty, especially to enable them to develop their research and to "work smart".

Another factor that had to be taken into account at that time was the pressure that was felt in NTU with the establishment of SMU with its downtown campus. Although not covering technical, engineering or science subjects, it was very much seen to be the "cool" place to study, and so not only were science, technology, engineering and mathematics (STEM) subjects losing out but also NTU was not able to attract many top students. The public images of the two institutions, NTU and SMU, could not be more contrasting. NTU was seen as dull, old-fashioned and boring.

It has to be said that the new global environment, at the turn of the millennium, presented challenges to universities not only in Singapore but everywhere, and demanded critical assessment of higher education for continued relevance in the 21st century. Social transformation had taken on a global scale, characterised not only by a knowledge-based and innovation-driven phenomenon, fast technological advancements and profound culture change but also by instability in the world economy, insecurity in international politics and the crisis of environmental sustainability. Teaching also had to adapt to the rapid technological changes taking place, especially the increased use of social media. For Singapore, careful and timely navigation through momentous changes in the global tide was, and remains, crucial for its internationalised economy. The government envisaged Singapore as a global city, a hub of creativity and innovation, talent and enterprise, and, as was said in its publicity material, one of the best places in Asia to "live, learn, work and play".

Adoption of the "knowledge economy" in Singapore meant that the national school system and the universities had to nurture young Singaporeans with greater breadth and flexibility, and with a willingness to experiment inculcated in them. In such a knowledge-based economy, Singapore's twin engines of growth in the manufacturing and service sectors were moving operations upstream into research and development of new products and services. All this meant that even with its diligent workforce, excellent physical infrastructure and first-rate legal and financial environment reputed for integrity and reliability, Singapore needed well-educated, creative and innovative individuals at all levels who could drive and steer the nation into the future. Therefore, it needed to educate its human capital to the fullest through a more flexible, diverse and holistic curriculum. Our intention was that this would foster a new mindset with the requisite skills, knowledge and motivation to operate in an increasingly interconnected and ever-changing world.

The Blue Ribbon Commission (BRC) — Its Finding, Philosophy and Implementation

If one looks at the changes in higher education that have taken place over the centuries, starting with the original European style of universities (very much religious institutions with instructions to small groups by learned monks), this evolved into the more modern university, especially with the greater dissemination of knowledge arising from the introduction of printing and moveable type by Gutenberg. In the 18th century, university education became linked to research through the Humboldtian philosophy. The next great revolution in learning, and the ubiquitous dissemination of knowledge, has been driven by new technologies such that one may describe the process as "Gutenberg to Gates". The changes driven by this latest revolution, especially with easily available tablets and smartphones and the increasing use of social media, came into their own just as NTU was reforming its undergraduate education. So, higher education has come a long way from the chalk and blackboard approach in formal lecture theatres, through whiteboards and pens, overhead projectors and similar aids to tablets and smartphones, group table settings rather than lecture theatres and all sorts of new electronic devices such as "clickers". The use of flipped classrooms and blended learning is now one of the mainstays of teaching. The Implementation Committee took on board these technological changes, and the resulting changed pedagogies, in drawing up its recommendations. In other words, our approach could be summed up as moving from a lecturing mode to that of a tutorial mode of learning. The idea was not new. The need for reform and change in education was recognised more than 60 years previously with American educator and philosopher John Dewey, whose attitude to education can be summed up in the often-quoted saying, "If we teach today's students as we taught yesterday's we rob them of tomorrow."

As already mentioned, the then NTU undergraduate curriculum remained heavily loaded. Over the years, more and more subjects and requirements had been added to the curriculum with students subjected to more and more hours of lectures, seminars, tutorials and laboratory/studio work. Apart from the resulting higher teaching workload for faculty, it had also caused fragmentation of teaching. For instance, large schools carried experts to teach in various non-core areas and these people had become somewhat isolated from their professional peers in other schools. The course load for the engineering programme (except for materials engineering) had risen to 153–160 academic units (AUs), compared to 144 AUs for other four-year programmes. With one academic unit for a laboratory session being equivalent to 3 hours per week, this translated to an average of 25–30 hours a week or 5–6 contact hours a day. With this high course load, it was difficult for students to actively engage in self-learning, reflection, research and pursuit of other interests and hobbies, which form part of a well-rounded education.

The Troika was aware that several top universities in the US, e.g., Harvard, MIT, Yale, Princeton and Berkeley, had carried out such reviews in recent years. With the release of the report "A Test of Leadership — Charting the Future of US Higher Education" by a Commission appointed by the US Secretary of Education, Margaret Spellings, in 2006, more US universities were expected to review and revamp their undergraduate education in the next few years. There was a similar trend developing elsewhere around the world, especially in institutions such as Imperial College London and Maastricht University in the Netherlands. Therefore, the Board agreed to go ahead with the BRC to comprehensively review undergraduate education at NTU.

The Commission, led by Haresh, included both external and internal experts, people from industry and recent alumni. It arranged to consult widely, especially including the student body. The Commission had the mandate to review and make recommendations on the desired attributes of NTU graduates, the type of curriculum that would elicit such attributes, the pedagogies to promote active and lifelong learning, including the assessment and examination system, and would look at how to tap into the key strengths of the university to enhance the undergraduate learning experience. Alongside this, it would also review the education and administrative load of faculty so that more space for research could be created. Thus, it had a wide-ranging freedom in its coverage in developing a blueprint to transform the very nature of undergraduate education at NTU.

Starting in September 2007, the Commission interviewed current students, many past students, all the Deans and many faculty members who were teaching undergraduate courses at NTU. Sub-committees of the BRC also visited major universities in Asia, the US and Europe to understand and learn from their experiences. The final report of the Commission was submitted to Guaning and Bertil at the end of March 2008 and thence to the Board, so the BRC had certainly worked rapidly, intensively and efficiently.

The BRC developed a holistic framework that identified five interrelated and mutually reinforcing attributes:

- *Ethical reasoning, integrity and moral character;*
- *Creativity, innovation and interdisciplinary synthesis;*
- *Self-discipline, disciplinary depth and lifelong learning;*
- *Leadership, teamwork, mutual respect and communication skills; and*
- *Professionalism, public service, social engagement and global citizenship.*

Recommendations were subsequently grouped under four key areas:

- *Academic culture;*
- *Academic experience;*
- *Student life; and*
- *Lifelong learning and employability, and institutional development.*

These aimed to enhance among other things the following:

- *The quality of faculty, excellence in teaching and effectiveness in learning;*
- *The undergraduate curriculum, learning beyond the classroom, campus life and residential education;*
- *Continuing education and learning; and*
- *Support to these educational imperatives.*

Both the full BRC report and that of the BRC Implementation Committee were exceedingly detailed and were, of course, specific to the situation at NTU.

As a result, undergraduate offerings have been changed within the teaching "envelope" being expanded still further and faster with a number of key initiatives:

- A new undergraduate curriculum, comprising at most 70% of depth and at least 30% of breadth and free electives, was introduced for new students from Academic Year (AY) 2011. Before that, the overall composition of the programme was much more traditional and weighted towards more formal lecturing. Guidelines were drawn up to manage double degrees in view of the additional complexities involved.
- NTU continues to update its curriculum and programmes to ensure that students have the relevant skill sets to contribute to the economy and society.
- Even before the BRC, the top-level students had to have more opportunities to undertake research projects and attend research seminars. There are various platforms for undergraduates to be exposed to research, independent study and team projects. Notably, there is the Undergraduate Research Experience on Campus (URECA) programme introduced by the then Vice President of Research Tony Woo. The students on this rather unique programme have published in reputable international journals, attended international conferences and taken part in research poster competitions. URECA is an important initiative in that we have been conscious, as has the government, of the low take up

of PhD opportunities by Singaporean students, who form a majority of the undergraduate intake. Hopefully, Singaporean students engaged in research through URECA may be persuaded to join the PhD programme. This is something that the 2015 QAFU report addressed.
- Beyond the establishment of new programmes, a diverse range of academic options and opportunities have been made available. More interdisciplinary content was introduced to add to the wide repertoire of options that students were already enjoying under the new curriculum. Schools progressively offered more courses with interdisciplinary content to meet increasing demand.
- To cultivate entrepreneurship in students, they have been empowered to take responsibility for establishing and running academic and services activities.
- The target of sending 50% of each cohort on overseas experiences has been achieved and we are now on track to reach the even more challenging target of 70% of each cohort that had been set.
- One of the major differences between schools, junior colleges and universities is that of the learning process itself. With our emphasis now on student-centric education, there is then a requirement of "learning-to-learn" programmes. Therefore, soon after the BRC was completed, we needed to introduce workshops specifically designed to give students support for generic learning needs including time management, academic integrity and note taking. At the same time, we strengthened pastoral care and counselling services together with methods to identify students who are at-risk or are facing social or psychological problems. The objective is to identify at-risk students early and provide them with the necessary assistance promptly. Finally, we needed to not only look after our graduating students with career advice and guidance but also introduce coaching to allow students to polish their resumes and engage in mock interviews to build confidence. All this has been facilitated by new Learning Centres, of which the Hive building is the most iconic.
- The BRC had started off on the basis that the whole of the undergraduate period at NTU was a learning experience. Education is about a holistic student experience that encompasses learning outside the

classroom. The development of such learning outside the classroom or formal structure is vital.
- Improvement of student life has been furthered with the engagement and empowerment of students in decision-making where appropriate. Actually, this is somewhat of a departure, given the social attitudes that prevail in the country.

The BRC conclusions and recommendations were strongly supported by the Board of Trustees during early 2008 and later presented to MOE, which expressed enthusiasm about the BRC approach and recommended that the concept be adopted by the other Singaporean universities. Therefore, with this support, NTU was all set to go.

Thus, the BRC was the key conceptual input to the reform of undergraduate education, paving the way for the future development of modernised NTU Education.

The main BRC recommendation was for a 20% cut in the AUs leading to a degree from the 150 or more AUs that counted towards a degree. This had to be taken as a guideline since, especially in engineering, it was necessary to take into account the views of the professional engineering accreditation bodies. Eventually, a compromise level of 130/135 AUs was agreed upon, although the course content was very much a matter for NTU, which pursued its objective of broadening the topics on offer. It also moved to a more student-centric approach to teaching. Professors are contradictory animals. They complain about too high a teaching load, but if you suggest reducing the content in their discipline, they object loudly! This was our experience at NTU as the BRC recommendation for reducing the AU content made public.

Arising from the BRC's philosophical recommendations, NTU needed a down-to-earth implementation scheme, and so a BRC Implementation Committee was set up in order to translate them into specific policies, plans, strategies and actions. The Committee was chaired by Bertil, as Provost, supported by the Senior Associate Provost, Professor Er Meng Hwa, who was, at that time, in charge of undergraduate education. The Committee communicated the philosophy and intent of the BRC to faculty, staff and students, and held dialogue sessions with the Students'

Union and other student leaders. After widespread consultation, the Committee completed its work by 2010.

This resulted in a final and comprehensive report with findings and recommendations, and thus NTU was ready to start the changes. Although the philosophical basis for undergraduate education had been laid out by the BRC, there were other influences at play, especially in terms of new pedagogies and new technological approaches, including "flipped" classrooms. All these factors had to be taken into account by the Implementation Committee.

It has to be said that there was quite a lot of pushback from faculty who were now under pressure to deliver more high-quality research at the same time as revamping their teaching. This followed from the rigorous and comprehensive promotion and tenure review, which had only just reached a steady state, and faculty morale was not high following this time of uncertainty. Much of this discontent about the pace of change in teaching and other reforms was channelled through the Senate and Academic Council. There was internal resistance from students who were concerned as to whether the new programmes would affect their future employability and some external resistance from both employers and some parents, especially those with a more traditionalist view of university education.

The whole NTU approach was summarised in the 5Cs for the attributes that an NTU graduate would be expected to have, namely character, creativity, communication, competence and civic-mindedness, shown diagrammatically in Colour Plate 10 (see page 139). An outcome-based approach to curriculum reform was adopted that also helped in terms of faculty assessment in teaching.

The rollout started in 2011 when Bertil took over the presidency and there was a major restructuring of the senior management in order to deliver the strategy (see Chapter 3) across the university as a whole. Under the new Provost, Freddy Boey, a number of different "commands" were created with Associate Provosts designated to look after undergraduate education and student life. Kam Chan Hin (now retired), who took over the education portfolio, had been responsible as the Associate Chair (Academic) in the School of Electrical and Electronic Engineering (EEE) for educational matters. Later, he became Chair of the school before becoming Associate Provost. He had the responsibility for undergraduate education, now as the Deputy Provost. Of course, the rollout started with the new 2011 cohort and so did not reach completion until 2014. One important aspect of the reform was that, as the programmes and student life at NTU became more interesting and exciting, it enabled NTU to improve its branding and attract more top students.

At that time, following a major revamp of the NIE educational programmes, its Director, the late Lee Sing Kong, took up the post of Vice President (Education) in NTU in 2014 and brought his experience of such changes into the mainstream of NTU, which eventually led to what is termed NTU Education. The aim was to take a holistic view of what we were doing — improving the student learning experience (including providing new intakes with a programme on "learning to learn"), rewarding teaching excellence, providing training in teaching for faculty and introducing new technologies with technology-assisted education and the resulting "flipped classroom" approach as well as the introduction of team-based learning enabled through technology. This meant a major infrastructural investment to convert all the tutorial rooms into the flipped classroom methodology to sustain group learning and discussion. This could only have happened with the full engagement and support of the Board of Trustees, which embraced and supported these changes and remained closely interested and involved as the programmes evolved. At the same time, the initiation of the Lee Kong Chian School of Medicine (LKC Medicine) (operated jointly with Imperial College London) provided an ideal test bed to develop this new mode of learning, drawing on both institutions' experience and desire to start a completely new approach to learning, and this gave an added impetus to the reform process.

Truly, it was one of the most remarkable changes in a university anywhere, philosophically, embracing new technologies, changing faculty attitudes to teaching and persuading students of the advantages in the new learning process, coupled with the determination to make it happen through major infrastructural investments.

All of the reforms described above require a financial investment and the Board strongly supported the plans to revamp the tutorial rooms turning them into flipped classrooms and installing the requisite technologies. However, the largest investment was in building a new learning centre for the students.

Below, we describe the two learning centres, the Hive (opened in 2014) and the Arc (opened 2018), which have been substantial investments in buildings with new flipped classrooms and learning spaces.

The Hive (named by the students), designed by Thomas Heatherwick, one of the celebrated architects of the London 2012 Olympics, was the first to be built. It has become an iconic building, but, as Bertil says, while the outside is spectacular, the inside is the most impressive with its flipped classrooms, spaces for individual study, a language centre and a place to coach students in writing reports and making presentations. More recently, NTU has added a second impressive learning centre — the Arc. The Arc has 56 new-generation smart classrooms with each equipped with multiple LED screens, wireless communication tools and flexible clustered seating designed for group discussions. With the completion of the Arc, NTU now has more than 280 smart classrooms. Together with other recently completed buildings such as the Clinical Sciences Building in Novena, 116 new smart classrooms have been built since 2015. In addition, NTU has converted 166 smart classrooms from existing tutorial rooms. This is a huge investment in modern advanced teaching and learning. Furthermore, everywhere, within the main academic areas, there are spaces (with sockets to charge tablets!) for the students to pursue their own studies. Every visitor must be impressed by the scene at NTU, which is very much one of learning in its truest sense. When it comes to modern learning spaces and taking advantage of digitalisation integrated into advanced pedagogics, NTU is second to none in the world. It is a challenge for universities in Europe and North America to follow this example of creating the classroom of tomorrow.

By the time that the Arc was officially opened in early 2018, NTU had set a bold target to redesign at least 50% of its programmes, over a three-year period, using the flipped classroom pedagogy by 2020. With all the encouragement that we gave our faculty, everyone is now fully committed to this new 21st century learning and teaching process. At the time of writing, NTU has completed 314 or 32% of courses already redesigned, with another 170 currently undergoing conversion. Ultimately all 2,000 courses will be converted.

This is another and different investment in faculty time and energy, but one which is paying off rapidly as it has enabled NTU to attract top students and turn out graduates with the all the skills needed for survival in the complex 21st century workplace. Although many universities are embracing these new pedagogies, these are often on a more piecemeal and fragmented approach. NTU is a leader and possibly unique in the way in which it has totally embraced the new pedagogies and has invested to support it. This was a very bold step and one which is paying off. It has been inspired by the BRC and then by the advent of LKC Medicine and championed from the outset by the late Professor Lee Sing Kong, former Director of NIE and Vice President for Education at NTU, whose wholehearted commitment was an inspiration to his colleagues.

Students and faculty are enthusiastic about the changed mode of learning. Students like the team-based experience and the teachers are appreciative of the positive responses that their new teaching engenders.

Improving the Quality of Teaching

All this meant a wholescale change in the methodology by which courses were delivered. In the chapter on faculty renewal and recruitment, we describe the changes that were implemented in 2007/2008. In these reviews, the emphasis was on research success, which is easier to assess through bibliometric and related measures, but how were we to assess teaching excellence? Following the decision in Bintan in 2007 to restart the Promotion and Tenure process, NTU had used a ratio of 6:4:2 between research, teaching and "service". Then, following the 2010 QAFU report, as well as the implementation of NTU Education, the "pendulum" was moved back to parity between research and teaching. Assessing teaching prowess and delivery took on a new importance. We still retained student feedback, but this was now put into context alongside a number of other measures.

Taking the lead from NIE, NTU instituted peer review with more experienced faculty sitting in on classes, as is done for school teacher training. This represented 20% of the assessment, and a further 20% was accorded to the teaching portfolio, including the teaching philosophy presented by the faculty member, with a third 20% given to academic supervision and mentoring. Now, the student feedback was reduced to 40% instead of being the main measure, although it remained a significant element in assessment.

A recognition system was put in place leading to the creation of a Teaching Excellence Academy to recognise and reward excellent teachers. Awards for good teaching were increased, especially in the schools. Awardees could then be recommended for college awards and eventually these awardees could qualify for university-level recognition and hence membership of the Academy. Not only did this provide a new incentive system but provided the university with a pool of really experienced and excellent teachers who could advise and mentor their colleagues as well as provide master classes. This formed the Teaching Council that was responsible for teaching appraisal committees for each faculty member. This Council reviewed teaching portfolios, assessed and advised on mentoring, as well as assessed a faculty member's student final year projects and any supervision of URECA projects.

Prior to 2007, NTU had established a Centre for Excellence in Learning and Teaching (CELT). At the time, this served a useful purpose in starting to introduce technology into teaching with all materials and lectures being recorded and put online. However, this was not enough and it was eventually replaced by a Teaching, Learning and Pedagogy Division to provide for faculty development and teaching support. One example of this is the Foundations of University Learning and Teaching programme, facilitated by experienced overseas faculty developers, as a course for new faculty. Another programme offers a suite of courses each semester covering fundamental issues in learning and teaching (such as assessment) and topical subjects such as threshold concepts and developing teaching portfolios for promotion.

In fact, in relation to technology, the BRC was reminded, forcefully, of the need for extensive faculty training in teaching and in using the new technologies during student focus groups conducted as part of the BRC review. We heard from students that, in their view, the uninspiring teacher was uninspiring whether in the flesh or viewed electronically, while the inspiring teacher would have students turn out at unsocial hours to hear such a teacher first-hand!

Now, there are structured courses on pedagogy and communications to help faculty and teaching assistants. A holistic view of teaching assessment has been adopted and there are grants and awards to promote and recognise excellent teaching. With regard to structured courses, Teaching-to-Teach programmes have been made available for different levels — for teaching assistants, new faculty and for experienced faculty.

One consequence of the flipped classroom is the increased need for teaching assistants, and here, as in most places, NTU relies on its graduate students. In fact, it is an expectation that such teaching is part of their own learning process for their advanced degrees. Therefore, to prepare the graduate students for this role, NTU introduced University Teaching for Teaching Assistants, which is a module course intended to prepare graduate students for teaching at NTU and as future faculty. This is very important as NTU has always considered it to be part of the research training that graduate students and fellows should help in teaching undergraduates. It is a truism being able to explain complex ideas to others also helps to clarify one's own thinking. It also bolsters teaching capacity and increases contact hours with students. Not everyone can be a good teacher, so only those who are identified as having an aptitude to be good in teaching are involved. This is in line with international practice and is a way of managing the teaching workload of faculty with these teaching assistant hours being confined to supervision of laboratory modules and tutorial sessions.

It has to be said that the arrival of the Medical School, which from the outset was based on the flipped classroom approach with the aid of "Professor iPad", was a key factor in promoting change within a quite structured environment. In addition, the Medical School introduced a "house" system to create more team bonding and a greater feeling of togetherness. This was a pioneering method of teaching students to become good doctors and, from the start, enabled these particular students to have built in more exposure to patients from their very early days in their student career.

In 2014, the opportunity to use technology in teaching arrived with massive open online courses (MOOCs). These were embraced by NTU, encouraged by the Board of Trustees, and NTU signed up to the Coursera delivery platform. Three MOOCs were developed — An introduction to Forensic Science; Beauty, Form and Function: An Exploration of Symmetry; and E-commerce and Technology. Not only were these very well received worldwide, but NTU, unlike most universities producing MOOCs, gave credits to its own students who completed the courses. This was really the start of Technology Enhanced Learning (TEL) that was more than just an adjunct to the learning process but became the heart of the teaching provision. Previously, we had not properly leveraged the advantages provided by technology. It is now our servant, not an adjunct nor our master! Very much encouraged and pushed by our Board of Trustees, we fully engaged in this activity with our faculty, working alongside professionals in multimedia, to improve visualisations and develop stimulating teaching, and alongside recording studio professionals, to advise on delivery and presentation. It was a massive "sea change" in our teaching, which really met the needs of the new smartphone generation. MOOCs had provided the stimulus, and the NTU experience shows that, if used in the right way, technology provides a quantum leap in quality, enables the flipped classroom and produces a really powerful pedagogy. MOOCs have also raised NTU's visibility locally, regionally and globally, with more than a quarter of a million participants registered from around the world.

The details given above show the time and attention that was devoted to changing the perception of what it meant to be a student at NTU. It was necessary not only to ensure that NTU's international reputation was enhanced but also to ensure that parents, and, in Singapore, it is the parents who usually make the final decisions, could see that the university was intent on providing a better all-round education and would look after and enhance the lives of the children whom they were entrusting to it. This was not always easy. For instance, Bertil had an encounter with the father of a student, who, after listening to the description of the changes to the NTU educational model, angrily said, "I want my daughter to be properly taught — that's what I pay for!" From NTU's own surveys, it has been found that, over the past few years, NTU has increased its "market share" of top students. The fact that NTU was able to consistently increase the percentage of the top students' choices demonstrated the impact that it has been able to exert on Singaporean society. However, there are still some perception barriers to be overcome as many parents still feel that only through traditional lectures are their children "being taught" rather than having to "learn to learn".

Premier Programmes for Top Students

Of course, NTU was very content to have increased its share of top students, but then it had to provide for them, above and beyond the usual programmes, even though these now offer a fantastic range of interesting opportunities. As is the case at all educational levels, and higher education is certainly no exception, there are a range of abilities in every cohort for which the university has to cater. That is only the start. Once at NTU, such students needed to be challenged by programmes that would "stretch" these top-performing intakes.

In the following paragraphs, we describe the elite programmes, not forgetting that the Lee Kong Chian School of Medicine is, itself, NTU's major elite programme. Table 1 shows the development of student recruitment over recent years.

Table 1: Recruitment of Top Students at NTU

Top A-level Students	SG	SG %	SPR	SPR %	IS	IS %	A-level	Total UG FT Intake	% Top Students
2015	345	86	22	5	35	9	402	6525	6
2016	384	83	24	5	53	11	461	6138	8
2017	403	86	27	6	36	8	466	5955	8
2018	469	84	35	6	53	10	557	6160	9
2019	438	92	25	5	13	3	476	6482	7
Top Polytechnic Students	SG	SG %	SPR	SPR %	IS	IS %	Poly	Total UG FT Intake	% Top Students
2015	151	70	12	6	52	24	215	6525	3
2016	146	73	15	8	39	20	200	6138	3
2017	125	74	7	4	36	21	168	5955	3
2018	118	84	4	3	18	13	140	6160	2
2019	110	73	11	7	29	19	150	6482	2

Notes: SG: Singaporeans; SPR: Singapore permanent residents; IS: international students; UG FT: undergraduate full-time students.

The Renaissance Engineering Programme (REP)

On Guaning's suggestion, REP was established because there was a perception that Singapore was not turning out the sort of engineers demanded by the industry and that we should be educating the industry leaders of the future. Not only that, but engineering was increasingly falling behind other disciplines in its ability to attract the top students to its courses. In other words, action was needed to address the criticism of our engineers made at the start of this chapter. In other words, we needed to be producing problem-solvers.

Engineering was ceasing to be regarded as "cool", and there was a perceived threat (actually enunciated by ministers) that the newly established Singapore University of Technology and Design (SUTD) (with its partnership with MIT) would soon outstrip NTU in its core area — engineering.

Thus, NTU started to develop a new programme in engineering that would include education not only in engineering but also in business, management and entrepreneurship, coupled with exposure to the full range of learning opportunities emerging from the Blue Ribbon recommendations. And so, the Renaissance Engineering Programme was born.

The programme is an integrated, rigorous and fully residential programme with a curriculum that covers a broad spectrum of multidisciplinary subjects bridging engineering, business and the liberal arts including science, mathematics, engineering technology management and interdisciplinary studies. Again, it was at the forefront of NTU's educational reform programme. This programme includes a one-year overseas experience at a partnering university. This partnering is based on carefully negotiated arrangements starting from the basis of "mutual academic esteem". This is coupled with an industrial orientation component, ending up with a dual degree comprising of a Bachelor of Engineering Science degree (with specialisation in a chosen engineering discipline) and a Master of Science in Technology Management in 4.5 years.

The programme includes specialisation drawn from the engineering programme of six Engineering Schools with students able to choose their specialisation in areas such as, for example, aerospace engineering, bioengineering, computer engineering and science or materials engineering.

The uniqueness of REP is that students get to do one year at an overseas partner university. The partners are as follows:

- University of California, Berkeley that specialises in engineering, research and entrepreneurship.
- Imperial College London, which specialises primarily in science, engineering, management and medicine.
- Northwestern University, which specialises in design courses offered by Segal Design Institute.
- University of British Columbia that specialises in engineering, research and cross-disciplinary collaboration.

Students may also conduct their professional attachment in the United States, the United Kingdom or the rest of Europe.

Therefore, NTU has been able to provide the engineering leaders that Singapore so urgently craved for and has been able to reverse the trend whereby top students ignored engineering for other disciplines. In the early part of this century, NTU had fallen behind NUS in both education and research, its core area and its original *raison d'être*. Then, we were faced with the new challenge from SUTD. The REP programme and the revamping of all the educational programmes have restored NTU to its rightful place as the premier engineering institution in the country. This has been recognised and appreciated by students and parents, the public in general, by employers and by politicians, and the programme itself is recognised as one of the leading top 10 programmes of its type in engineering in the world.

NTU's Other "Elite" Programmes

As described on the NTU website, the REP and the other elite programmes — the NTU Premier Scholars Programmes (PSP), comprising the University Scholars Programme (NTU-USP), the CN Yang Scholars Programme (CNYSP) and NTU-NIE Teaching Scholars Programme

(TSP) — aim to attract high-achieving post-secondary students with outstanding curricular records, leadership qualities and a strong passion to contribute to society. These programmes are specially developed for exceptional students who look forward to developing their potential through a high-quality education that goes beyond their regular undergraduate programme and prepares them well for the rising demands of the highly volatile 21st century workplace. On top of a multidisciplinary and broad-based curriculum, these students have personal guidance by top faculty, interdisciplinary and intensive research opportunities, overseas exposure, as well as the opportunity to meet renowned Nobel laureates and other world-class leading scientists, politicians and industry leaders. Students who are under the CNYSP, USP and TSP will, upon their graduation, be awarded a special certificate in addition to their degree certificate.

CN Yang Scholars Programme

Recognising the need to cater to top students early on in his presidency, Guaning instituted a new programme, the CN Yang Scholars programme (CNYSP). It was launched at the 2006 International Physics Olympiad hosted by NTU/NIE by Yang Chen-Ning (C N Yang, 杨振宁) himself, perhaps the best known Nobel laureate of Chinese origin and who has had a strong link with NTU dating back to *Nantah*, and, more recently, as a member of the Institute of Advanced Studies International Advisory Panel at NTU. CNYSP is an elite programme modelled on the curriculum of MIT and Caltech, aiming to provide C N Yang Scholars with a solid foundation to succeed in graduate studies and research.

Initially, more of an "add-on" to the normal undergraduate programme, it has now become an elite programme *ab initio*. Again, to quote from the NTU website, "the CNYSP is tailored to provide students with intensive opportunities in research, be it locally or overseas. The CNYSP aims to broaden the scholars' global research experience by engaging them in the overseas summer research attachment and overseas final year project." At the end of the undergraduate study, CNYSP graduates are given an option to pursue postgraduate study (PhD) with a scholarship in NTU or in a joint PhD overseas.

In detail, the CNYSP provides knowledge for the 21st century, promoting individual and unique talents and encouraging proactive global citizenship. This includes undertaking multidisciplinary courses in the basic scientific disciplines as well as introducing topics such as global climate change and the first exposure to the research experience. There is also a residential learning experience plus an initial research attachment in research institutes or external laboratories. This is followed by an overseas final year project accompanied by courses on topics such as writing and reasoning, ethics and enterprise, and innovation and leadership. It is highly competitive with only 50 students selected every year.

Ultimately, one aim is to attract such students, on graduation, to remain at the university and become graduate students. One of the difficulties for universities in Singapore is the dearth of Singaporeans and permanent residents to embark on a PhD. We all have an obligation to attract more Singaporeans into research to make this sector sustainable and it is one of the university's key performance indicators. A shining example of success in this aim is that of Nelly Ng Huei Ying, a specialist in quantum computing. She started out as one of the 2007 freshman class of CN Yang scholars graduating in 2012 as a Koh Boon Hwee Scholar and was awarded the Shell Eastern Petroleum Gold Medal as the top student in physics. She then joined the Centre for Quantum Technologies, NUS as a Research Assistant, going on, in 2017, to receive her PhD from Delft University of Technology in the Netherlands. This was followed by an Alexander von Humboldt Postdoctoral Research Fellow at the Free University of Berlin. Then, in 2020, she returned to NTU as a Nanyang Assistant Professor, completing a 14 year journey. This demonstrates the value of such "elite" programmes in developing Singapore's own academics of the future.

University Scholars Programme

The need to provide for the best students in disciplines outside engineering and science was the main driver behind this initiative. Catering principally to the arts, humanities, and social sciences, the University Scholars Programme (NTU-USP) leads a university-wide commitment to provide an intellectually stimulating and enriching academic environment for the best students of NTU. The programme includes an exciting multidisciplinary curriculum that complements their core curriculum and supplements their general education programme. From ethics to quantitative reasoning, from religions of the world to astronomy, NTU-USP offers a wide range of courses, special events and learning opportunities each year that promise to broaden students' perspectives and challenge their creative thinking and analytical ability.

NTU-NIE Teaching Scholars Programme (TSP)

The NTU-NIE TSP is the latest addition to the existing suite of scholar programmes in NTU. It is a premier scholars programme aimed at preparing tomorrow's leaders of education who possess the passion and aspiration to inspire, nurture and lead our next generation. NTU, as the host for NIE, has to attract the best students to all its programmes, but especially to NIE. After all, Singapore school education is held in high esteem worldwide, and nationally, the profession is an honoured and well-rewarded one. It was important that NTU, and NIE, had the ability to be able to attract top students into education and so become future leaders in the teaching profession.

The programme offers a unique opportunity for both personal development and international exposure in interdisciplinary training through seminars, conference presentations, research assignments and mentorship, internships and overseas programmes. Graduates of TSP will be well equipped with intellectual rigour, strong leadership and global perspectives — ready to fulfil their aspirations in education and make their contribution to shaping the future of the nation.

Residential Education Enhancing Student Life

NTU has been very privileged to have had a large campus on which to develop and this has given it the ability to become a residential university. It is not just residential for students but also for faculty and senior staff, of which around 1000 of them, with their families, live on campus. There are food outlets, shops, sports facilities and a nursery school. It is an educational and social community in its own right. All parties contribute to the

NTU "town" to provide a multigenerational and international community that is rarely found in universities. Together with the staff residing on campus and all the other people working on the campus — caterers, gardeners, maintenance contractors and many others — NTU is a small city of between 45,000 and 50,000 people during any workday in term time. Thus, the President of NTU was also the "Mayor of the Yunnan Garden Campus City"!

Even with quite extensive building programmes in the past, the provision was far less than the demand. Driven both by this demand and the intellectual case made by the Blue Ribbon Commission for a holistic experience for the students, NTU embarked on a major investment of US$1.8 billion to provide for a majority of the students, if not for all. One aim was to ensure that all freshmen would have the opportunity, and would be encouraged, to stay on campus and start to participate in all the activities that a residential experience provides. The campus has extensive sports facilities including a major new sports hall, the Wave, that can seat 3,000 and is the largest all-wood building in Singapore. Now, at the time of writing, some 16,000 students live on campus in the thriving community called NTU.

Eight new halls have been built, which increased our residential capacity by some 5,000 extra places. In the past, the halls were just given numbers, but now each hall has an interesting name with the new halls being named after the major tree species (following Bertil's suggestion) to be found on the island such as Saraca, Tamarind and Meranti — the latest of the halls. The second Graduate Hall (800 beds) was completed in early 2013. The new halls were designed with environmental sustainability in mind and are the latest buildings on campus to get top marks for being "green". This also gives the occupants a feeling that they are contributing to a better environment. At a time of increasing concern about the rise of nationalism around the world, the residential approach of NTU fosters racial and cultural integration in a meaningful way.

With such provision, Bertil, in one of his first actions as President, appointed an Associate Provost for Student Life (Professor Kwok Kian Woon) to start to engage with the Students' Union, the Graduate Students' Council and with the various school clubs, and through this student engagement to develop on many fronts not least that of residential learning. Not only is staying on campus convenient but it has enabled the development of new programmes specifically designed to enhance the student experience. This is the Residential Education (RE) programme with courses well away from the formal curriculum such as culinary appreciation, gardening, art, financial planning and healthy living. Many of the courses have a focus on developing practical skills for the future such as in developing entrepreneurship and learning how to invest and budget wisely, surely a core skill for everyone! Courses are not yet credit bearing, although this may be the case elsewhere.

Being able to meet the physical needs of staff and students is most important and NTU has upgraded its sports facilities to a very high standard. Adding to this, at Bertil's initiative, there is a jogging track around the campus, highly visible as it is made of a bright blue special running surface.

At the same time, having so many young people in our care means that we have pastoral duties to mesh in with residential education. This has to be both preemptive and proactive while not being intrusive.

Of course, with so much else besides the formal courses, there are also overseas exchanges, internships and industrial attachments, and final year projects. Therefore, with sports and community activities as well as residential education, students' lives are as packed and as busy as ever, but now in a far more holistic way than it was pre-BRC.

The university, through NTU Education and all the many other reforms instituted over the past decade or so, is now able to produce the graduate of the future. This is someone with high-quality education in a wide variety of topics, as well as their specialism. This includes language skills, grooming, how to conduct oneself in interviews or how to make interesting and succinct presentations. In the end, the graduate will encompass the five NTU Graduate attributes (the 5Cs), namely competence, creativity, communication, character and civic-mindedness.

At the end of the process, NTU produces graduates who are our alumni and our global family. Not everyone joins alumni associations, but NTU has an impressive nearly quarter of a million alumni registered in the various chapters in Singapore, China, the US, and Europe. Again, an impressive achievement for such a young university. This is discussed further in the chapter on alumni.

The Outcome

With the reforms introduced by the Blue Ribbon Commission, the investment in technology-enabled teaching and learning, the development of tutorials, group learning, flipped classrooms based on modern technology, a huge expansion of residential living and the ability to meet the needs of all students, from the most disadvantaged to the most gifted, have totally transformed the NTU student experience. Now, we are able to attract the best students, including provision for the very top students through the specialist programmes. In fact, we have increased our share of top students so that NTU is no longer seen as the "poor relation" of NUS, but as an equally desirable place at which to study. At the same time, for those students who see clearly their "life path" into employment, over 90% of NTU's graduates gain full-time employment within six months of graduation — quite an achievement compared with European universities! In NIE, there is a programme especially devoted to training teachers for early childhood and those with special educational needs. Playing on the acronym of the educational research programme (CRADLE), the early childhood programmes, and with continuing education, one could say that NTU is now educating Singapore from "the cradle to the grave"!

With all our new programmes and pedagogies and the use of the latest technologies and flipped classrooms, which have led to a renaissance of the tutorial system, NTU has become not just the "Oxbridge" or "Ivy League" of the tropics but is now an educational establishment of the future, with its wholehearted commitment to 21st century pedagogy.

Yet, challenges remain. Even though the Troika has tried, it has not succeeded in embedding a seminar culture within the university. Even Nobel Prize winner Richard Feynman would have found it hard to attract a full house at NTU! Singapore needs sustainability in its higher education sector, which means "growing" its own professors. That is what NTU's elite programmes are about, but only time will tell whether these efforts have borne fruit. What is clear is that over the past 15 years, NTU has advanced hugely and no more so that in its undergraduate teaching where it has fundamentally restructured itself and has now achieved a preeminence among the world's leading institutions.

When the unusual rapid progress of NTU is considered, one tends to think about the research developments, but the ambition to reform education was also both very ambitious and successful and has enabled NTU to take a major leap forward and become a model for others to follow.

Chapter 14

Elephants and Gazelles: The People Factor

Bertil likes to say, a university is "brains more than bricks". There is an equivalent saying in Chinese: to build a university, bring in the masters rather than build big buildings.

In this chapter, we show how true this is and how, in NTU's case, appointment (recruitment), promotion and tenure (APT) were the key factors in its success story. What was achieved at NTU in terms of faculty renewal, and its rapidity, has amazed many people. Possibly the single most important key factor was the manner in which a new promotion and tenure system was introduced, leading to the revitalisation of faculty and the release of their potential, a process that is described below.

From day 1 of the first Troika meeting, we had put faculty renewal at the top of our agenda.

In the month prior to taking up his appointment as President in January 2003, Guaning was shocked to be presented with a mountain of files, all of which related to the performance assessment and pay adjustment of NTU faculty. Without international references and reasoned submissions, this was reminiscent of the civil service of the past, but even the civil service had a hierarchy and a system of appraisal. Guaning refused to make decisions on the mountain of files, most of whose subject he did not know, and this convinced him that the system had to change.

With autonomy in 2005 came accountability in the form of the first QAFU report. Its External Review Panel (ERP), made up of senior academic leaders from around the world, identified a number of issues that needed to be addressed in what it described as "mission critical", one of which was the promotion and tenure (PT) system at NTU. The whole process of APT became a very crucial matter in that NTU was being faced with a big increase of student numbers requiring more faculty, and the ERP identified serious flaws in the PT part of the process.

The 2005 QAFU exercise, while bruising to the ego, pointed the way ahead. Faced with the possible extension of tenure to 65 years (it was previously only to 55 years followed by a rolling contract up to retirement age), Guaning resisted pressure from the ground to implement tenure extension. He wanted to reserve tenure to 65 years for those who qualified by having a high standard of achievement in which research played a critical role. This was also consistent with Haresh's observation during his sabbatical in 1992. Thus, Guaning and Haresh agreed that of the QAFU recommendations, the redesign of the APT process was the number one priority.

Its report started by saying that the elements of a good PT system include the following:

- Clear criteria for promotion and tenure, including the weightage for performance in teaching, research and service;
- Transparency in the assessment process;
- Robust peer review including by external assessors; and
- Consistency in application of the process and criteria across the institution.

Having identified these basic requirements, the QAFU report continued by observing that "NTU's PT system lacks transparency and consistent application across the university. The current process in which the final decision on PT matters (subject to endorsement by the Establishment Committee of the Council) is made by the University Academic Personnel Board (UAPB) which comprises the President, the Deputy Presidents, Director NIE and all the Deans of Schools, does not optimise outcomes. Faculty should be considered for tenure after 6 to 7 years of service, and external peer review should be done at this stage and not only at the point of consideration for promotion to the position of full

Professor." Clearly, this was not the case during the 2005 QAFU. The review further recommended that NTU should adopt and apply current international best practice. With Haresh on board, the obvious choice as a model was Stanford.

The ERP observed that at the time of review (2005), tenure at NTU was up to 55 years of age, and thereafter faculty could move on to a system of time-limited "rolling" contracts or retire from NTU to seek employment elsewhere. There was also the phenomenon of "eternal" assistant professors as there was no tenure clock to incentivise progress in the manner of the American system of a real tenure track. Singaporean universities had moved from a British system to an American structure of Assistant/Associate/Full Professors in the 1990s, but the system of tenure clocks for Assistant Professors had not been implemented and the number of Full Professors in the system was far short of the norm in American, European and other universities around the world. Many of the Full Professors were now in senior administrative positions, reducing further those fully involved in teaching and research. Indeed, this was not a problem for NTU alone as the situation was similar in NUS and in Hong Kong universities. The current Provost of NTU, Professor Ling San, when an Associate Professor at NUS where he had been departmental Deputy Head for a few years, was offered a post by NTU to head the Division of Mathematical Sciences at the School of Physical and Mathematical Sciences (SPMS), but still as an Associate Professor. NTU was going through its internal and external processes for his appointment as a Full Professor. However, he was very clear that he wanted the full professorship on academic merit ahead of headship or other administrative roles. He did not accept the offer. He recounts that, at the NTU interview, some senior academic leaders told him that at NTU he could be promoted to full professor, recognising his contribution to leadership and service, instead of research and teaching. He did not agree with that position, and he still does not agree. Academic merit is important. Later, following a complete academic appraisal, Ling San was appointed a Full Professor and was happy to accept this recognition of his academic merit.

It is worth quoting the QAFU report as this deals with the major change of tenure that NTU was facing at the time. The QAFU report said,

"The ERP notes that NTU is hesitant to raise the age limit because it will delay the exit of existing under-performing tenured faculty. NTU has also shared that newly appointed faculty are informed that, when they are up for consideration for tenure, this will be to an extended age of 65 years. While this does go some way to addressing the situation for new faculty, NTU needs to consider how it can maintain the morale of and retain good performers in the cohorts of previously employed faculty still subject to the 55 year age limit. There are other ways to manage performance short of outright dismissal and ultimately if NTU wants to move ahead and not continue to lose time, it must overcome its reluctance to take a tough stand with underperformers." This was a misunderstanding on the part of the ERP of the real reason for holding on to tenure at 55 years. It was not to manage underperformers, but to put everyone through quality control again, measuring against much higher standards. Only Haresh and Guaning knew this was the plan. They were not ready to announce this at the time of the QAFU because it was sensitive to morale and they needed an appropriate leader (a Provost) to execute the action. The QAFU report was in November 2005, one and a half years before the arrival of Bertil and nearly two years before the first promotion and tenure review took shape.

The report had indeed highlighted the fact that the whole tenure system in the university was ad hoc with different schools having different practices and there was a suspicion that there was a degree of favouritism in the system. These characteristics are often consequences of a highly top-down system.

The first step in following up the QAFU recommendation was done by Haresh using the Stanford PT template. Any faculty who wished to be awarded tenure to age 65 would have to go through an evaluation process. Assistant Professors had six to seven years to go pass the tenure hurdle. In cases where they had been misused (this was quite common) by overloading them with teaching and administration duties which restricted their research time, those concerned could be allowed up nine years prior to the tenure assessment.

This would entail the review of 1,200 or so faculty members — a huge task to undertake, especially when so much else was happening.

In starting the reform process in 2005, Guaning had asked Haresh to lead a committee to create the processes for appointment, reappointment, promotion and tenure and this had been approved by the Board and started by the time that Bertil came on board as Provost. One of Bertil's first tasks was to implement this decision, but with a number of changes that were subsequently agreed upon and are described below.

As Haresh recalls it, in starting to consider how best to create a fair, transparent and consistent system for APT, there was much confusion among the committee members. They were all used to dealing in an ad hoc and somewhat secretive way of conducting this most important function for academic excellence that they could not understand what Haresh was trying to implement. Haresh says, "*I gave them examples of how these processes were carried out at Stanford and other major US public and private universities. The Committee members were somewhat timid and reluctant to go along with the proposed changes. I stood firm and threatened them with grave consequences to the quality of NTU faculty if we did not make 'radical' changes (at least to their eyes).*" Eventually, Haresh prevailed and developed a scheme, based on the Stanford "best practice blueprint", with which Haresh was very familiar. The new system was used experimentally on a few appointments in 2006, and some minor modifications were made. Now, it was up to the new Provost to take this forward and implement the system. In fact, in 2007, there was still a lot of scepticism about whether there would really be any changes and many people assumed that this was more of a routine activity without any dramatic changes. In other words, the assumption was that everything would remain as "business as usual", but they were proved to be very wrong!

In early 2007, the process was started and so, by the time Bertil arrived in April that year, the system was already in place. First of all, one could not ask to be considered for tenure, one had to be nominated within the school. Then, a School Review Committee for PT (SRCPT), made up of peers from the school, reviewed the cases and agreed on the cases that were sufficiently mature and good enough to go forward. The cases were then forwarded to the School Chair and onward to the College Dean's committee, at which recommendations would come forward for approval. The overall scheme was strongly supported by the Board and this gave added authority to the changes underway.

Bertil considered that the implementation needed to be made even more rigorous and concrete, and that it was necessary to implicate the Deans in any upgrade that needed to be made.

On this latter point, Bertil remembers that, soon after his arrival at NTU, one of the Deans sent his secretary to see the new Provost with papers for tenure which he expected the Provost to rubber-stamp, without even a face-to-face discussion, for forwarding to the Academic Affairs Committee (AAC) of the Board of Trustees. This was a total anathema and Bertil quickly realised that he had to insist that there would be no shortcuts to proper discussion and consideration of all appointments, in addition to the review of tenure cases.

We had previously explained why the Board of Trustees reference for tenure cases is necessary here as this may be seen as micromanagement by the Board. It is worth repeating that the award of tenure is a major investment in a person as well as being a lengthy financial commitment of taxpayer's money (some receiving tenure at, say, 40 would imply a salary commitment of a quarter of a century), it was considered that the Board of Trustees had a duty to vet all such appointments through its Academic Affairs Committee, at that time chaired by Haresh.

One of the most important barriers for any programme to get their candidates either approved for appointment, promotion or tenure was the work done by the AAC. Even after all the previous reviews carried out by the divisions, schools, Deans and the Provosts and Deans Group (PDG), it was not uncommon that the AAC would send the case under consideration back to the school where it originated. The Troika was aware of the frustrations felt by the Deans and other leadership academics, but there were always gaps in the quality of the prepared and presented cases. The AAC took a "no exception" stance in sending back those cases that needed more information or for a better case to be made. It was due to this last filter that the Provost, Deans and the Chairs made sure that their cases were flawless. Over time, this resulted in better quality of papers and more robust collection and presentation of their arguments for approval. Haresh says, *"I believe that over the eight years of my personal observations and experience, this final approval process tremendously improved the quality of faculty we recruited, retained, promoted and gave tenure to. This was an important step that the Troika had agreed upon to ensure that all cases were complete, well-argued and presented."*

We describe, elsewhere, the creation of the PDG which became a key instrument for the reform not only of APT but also for the many other changes that were made at that time. The aim was to have common standards across the colleges and university with the same high-level threshold bar in place and with shared decision-making. Thus, the PDG became a very high-level university advisory board to top management. It was a key milestone in the development of NTU and a radical change from the past.

At a retreat meeting of the PDG on the neighbouring resort island of Bintan, Indonesia, in June 2007, there was a lengthy discussion of the weighting that should be given to the evaluations for teaching, research and "service". Eventually, all present accepted and agreed that this should be in the ratio of four for teaching, six for research and two for service. It was generally accepted that, at this juncture, in the ambitious plans for the evolution of NTU, research had to be accorded the highest priority. It was also accepted that the system really had to be based on peer review so that each case could only go forward once six external referee comments had been sought, and received, in support of a candidate. For promotion to Full Professors, there was a requirement for 10 external assessments with the bar commensurately higher. Finally, to ensure consistency across the university, the final decision on whether to recommend tenure would be taken by the PDG itself. This was a vital step in meeting the QAFU demands for rigour, consistency and, especially, transparency. People had to realise that this was not going to be business as usual. There was some opposition from the Chairs as it diminished their powers of patronage and influence. However, it was vital that the Deans were made part of the decision and the process and, therefore, it gave a new impetus to the college structure that was then still in its infancy.

It was important to set the bar at a significantly higher level so as to achieve parity with high-level international norms and it was this that sent shockwaves through the system. However, with hindsight, most of those who qualified under the new tenure arrangements were proud that their tenure was equivalent to that at the top universities and that they were very much equivalent to their peers in these elite institutions.

It was also agreed that, should faculty not jump over the new bar, which had been set high, then the university had to look at the implications for delivery of teaching on the one hand and how to deal with those who failed on the other. The PDG agreed that all contracts to age 55 would be honoured and that anyone close to this age who did not clear the hurdle would be guaranteed, for compassionate reasons, at least 12 months at NTU before they had to leave. There was also a system for those who just failed in the new tenure assessment to have some time to try to correct weaknesses and be reconsidered — these were what came to be termed the "soft nos".

With some 1,000 candidates in the first two rounds, this review became a mammoth task during 2007 and 2008 and little did the PDG realise the workload they were giving themselves when its members agreed to embark on this process!

However, following the seminal meeting of the PDG in Bintan, Bertil had to pause the implementation process, which was done immediately on his return. The Office of Human Resources had taken it for granted that it would supervise the tenure review process and not that the Provost should lead the process. Bertil quickly disabused them of this assumption. Now, everyone had to set about getting the external reviews that would be followed by the internal committee assessments. It has a necessary shock to the system. Getting all the external assessments measured against the new criteria weightings took some time, so it was not until September of that year that it was ready and the process started in earnest for the PDG. Frequent meetings were held in the evenings and over weekends in which the SRCPT Chairs and the School Chairs appeared before the PDG to defend their recommendations. This was a long process. Food and drinks were arranged for the PDG and very many pizzas were consumed and cups of coffee drunk over the next six months or so! Meeting during the weekends was necessary as the other work of the university had to continue.

This became known as PT1 and the whole process created much uncertainty and a lowering of morale among the faculty. It became clear to everyone that the bar for promotion and tenure had moved up. *It was not business as usual!*

However, the process was gradually accepted, as it became known that it was fair and that the same standards were being applied consistently across the institution. A second PT (PT2) followed with about 200 cases to review so it was again quite onerous, although less so than in 2007/2008.

Naturally, there were criticisms of the process as many felt unclear without any formal feedback. Possibly, this had resulted from the decision that this was a matter for the School Chairs and it was this failure of communication on their part that was the cause of much unhappiness. They did not want to carry the bad news and it was so much easier to blame the top university management for the tough decisions.

Many people had taken their promotion or tenure for granted or had already been promised it by their Chair. Now, this did not happen because of the much higher bar that had been set. Some people disagreed with the weighting given to research and others criticised the teaching assessment that was too heavily dependent on student feedback. This latter point was something that the Troika agreed with and in the chapter on reforming education, we describe how this particular concern was addressed and dealt with.

The result was traumatic. In the end, some 250 faculty (20%) lost their positions at NTU with some remaining in temporary positions in teaching-only roles. Naturally, such a dramatic change shocked both NTU and Singapore and not only made the local press but also raised questions from ministers in response to faculty who were their constituents. Bertil and Guaning had to publicly defend the rigour of the process that was now operating at the highest level of international best practice. Of course, there was a small element of "rough justice", but the overall process was transparent with clear criteria. However, a lot of antagonism remained, resulting in Bertil being threatened and his car tyres being slashed. It shows the virulence with which these changes were greeted in some quarters. However, interestingly, all those affected eventually found posts in the Singaporean education system or became faculty members in other institutions in the region. The great benefit for NTU was that it created the space for new recruitment and the essential revitalisation of the faculty body. It was probably the biggest single reason why NTU progressed as it did. It was a case of "not changing the car" but "changing the engine in the car", while the car was running!

Initially, some 40% of faculty were rejected, with half being termed "soft" rejects with detailed improvement points identified so that those concerned could address these criticisms and reapply, which they did over the next two to three years. While this rate of rejection came from the PDG, it is interesting to note that the school-level assessment had resulted in only a 10% rejection rate. Clearly, one could only have high standards rigorously enforced by taking the decisions to a higher level, as had been recommended by the 2005 QAFU report. This would not have been possible if it had not been for strong top-down action. In a bottom-up process, there may be too many collegialities and loyalties to overcome.

What was the overall outcome? While there had been a significant dip in morale throughout this process, by the end of the second review, morale was increasing as those who remained had passed this high academic bar. The 75% of faculty who had succeeded were now empowered and had renewed confidence that released potential in both research and teaching — a very important factor in NTU's future rise. One example is of someone who today is a very successful academic researcher and yet in 2007, before PT1, said that he would not respond to competitive calls for proposals as "there is no point as NUS academics always get the money". Now, he outcompetes the other institutions. The result was that it gave renewed confidence to those who passed the rigours of the PT review and, in addition, it created the space for new recruitment that is discussed below. It had released NTU's existing potential in a very big way.

Now, we turn to our exotic menagerie of "elephants" and "gazelles", metaphors invented by the Troika. To mix metaphors, we had to prune the forests (PT process) to provide light for a replanting scheme (elephants and gazelles). The Troika had already prioritised this, at its first meeting, as being a key factor in the development of the university. Without having a successful, and again rigorous, recruiting process, much of the effort in the PT review would have been nugatory. Thus, firing and hiring were the two essential keys to NTU's future success.

Elephants are leading academic professors who have been recruited to NTU to nucleate new and competitive research and give us a much-needed kick-start in a particular area. We wanted world leaders with proven academic brilliance and leadership to come to NTU. They would set new standards and become role models, especially for local faculty and for students. Such successful and senior academics would pave the way for NTU to become competitive in research and increase its share of the funds available.

One such "big elephant" was Kerry Sieh. Kerry, a world-leading expert on earthquakes and their origin, a member of the US National

Academy of Sciences, and holding an endowed chair at the California Institute of Technology, had come to NTU as a Visiting Professor in order to study the subduction megathrust that has been producing great earthquakes offshore Sumatra. How was NTU to secure Kerry's continuing presence? Initially, the thoughts of Guaning and Haresh turned to the issue of security in its broadest sense, especially including seismic risk. President S. R. Nathan was very much involved, formerly being in charge of what is now the S. Rajaratnam School of International Studies (RSIS) and having known Haresh from the latter's Stanford days. Haresh and Guaning spent many pleasant afternoons having tea with the President, discussing how to take a security-orientated research institute forward. This evolved over time and eventually led to the Earth Observatory of Singapore (EOS). The answer was the NRF Research Centres of Excellence (RCE) opportunity worth S$150 million over 10 years, which is discussed in Chapter 16. Bertil was charged with encouraging Kerry to submit an application and to assist him in preparing the submission, bringing in other elephants including leading researchers such as Paul Tapponnier from Paris, a member of the French Academy of Sciences and one of the top tectonicists in the world to the RCE. The success in recruiting such top scientists and in gaining an RCE was a real milestone in NTU starting to become a truly research-intensive university.

Another big recruit was Staffan Kjelleberg, an internationally recognised expert in studies of bacterial adaptive responses, signalling-based communication between bacteria, bacterial biofilm biology and chemically mediated interactions between bacteria and marine organisms. Again, this was based on successfully bidding to the RCE scheme (see also Chapter 16). With this recruitment, we not only enticed an elephant to NTU but also, with the RCE approval, he was able to attract other elephants such Stephan Schuster, a world-leading genomicist. This not only brought top academics to NTU but also enabled it to establish new disciplines both new to NTU and new to Singapore. Especially significant was the establishment of a high-level genomics and metagenomics research capability. This is what happened with the RCEs as we brought in advanced earth sciences and global environmental change on the one hand and environmental microbiology and biofilms on the other.

In taking the recruitment forward, the Troika recommended that to pursue this policy we needed a special recruitment fund to attract the "elephants". This was taken to the Board that approved the idea early in 2008 as part of the university's budget process. Through the PDG system, Bertil asked the Deans to come up with suggestions for "elephant" recruitment, but the answer came there were none, except for Jitendra Singh, the Dean of the Nanyang Business School who was able to attract "business school elephants" such as Chiu Chi-Yue and Hong Ying Yi. In the end, the job was left to Bertil to hunt down the elephants using the recruitment fund as an incentive and using the high-level network that he had established through his involvement with the Nobel Committee and, in Europe, through the European Science Foundation.

Later, another initiative was in structural biology with, at the start, the recruitment of Pär Nordlund, a leading X-ray structural biologist, formerly working at Oxford University and then at the Karolinska Institute, Stockholm. Second, Bertil recruited Daniela Rhodes, a Fellow of the Royal Society from the Cambridge-based Laboratory for Molecular Biology (LMB), a location which had produced 13 Nobel Prize winners and a further 11 alumni who have become Nobel Prize winners. Bertil recalls that he met Daniela at a farewell dinner in Heidelberg for the Director of the European Molecular Biology Organisation (EMBO). He followed this up at another dinner, this time at Trinity College Cambridge attended by Nobel Prize winners, Venki Ramakrishnan (now President of the Royal Society) and Amartya Sen. Daniela was persuaded and came to NTU, later winning a high-value Tier 3 grant with which to establish the Nanyang Institute of Structural Biology, based around advanced electron microscopy.

In other areas, NTU recruited Zhang Hua and David Lou, later named by Thomson Reuters in the 2015 list of the World's Hottest Researchers. We recruited Nickolay Zheludev, FRS who won another Tier 3 grant and who, with Sir David Payne from Southampton University, developed the joint activity in photonics which has led to the establishment of the NTU Photonics Institute, one of the major success stories of NTU and Singapore.

We did not only confine ourselves to engineering and science, but hunted elephants in medicine, sociology and the humanities. One such person is Charles Salmon, an eminent American expert in mass communications from Michigan State University. Another was the University of California, Los Angeles (UCLA) behavioural sociologist Zhou Min.

Of course, the advent of the Medical School brought new challenges and opportunities, and we were able to use this brand-new and exciting development to "lure" other big elephants such as George Augustine, a reputed clinician scientist in the neurosciences; John Chambers from Imperial College, working in the public health area; and from the Karolinska Institute, NTU was also able to attract Per-Olof Berggren, a renowned endocrinologist.

During this process, we have always been mindful to try to find leading Singaporean academics. This was not an easy task as this is, again to mix metaphors, fishing in a small pool, as too few Singaporeans enter academia. This remains a continuing problem for Singapore. Even if one is able to "hook" someone, they may not be very mobile from their overseas institutions. Nevertheless, it remains a key point, high on NTU's future agenda, to have high-level Singaporeans on the faculty to ensure the sustainability of the university.

Using visiting professorships was another means of attracting leading academics to NTU and several later took up positions within NTU. Here, we must mention Stephen Lansing from the University of Arizona and Peter Sloot from the Vrije Universiteit, Amsterdam, who established our Complexity Institute; Rudy Markus, a Nobel Prize winner in chemistry; Maria Michel-Beyerle, a well-known physicist who was not only a faculty member of NTU but also headed the Technical University of Munich CREATE project; and the last was the late James Barber, FRS from Imperial College London.

Again, to pursue the animal metaphor, having completed our elephant hunt, we went trapping for the gazelles — the brightest young researchers intent on making an academic career for themselves whom we wished to entice to NTU.

During 2006, and following from earlier advice from the NRF Science Advisory Board, NRF introduced its call for proposals for NRF Fellows. At Bertil's instigation, while he was a member of this Board, NRF had established a scheme for support for the best young researchers, modelled closely on the European Young Investigator Awards (EURYI) operated by the European Science Foundation (ESF) and later incorporated into the European Research Council (ERC) — now the ERC Starting Grants scheme. All addressed the difficult transition from a post-doctoral fellow to a truly independent researcher and Principal Investigator (PI). The NRF scheme was generous, initially with a US$1.5 million grant to be held at a Singaporean institution which would be the host and provide the awardee with an academic position.

The Troika had been concerned that junior faculty appointments were being made with a low ambition, merely replacing faculty who had left for whatever reason and with the intention of plugging teaching gaps. This was, as Bertil phrases it, "being confined to the 'salt mines' of teaching" without the scope to develop, both as a researcher and as a teacher, nor to become a fully functioning academic.

NTU had to break this mould and, early on, it was agreed that all new academic hires, at whatever level, would have a Start-up Grant (SUG) from the university. At the famous Bintan retreat (see earlier), the PDG had considered this problem and had not only recommended the SUG system but also gave instructions that new Assistant Professors, on a three-times three-year tenure track, had to be protected somewhat from the normal academic chores with reduced teaching and minimal service during the first three-year tranche of the tenure track. In this way, we would give all new junior hires the opportunity to establish themselves. Unusually, this common sense and international best practice policy created resistance from established faculty who saw this as impinging on their rights as senior academics. With a strategic fund to carry out this policy in the name of the Provost rather than the schools, NTU was able to move ahead.

Turning back to the NRF Fellows, here NTU was now operating at the top world level. This was another great opportunity for NTU. Initially, it had been expected that the young NRF Fellows would naturally select NUS to host them. The procedure was that, during a week-long visit to Singapore, the short-listed candidates from the world's leading institutions would visit the various institutions in Singapore, meet academic leaders and faculty in their chosen area of study, as well as make presentations to the NRF Science Advisory Board, which would make the selection. Although time-consuming, it ensured that only the very best would get past this rigorous filter. To everyone's surprise, but maybe not those at

NTU, half the successful candidates chose NTU. This result was repeated in the following years when NTU, at times, even had the majority of candidates choosing to come to our university. It was a mark of growing confidence in and external visibility of the institution. We were now competing as equals with NUS and Singapore was achieving its original aim, when NTU was founded, to have two major internationally recognised universities in the country. Over the last decade, NTU has cumulatively continued to secure almost half of the NRF Fellows with the remainder shared between the other Singaporean research institutions.

It is noteworthy that two of the successful NRF Fellows were previously EURYI awardees — Christos Panagopoulos and Hilmi Volkan Demir, both now Full Professors in the university and examples of what could be achieved here. Another later recruit who had held an ERC Starting Grant was Ayumi Tashiro. It was somewhat disconcerting for the European institutions to find that they were now less attractive, despite trying their best, than institutions in Singapore in being able to attract the best to its shores.

At the same time, there were only a limited number of NRF fellowships available of which NTU was gaining one half. However, this was only five or six "gazelles" per year. We needed to increase our trapping rate! Furthermore, the NRF Fellowships were confined to the science, technology, engineering and mathematics (STEM) subjects and medicine and we needed to recruit on a wider basis.

Again, following discussions in the Troika and the PDG, NTU instituted a new recruitment category, namely the Nanyang Assistant Professorships (NAPs), covering all disciplines. These would be recruited competitively from across the world and would be subject to a high-level review system within the university. Essentially, the system consisted of shortlisting proposals and then assessing candidates on the basis of their presentations and detailed questioning by a panel and was similar to the model first introduced in ESF under Bertil's leadership. In the chapter on research, we refer to the creation of the NTU Research Council chaired by Bengt Nordén from Chalmers University, Gothenburg, Sweden, and previously a Chairman of the Nobel Chemistry Committee. The decision to use this mechanism, which we also used to assess Tier 2 grant applications, was primarily to provide a high-level assessment process for the NAP candidates. It was also agreed that NAPs would receive a much higher start-up grant than that to be accorded to the standard recruitment with up to S$1 million being made available.

Having announced the call for NAP proposals, and with around 10 appointments in mind, we were gratified and overwhelmingly surprised by the number (over 600 applications) that we received from young researchers, mainly at prestigious universities who wanted to join NTU. These included many "westerners" as well as "Asian returnees". We have continued to recruit 10 or so NAPs each year and gradually attracting applicants not only for science and engineering but also for arts, humanities and social science. Professor Steven Boxer, from Stanford University and a member of our selection committee, commented that he had never seen such a high calibre of applicants as those applying for NAPs, even though he had served on high-level selection panels for the US National Institutes of Health (NIH) and the National Science Foundation (NSF). Selection for such appointments is tough and rigorous and this has helped to raise the overall recruitment bar. Candidates were expected to give mock lectures and produce evidence of a high level of research and good teaching practice.

Now, the designation "Nanyang Assistant Professor" is an important and much sought-after accolade in NTU and now recognised internationally as a quality label. Over a decade of its operation, NTU has received more than 4,000 applications and has made over 100 appointments for this much sought-after title. It has been immensely satisfying and successful and has led to the renewal of faculty with the brightest and best young and aspiring (and hungry for success) academics from around the world. Now, other universities around the world are imitating our highly successful recruiting scheme.

As described elsewhere, the NRF fellows and the NAPs represent only 5% of the total faculty and yet they produce 40% of our high-impact papers especially in *Nature* and *Science*. Almost all the NRF Fellows and the NAPs attain tenure with relative ease. It really is an investment in the future and a legacy of which we in the Troika are naturally very proud. We have great confidence that these young gazelles will drive NTU forward as a place of high academic esteem. They represent the NTU of tomorrow.

Chapter 15

A Unique Medical School

Most universities want not only to have good schools and top-class professors but also to host two schools that are deemed to be very prestigious. One is a Business School and the other a Medical School. Nanyang Technological University (NTU) was fortunate that, from almost its inception, as related Chapter 3, it had a Business School. This, the Nanyang Business School, with its specialism in accountancy, is now highly thought of as one of Asia's top business schools and is now ranked 22 in the world according to the *Financial Times* rankings.

In the region, several of the top universities had started out as Medical Schools. That was the case with NUS (it started in 1905 as the Straits Settlements and Federated Malay States Government Medical School). The school was renamed King Edward VII Medical School in 1912 and was the first institution of higher learning in Singapore. Hong Kong University and Yonsei University in Korea have had similar trajectories. All developed from the need to meet the basic demand for doctors at the end of the 19th century.

Around the turn of the millennium, with an increasing need for medical doctors, Singapore started to plan an expansion of its medical training capacity. The only medical school at that time at NUS did not have sufficient capacity to train the requisite number to meet these needs.

Actually, this was the time when Singapore announced its Biomedical Sciences Initiative (BSI) designed to make the country the biomedical hub of Asia and to attract both research and health sector manufacturing capabilities to Singapore. This was very much inspired by Nobel Prize winner, the late Sydney Brenner, whose idea was that Singapore would be a hub for such research in Southeast Asia.

The 2001 Medical Education Review Panel, chaired by Lord Ron Oxburgh (a leading geophysicist who was to be later a member of the 2010 QAFU), recommended that Singapore should establish a graduate medical school to produce the highly trained medical leaders needed to support the BSI. It endorsed a partnership with Duke University proposed by Singapore Health Services (SingHealth — the largest group of medical institutions in the country), but it needed an academic host and this was somewhat foisted onto NUS to provide the necessary local degree validation. The Duke–NUS partnership commenced in 2005 with the aim to produce clinician-scientists with an American-style graduate entry. Although the aim was to produce clinician-scientists for the BSI, it was only partially successful as many of these graduates became doctors within the general health service.

As the only other "big" university, NTU worked with the Singapore General Hospital (SGH) to propose setting up a medical school. The aim, at that time, was to establish a second medical school in partnership with an American university, and the University of Washington in Seattle was chosen as the academic partner. Unfortunately, the working relationship between NTU and SGH was not seamless. SGH's senior representative at that time, Dr. Soo Khee Chee, related to Guaning his experience working with NTU. Essentially, SGH found NTU was very protective of the project and did not work with its partner in an open and transparent manner. For example, SGH had not been kept informed of the visit of the external panel assessing NTU's proposal and so did not have a chance to provide their inputs for the presentation. This was probably the consequence of the top-down culture at NTU as well as considering it unnecessary to have external help, even from the medical partner. Without the medical input from SGH, the panel found the proposal not up to mark.

Eventually, the second medical school in Singapore was set up as an American-style graduate programme structured more for research and training clinician-scientists on the SGH campus. This was the partnership between NUS and Duke University and, thus, NUS became unusual as a university with two medical schools.

What of NTU? In 2001, the review panel concluded that NTU was not ready for a medical school. It was in its first decade and still dominantly an engineering institution without a sufficient natural sciences base to host a medical school. Provided that NTU took steps to develop the natural sciences, it could be considered as a possible host for a medical school at some later stage. In order to prepare for this eventuality, it was proposed to expand NTU to include a School of Biological Sciences (SBS). This occurred in 2002, to be followed three years later by the School of Physical and Mathematical Sciences (SPMS). It was not until nearly a decade later that NTU was finally able to set up a medical school. The then second Minister for Education Ng Eng Hen, who was later to play a crucial role in establishing the medical school, was heavily involved in supporting and encouraging NTU's "science expansion". Remember that, at that time, it was before autonomy and NTU was governed by a governing Council appointed by the Ministry of Education (MOE).

As the decade progressed, Singapore's continued population growth and the anticipated medical demands of a rapidly ageing population became key factors in reviewing the case for increasing the supply of medical doctors in the country.

In late 2007, the government, concerned about its provision for higher education and, in comparison with similar populations elsewhere, with the age cohort going to university being well below the average in the developed world, set up a Committee for the Expansion of the University Sector in Singapore (CEUS). This led to the creation of Singapore's fourth university — the Singapore University of Technology and Design (SUTD) and the Yale-NUS Liberal Arts College. Bertil was the member from NTU as was the Chairman of the Board of Trustees, Koh Boon Hwee.

Bertil recalls that he was at the Troika meeting in Rigi-Kulm when he received an SMS message asking him to join CEUS, and for him it was the start of the medical school story. Later, he donated this Nokia phone to a time capsule buried at the official opening of the Medical School building in Novena in August 2017.

In November 2007, in a memorandum addressed to the Committee, statistics provided by the Ministries of Health and Manpower indicated that the projected population increase coupled with demographical changes in the ageing population would lead to a resource shortage and growing strain on the existing healthcare resources in the coming decades. Based on the statistical analysis, it concluded that Singapore would be required to double the number of doctors it produced by 2020. It estimated that Singapore needed an input of new doctors of around 800 per year, of which a majority were at that time recruited from abroad. Other than NUS, which had increased its student intake from 250 to 300 (an output considered high by international standards), the balance was being made up with foreign graduates and there were concerns about the quality of such recruits. At that time, none had graduated as a qualified doctor from Duke-NUS (it was formally established in 2005, taking its first intake of students in 2007 and passing out as doctors in 2011). It was on course to produce 54 doctors per year, who were trained as clinician-scientists rather than meeting the demand for primary care. The memorandum concluded that Singapore's capacity was inadequate to meet the projected demand as outlined by the Ministries. This indicated the need to reexamine the case for establishing Singapore's third medical school (as the second school with an undergraduate intake) with the aim of producing practitioners for the public health system and that this would be the key to resolving the national shortage of trained doctors.

This was the opportunity for NTU. Guaning and Bertil had already discussed this as a key priority for the university and were ready to respond.

NTU immediately replied positively in a short paper presented to the Committee. In an effort to evaluate NTU's academic and resource capabilities to support our proposal to host a medical school, and, following on from our initial response to the CEUS paper, Guaning asked Bertil to produce a feasibility and scoping study. Bertil then turned to and engaged Professor Jan Carlstedt-Duke, who had had a central strategic role as the former Dean of Research at the Karolinska Institutet in Stockholm and had worked at a high level in the Swedish system, to work on this project. In this study, conducted in 2008 and 2009, Professor Carlstedt-Duke identified several schools across NTU working in areas relevant to medical science and in ongoing collaboration with hospitals and clinical research labs. It transpired that more than 300 ongoing medically relevant projects were underway with faculty involvement from the Schools of Biological Sciences, Chemical and Biomedical Engineering, Materials Sciences and

Engineering, Physical and Mathematical Sciences, Computer Engineering, Electrical and Electronic Engineering, and Humanities and Social Sciences. Jan was also introduced by Guaning to Karen Koh, former Deputy Chief Executive Officer (CEO) of SingHealth, who provided much of the background information that Jan needed. Later, Jan was instrumental in the practical implementation of the Medical School and the creation of an institute (Nanyang Institute of Technology in Health and Medicine (NITHM)) to bring medicine, engineering and other disciplines into alignment, and he was a member of the Medical School's governing board.

Further discussions were held with the Chairman of the Board of Trustees and, in June 2008, the proposal was put to the full Board and the decision was "Let's go for it!", although some members, including Haresh, were cautious. This was because, in the US, universities with medical schools run the associated hospital carrying the medical liabilities. This is not the case in Singapore as it followed the British model.

Work continued on fleshing out the proposal, again debated by the Board of Trustees in February 2009, following which NTU's proposal for the new Medical School was formally submitted to MOE.

The proposal outlined a response to the contextual challenges of Singapore's healthcare needs, including a rapidly ageing population, as well as proposed outcomes that sought to bridge the gaps in current local practice. The proposal would also go on to provide key recommendations to shape the design and composition of the school's management framework, faculty recruitment strategy, pedagogic approach and curriculum content. Strong governmental support notwithstanding, establishing the medical school remained a significant undertaking that required a careful assessment of both the university's resources and the healthcare needs of the community it sought to serve. It was also recognised that the new medical school would lead to a series of beneficial impacts such as enhancing NTU's research activity as well as serving the community through provision of supply and access to better trained doctors and quality healthcare services. The proposal identified the need to develop further community-based medicine initiatives and proposed a programme designed to respond to the needs of the healthcare system of the future and to establish wider practice of doctors working in multi-professional teams.

These planning efforts also had to take into consideration that the new medical school would be acting in concert with the NUS Medical School, Duke–NUS Graduate Medical School and with the Singapore Ministry of Health's clinical transformation strategy. In addition, the study also recommended establishing an affiliation with a clinical partner as a priority, as well as the need to create interfacing platforms between the proposed Medical School and the existing NTU faculty and schools. Finally, another key recommendation in the proposal suggested seeking out partnerships and sustained engagement with leading universities strong in medical research and education to further boost the capacity and assist in the quality assurance processes.

Four international academic partners were under consideration. As research partners, Imperial College London and Karolinska Institutet were considered because of their strong medical schools as well as because there were ongoing research collaborations between NTU and these institutions. For teaching partners, NTU looked at the University of Warwick, UK and the University of Sydney, Australia. These were considered because, first, University of Warwick was a young school and had recent experience of the setting-up phase of a medical school. It concentrated on the area of primary care, an area in which NTU saw itself in meeting national needs, and it had a strong life sciences department linked to the medical school and with which NTU was developing a research collaboration in neurosciences. University of Sydney, on the other hand, was a well-established and renowned school with an exciting curriculum and with many novel and modern approaches to medical training.

By this time, Ng Eng Hen had become the Minister for Education, and as a medical doctor, took a leading role in approving the NTU proposal and taking it forward. His role in the founding of the school cannot be understated. He felt that the Singaporean medical establishment was not fully supportive and that NTU needed a prestigious partner to be associated with the school. He considered that Imperial College London fitted the bill best as Singaporeans knew the Imperial College branding. Given this, he fully supported the aims of NTU and, having obtained firm political endorsement from the Singapore Cabinet, gave NTU the go ahead to develop a five-year, undergraduate-intake programme. Thus, we were able to go to the next stage with firm political support. This time, Bertil received another SMS message to inform him of the Cabinet decision. This closed the loop between the first and second SMS texts!

By happenchance, in 2009, the then Rector of Imperial College, Roy Anderson, was visiting Singapore to take part in the inaugural meeting of the Global Alliance of Technological Universities (GlobalTech) that had been formed following an initiative by Guaning. He met the Minister and other senior figures in Singapore and, a few months later, Imperial College agreed to go forward with NTU, and formal negotiations commenced in August 2009. Minister Ng followed up with a visit to Imperial College to get the College's agreement.

Imperial College was relatively new in the medical field. Previously devoted to engineering and science, it added St Mary's Medical School to its portfolio only in 1988. In the mid to late 1990s, it incorporated the National Heart and Lung Institute, the Charing Cross and Westminster Medical School, the Royal Postgraduate Medical School (RPMS) and the Institute of Obstetrics and Gynaecology. Thus, in a short time, it had become a powerhouse in medical education. For Imperial College, linking with NTU was an unprecedented opportunity for a landmark collaboration to establish a joint medical school abroad in Singapore. There was consensus among us, the Board and MOE that Imperial's leading expertise in engineering and technology, shared research profile and strong integrated platforms to promote interfacing between engineering and medicine research were similar and would work to complement NTU's research profile and efforts. These attributes were further supported by an existing alliance between NTU and Imperial College built on strong, long-standing collaborations across education and research, and, importantly, based on mutual academic esteem.

Negotiations, often hard and complex, took place with Bertil and Jan Carlstedt-Duke from NTU, together with the Deputy Permanent Secretary from MOE and a senior official from the Ministry of Health meeting with the Imperial team led by Mary Ritter, then Pro-Rector International, and other key colleagues from Imperial. These negotiations continued through 2009 during which time Keith O'Nions[1] had replaced Roy Anderson as

---

[1] Sir Keith later joined the NTU Board of Trustees and, in 2019, was granted an Honorary doctorate by NTU.

Rector, initially on an acting basis and later as the definitive appointment. Bertil flew to London to meet Keith who enthusiastically backed the joint project. He was a pillar of strength in the creation of the joint project and, sometime later, he was invited to join the NTU Board of Trustees. The negotiations were very intense and, occasionally, were stuck, but, with good will on both sides, a final agreement was signed in August 2010 lasting for an unprecedented 18 years. Koh Boon Wee played a major role during the negotiations when they became somewhat bogged down. Together with Bertil, who had a long-standing affiliation with Imperial as a Fellow of the College and a Visiting Professor, he played a critical role at such junctures. Later, Lim Chuan Poh, the then Chairman of A*STAR, Board of Trustees member and also a Fellow of Imperial College, was persuaded by Bertil (when they travelled together to Mexico) and Mary Ritter to chair the pro-tem and then the full Governing Board of the new school.

The intention to create the medical school was announced by the Prime Minister of Singapore in his speech at the Singapore 2010 National Day Rally earlier that month. It had become a "juicy morsel" for such a senior politician to include in this important speech. From then on, it was implementation!

Such a lengthy academic agreement is most unusual and the 18 years consisted of a three-year development phase, a five-year operational phase during which the first cohort of students would be admitted, a further five years of operations and then a final five years of ramp down after which the medical school would be solely NTU. There is an option to prolong the operational phase in successive five-year periods if the partners mutually agree.

There were a number of crucial developments during this gestation. Imperial College had proposed that teaching should be based on e-learning. Koh Bon Hwee then proposed that this should be instrumental in developing e-learning throughout NTU and proposed to the Board that NTU should put up US$20 million to support such a move. MOE allocated US$90 million including a component for research (a most unusual move by the Ministry), which NTU augmented by a further US$25 million from its own budget. These figures demonstrated the importance with which the project was regarded in Singapore.

Meanwhile, Guaning and Director of Development Marina Tan Harper had been working on developing the possibility of a generous Lee Foundation donation for the medical school in honour of the founder, Tan Sri Dato Lee Kong Chian. Guaning had been working on fund-raising since 2005 and had established a close relationship with the Lee Foundation, Singapore's largest charitable foundation, established by the late philanthropist Lee Kong Chian. The Foundation was chaired by the late Dr. Lee Seng Gee. Dr. Lee had approved the first big donation of S$10 million towards establishing the Institute of Advanced Studies at NTU. This time, we are asking for S$150 million, the biggest ever donation in Singapore. The naming rights offered were likely to be the last medical school to be set up in Singapore. The Lee Foundation did not like giving big donations, preferring to champion smaller organisations closer to those needing assistance. The possibility of honouring their father with a medical school was, at least, tantalising. We were aware that Dr. Lee Seng Gee, the eldest son of Lee Kong Chian, was not well and relied on his wife, Dr. Della Lee, to attend to his needs. Marina had by then established a close friendship with Mrs. Lee. Meanwhile, Guaning sent KC Chew, the Chief Development Officer, to work on the other members of the Lee Foundation Board, chaired by Acting Chairman Dr. Lee Seng Tee and including five third-generation descendants. The Foundation used to be run top-down by Dr. Lee Seng Gee such that he was the final arbiter on whether the petitioner request was granted. Now that he was not well, the other voices on the board counted more than ever. The details of the medical school were presented to the Lee Foundation Board with the full complement of NTU and Imperial leadership present. In particular, Bertil and the Principal of Imperial College Faculty of Medicine, Professor Stephen Smith, had to provide in-depth academic and medical details in quite intensive discussions. After that, we could only keep our fingers crossed as the Lee Foundation debated on this naming opportunity.

When word came that the Lee Foundation had approved the gift, there was a collective sigh of relief. We had secured the largest ever donation to an academic institution in Singapore. The school was named the Lee Kong Chian Medical School or LKC Medicine in short. The late Tan Sri Dato Lee Kong Chian, a key figure in the post-war development of

Singapore, had been involved in the founding of *Nantah*. In a way, we had come full circle.

Charitable giving in Singapore is highly encouraged by the government, which matches such donations in the case of universities and especially if it is a new area. Thus, overnight, the donation jumped to S$400 million Nowhere else would we have received such a generous "start-up" fund — we really were in business!

LKC Medicine was established to add to Singapore's healthcare capacity, and built upon NTU's academic portfolio that had developed over the course of the past few years. Its development also played an important role in casting pertinent questions to shape the country's long-range roadmap for healthcare delivery. It also emphasised the need to re-examine the alignment of competencies among the existing medical schools. LKC Medicine's development has provided an opportunity for the introduction of the latest pedagogic approaches, especially using new technologies, implementation of a tailored educational agenda for the local context, as well as advance solutions for the healthcare challenges of the future.

We had to select a clinical partner for the school and our choice fell on the Tan Tock Seng Hospital (TTSH), located in the Novena district of Singapore, one of Singapore's largest multidisciplinary hospitals with 45 clinical and allied health departments and 16 specialist centres. Tan Tock Seng is part of the National Healthcare Group (NHG). It is located in what has become Health City Novena, an incredible concentration of integrated medical and healthcare operations with not only Tan Tock Seng Hospital and LKC Medicine (housed in spectacular new buildings) but also the National Skin Centre and the National Centre for Infectious Diseases and with, alongside, the private Mount Elizabeth Novena Hospital.

Thus, Novena became our third and very significant medical campus consisting of three buildings. The first is the heritage building, originally a hostel for medical students that subsequently became residential quarters for nurses and is now the headquarters of the Medical School. The second is a new Annex to that building housing the auditorium, the Toh Kian Chui Annex. The third building is the 20-storey Clinical Sciences Building.

These are described in the chapter about the campus. The Clinical Sciences Building is equipped with the latest information technology (IT)-enabled teaching and with consulting rooms and operation theatres in which the teachers can observe the students in action. On the main Yunnan Garden campus, NTU has built an Experimental Medicine Building with advanced research laboratories and flipped classrooms including a large "learning studio". To this end, the dual-campus model with the Experimental Medicine Building adjacent to the School of Biological Sciences has served to promote opportunities for interaction and convergence to better drive basic biomedical science research efforts.

The NHG was identified as the primary clinical partner when the school was first established. NHG was very active in the initial planning and implementation of the medical programme. Our key hospital partner is TTSH which provides its undergraduate students with early and extensive exposure to patients and clinical care conditions. With the curriculum's emphasis on patient-centred care, the clinical education arrangements seek to expose students to the whole pathway of care and encourage deeper understanding of patients' needs within a holistic framework. The various components in the learning curricula combine to create a transformative learning experience designed to produce thinking, collaborative and empathetic doctors essential to an evolving and challenging healthcare delivery landscape. As an example of novel approaches to enhance these qualities is the long-term patient project. Pairs of students follow a patient with a chronic disease during Years 1 and 2 with regular contact with the family. Also, they follow the clinical and social implications of the disease. This approach is a crucial component of the curriculum, providing a service-learning experience for the students, and serves to facilitate collaborative teamwork and simulate patient-centred care. In contrast to existing medical schools, LKC Medicine exposes students to patients at a very early stage in their learning. Students not only meet "real" patients, but through "mock" consulting areas, the students can practice on actor-patients under close observation.

The decision was made for LKC Medicine to be established as an autonomous school of NTU, with formalised affiliations to the two universities. Over the course of the negotiations, one of the major challenges that emerged was the way in which the decision-making framework could be designed to ensure an equal partnership across governance and administrative decisions. This eventually led to establishing a Governing Board, which would formally institute joint decision-making and play an important function in ensuring that existing quality benchmarks and standards were being upheld. The Board, chaired by Lim Chuan Poh, has two representatives each from Imperial College and NTU plus representatives from the Ministries of Education and Health as well as representatives from Singaporean business/industry and from society. Each partner is accorded equal weight in decision-making with the power of veto with respect to a predetermined set of reserved matters. The reserve matters were jointly identified and agreed upon by both partners and relate to important issues such as governance and administration, faculty recruitment, research matters and curriculum, among others. This governance framework proved to be an integral feature of the partnership between the two universities, providing a systematic method to take into account strategic restraints of either partner in the event of key decisions.

The engagement and representation of Imperial College leadership was also a critical feature of the composition of LKC Medicine's academic leadership. The arrangement agreed upon was for the Dean of the Imperial College Medical School to be the LKC Medicine Dean on a part-time basis with a Senior Vice Dean recruited from Imperial to take on a full-time appointment at LKC Medicine. Core faculty would be recruited on a joint appointment basis, although, in the end, LKC Medicine staff were only granted "visiting faculty" status at Imperial. Professor Stephen Smith, then Principal of Imperial College's Faculty of Medicine, became, ex officio, the Founding Dean of LKC Medicine. His appointment was followed by a series of joint senior appointments from Imperial College including Professor Jenny Higham, Deputy Principal for Education at Imperial College's Faculty of Medicine (now the Principal of St George's Medical School, London), as LKC Medicine Senior Vice Dean responsible for curriculum development. Following Stephen Smith, and after an interim appointment, Professor Dermot Kelleher took over the position and was significantly instrumental in consolidating the success of the joint enterprise. This senior representation in governance and administrative arrangements from Imperial College was crucial in ensuring that the school received the necessary expertise and advice. Now, there is a Dean recruited directly to Singapore (James Best from Melbourne). During this early development period, Imperial College hosted an NTU office to deal with medical school matters at its South Kensington campus.

The design of LKC Medicine's curriculum entailed the consideration of several key factors, which among others include delivery methods, learning material and technology capacities. Unencumbered by tradition and given a strong mandate for innovation, LKC Medicine's curriculum was envisaged to distinguish itself from the current offerings around the world by providing a strong grounding in community-based medicine while employing pioneering pedagogical approaches and the latest e-learning technologies. At the heart of LKC Medicine's educational mission is the successful training of high-quality doctors who were adapted to respond to future medical challenges. In view of this, LKC Medicine's Curriculum Development Team worked closely with the Imperial Curriculum Team to adapt the latter's existing curriculum within the context of Singapore with a focus on team-based learning. The new curriculum was jointly developed with Imperial colleagues (of which Professor Martyn Partridge took a leading role) and over the next few years, making use of a pedagogic shift towards team-based learning. This team-based learning pedagogic approach remains a distinguishing feature of LKC Medicine's curriculum, heavily incorporating the use of information technology and electronic tablets for delivery and assessment. As the first undergraduate medical school to completely replace classroom lectures with pre-recorded lessons, the move to adopt team-based learning was chosen due to its interactive and collaborative nature and the learning strategy's emphasis on comprehension and application. "Professor iPad" is an important member of our faculty! As we have said, she is also very busy elsewhere in NTU! It was also made possible by NTU's prior investments in IT infrastructure and enhanced by the NTU Board of Trustees' decision to ring fence a budget of S$20 million to further support e-learning investments at LKC Medicine and subsequently to be rolled out across the university (see Chapter 13).

Interestingly, Imperial College had had the ambition to introduce IT-enabled learning in its own medical school in London, but this had foundered on "tradition" and the inertia that is found in universities. The opportunity to start here in Singapore with a clean slate was especially welcomed by the Imperial College faculty involved with us. Its success in LKC Medicine has resulted in it being "re-exported" back to the UK in a kind of "feedback loop".

In addition to clinical education and training and in line with the Humboldtian notion of linking research to education, LKC Medicine is equally committed to pursuing the development of its clinical and translational research programmes. LKC Medicine's research strategy straddles four key thematic areas (metabolic disorders, neuroscience and mental health, infection and immunity, and dermatology and skin biology) in population health with a strong focus on addressing the healthcare challenges of the community. LKC Medicine's research strategy also represents a significant opportunity to leverage the other research strengths at NTU and generate greater interdisciplinary collaboration between medicine and engineering. This was further advanced by the establishment of a virtual institute, the Nanyang Institute in Health and Medicine (NITHM), that acted as an interdisciplinary focus across all colleges and schools to enhance medically-related research across the university under the leadership of its first director, Director Jan Carlstedt-Duke. Thus, the two academic partners (Imperial College and NTU) mirrored each other in having medical schools embedded within predominantly engineering institutions.

Over the course of bringing LKC Medicine's blueprint to life, the management and implementation team encountered their share of challenges as documented in this chapter. Since the enrolment of its first cohort of students in 2013, the student cohort has seen subsequent enlargements as manpower projections for medical professionals continue to rise. This was further compounded by the significant constraints posed by the scarcity of manpower and tensions in adapting Imperial College content for the local context and delivery. One of the key lessons that emerged from these tensions was the need to coordinate and build a dedicated staff team in curriculum development to ensure that the quality of education remains uncompromised. Fortunately, these pressures were partially eased by the emergence of positive developments in the healthcare delivery landscape, such as a growing base of clinical partners and a larger pool of clinical educators from which to draw upon. Furthermore, information and communications technology (ICT) has played a significant role in curriculum delivery, and its rapid development continues to present vast opportunities for transformative changes and innovation in both future content and delivery.

LKC Medicine has also met with tremendous success in attracting outstanding and engaged students at a similar level to those going to the NUS Medical School, forming a highly competent student body set to have a positive impact as future advocates for civic engagement through medicine. Of the students who have enrolled, 98% are Singaporeans — a very welcome development. The joint involvement of these two world-class universities has been very attractive to top students, especially upon graduation as they receive certificates from both institutions. However, the rising costs of a medical education continue to pose as a challenge of access and may pose serious implications on the supply and diversity of doctors in the future. Here, the big Lee Foundation endowment had stipulated that half of their donation, S$75 million be devoted to making the school accessible to families of limited financial means.

In research, LKC Medicine continues to face important future challenges. The first ongoing challenge is to ensure that the framework conditions and mechanisms are sustained to optimise and encourage ongoing academic interaction between LKC Medicine and the rest of NTU. In a bid to promote greater interaction between LKC Medicine and other schools and major research institutes, NTU has sought to incorporate transdisciplinary structures and research institutes that provide both a joint platform for research and unique capabilities for translation of basic medical research into technologies. To this end, NITHM continues to play an important role in creating strategies to address collaborative gaps and facilitate cooperation between LKC Medicine and the rest of NTU.

LKC Medicine's recruitment efforts were not without its problems that saw the school stretched to provide faculty and clinical educators in the early stages of what has been a uniquely rapid setup phase. The school addressed the challenge by embarking on a strategy to leverage Imperial College and Karolinska Institutet (KI) as resources of academic experience and joint faculty appointments, which, to a certain degree, was effective in serving to ease and abate the burden. Initially, more faculty were recruited from KI. It is only recently that NTU has been more successful in recruiting faculty from Imperial College. Both were identified as key research partners when the school was first envisaged. The joint appointments were also key to fostering and sustaining the academic ties and relationships between the two universities. Despite the challenge of being a new medical school, LKC Medicine was also successful in recruiting leading international academics who helped to propel the rapid development of strong research competencies and augment the existing research clusters and capacity. With the key resources in place, LKC Medicine is becoming a stable, sustainable and forefront medical school within the global medical community.

Locally, by linking with TTSH, NTU is engaged with NHG. At the same time, it has had to become part of the overall Singaporean health network including the other major hospital grouping (SingHealth) as well as with the National University Healthcare System (NUHS) and the Duke–NUS Medical School. The first Executive Vice-Dean, Professor Lionel Lee, was instrumental in forging networks across this pan-Singaporean health landscape.

The events that have unfolded over the course of establishing LKC Medicine have played an instrumental role in strengthening the school's ability to contend with the challenges. The overarching lesson to be drawn from LKC Medicine's experience, however, is the successful adoption of a strong collaborative approach across various aspects of governance, education, research and funding. The management's ability to effectively gain support while maintaining a degree of autonomy from their stakeholders in government and their clinical partners has put them in good stead to accomplish their research and education missions. As noted previously, the consensus to establish a clear, equal and effective management structure to address issues and conflicts has played a substantial role in supporting the successful delivery of the school's educational and research outcomes. Now, at the time of writing, the first cohorts of doctors have graduated from LKC Medicine and are now contributing to the medical services of Singapore. While the challenges may vary as a result of circumstantial and contextual differences, this chapter attempts to offer some insights into the approaches adopted by LKC Medicine in overcoming its major hurdles that could be adapted by university administrators when developing future blueprints for a medical school and answering social imperatives.

It really has been a unique and rewarding experience. There are many research collaborations between universities and frequent student exchange programmes. However, it is exceedingly rare to have such an intimate educational and research collaboration as exemplified in this story and one that spans half the world.

Of course, the ultimate test as to whether we have succeeded will be the quality of doctors that are produced and who will care for their fellow citizens. The intense competition of top students for places at LKC Medicine bodes well in this respect. Remarkably, it will be the first time in over a century that a Singapore-trained doctor will be without an NUS label.

This joint institution has pioneered new educational models that have been adopted throughout NTU and will serve as a model for others. It is truly a unique international academic collaborative arrangement. It has become a pioneer and exemplar of what can be achieved when two such eminent institutions work together in their common interest.

Chapter 16

The Research Powerhouse Part 1: The Big Picture

All the leading universities in the world combine both education and research and describe themselves as "research-intensive". This is the philosophy first enunciated by Wilhelm von Humboldt, an educationalist and reformer in Prussia in the late 18th and early 19th century. This philosophy, the Humboldtian model of higher education (German: *Humboldtsches Bildungsideal*), has, at its core, the holistic combination of research and education. All three members of the Troika recall that the professors who followed this in their student days were those who were remembered as generating the excitement that everyone felt when exposed to new knowledge. While faculty in almost all universities carry out research to some degree, what is meant by "research-intensive" is that universities put major resources into both research and education.

A Changing Research Climate

Chapter 2 covered in detail Singapore's journey from a poor third world city to one of the world's leading economies with the associated progression of its universities and research environment. The Singapore of 1965, with its share of slums and poverty, was a place where university, let alone research-intensive world-class universities, was a luxury affordable to only the fortunate few. Chapter 2 also described how the university scene has been transformed along with Singapore's economic progress. In 1998, Singapore took the first step towards hosting world-class research with the creation of the Singapore–Massachusetts Institute of Technology (MIT) Alliance (SMA). That programme, completely funded by Singapore, involved both NUS and NTU in collaborative projects with MIT faculty. By the turn of the millennium, a flurry of moves by the government saw the relaunch of A*STAR in 2002 with the institute's leadership readings like a "Who's Who" of world research, the inauguration of a new president at NUS determined to make up for lost time and, in 2003, Guaning's inauguration at NTU with his ambition to fundamentally change NTU from a teaching-focused, practice-orientated, engineering-dominated institution to a world-class research-intensive university that would be a worthy rival to NUS. From this time on, the city-state emerged as a centre of research excellence.

This was very much fronted by A*STAR, led by Philip Yeo,[1] and influenced by the late Sydney Brenner.[2] Thus, under Philip Yeo's leadership, A*STAR and Singapore became the go-to place for biomedical research and development in Asia in areas such as infectious diseases, functional genomics and stem cells. It became a magnet for leading researchers in the world to come to Singapore. A*STAR's second pillar was its already existing engineering- and science-based institutes.

This early A*STAR "effect" had a most significant impact on NUS, located close by, in a manner akin to what happens in France through *Centre national de la recherche scientifique's* (CNRS, French National Centre for Scientific Research) interaction with French universities. Although itself a renowned research organisation and although its research units were located in universities (the *Unité Mixte* concept), it actually "defoliated" the universities of their best research talent, leaving French universities as mainly teaching institutions.

---

[1] Phillip Yeo (Noel Philip Yeo Liat Kok) is a highly regarded civil servant who served as Permanent Secretary, Ministry of Defence; chaired the Economic Development Board; and served as A*STAR Chairman from 2000 until 2007.
[2] Sydney Brenner, FRS (1927–2019) was a South African molecular biologist and a joint Nobel Prize winner in Physiology (2002).

In Singapore, the emphasis on A*STAR resulted in a lack of resource at the universities and a relatively lower standard of scientific research.

In order to develop a world-class molecular biology centre, Sydney Brenner convinced the then Deputy Prime Minister Dr. Goh Keng Swee, to agree to create the Institute of Molecular and Cell Biology (IMCB) headed by a heavyweight researcher, Chris Tan, a Singaporean. Brenner chose to locate IMCB in the NUS campus, nominally part of NUS, but with separate administrative reporting. This went to the extent that IMCB was independently awarding its own (NUS branded) PhD degrees, considered to be at a higher level than an ordinary NUS PhD. This situation, created because "basic research was a dirty word" under the mantra of industrial relevance, dominated budgetary thinking.

A*STAR, under Philip Yeo, was not prepared to risk the hard-earned excellence of its research institutes by leaving it to NUS to run. Thus, the universities were funded for research at a "subsistence level" compared to the A*STAR life sciences institutes in the newly built Biopolis.

As for A*STAR, with successive research and innovation five-year plans, it became a much more "downstream" research organisation, leaving "upstream" research to the university sector. Bertil describes this process, which took place over more than a decade, as moving from the German "Max Planck" equivalent to a "Fraunhofer" model, and in more national terms as moving from the French system described above to the German system in which research-performing organisations work alongside research-intensive universities for mutual benefit. At the same time, the universities were empowered by the creation of the NRF, described elsewhere.

As set out in earlier chapters, NTU started out as very much a teaching institution in which research was "tolerated" rather than encouraged. At that time, faculty were primarily recruited to teach. This was the level the economy needed in NTU's early days that limited the growth in quality of the university. The ability to hire the best faculty to teach depends on providing them with the freedom and wherewithal to remain active researchers, imparting their forefront knowledge to their students. What research that was conducted at NTU then tended to be in engineering (especially in electrical and electronic engineering related to defence). Professor Er Meng Hwa (later Vice President of NTU) was recruited to

Nanyang Technological Institute (NTI) in 1985, having completed his PhD in a top-level research department under the aegis of Professor Brian Anderson[3] at the University of Newcastle, Australia. Yet, he recounts that, soon after his return, in one interview with a senior faculty member, he was told "continuation of your PhD research is NOT encouraged" and yet he had arrived at NTU as an excellent young researcher who completed his thesis in three years and published seven papers. With such a background, he was still not encouraged in his research career. Gradually, the amount and level of research conducted at NTU increased during its first decade with a few pockets of special expertise emerging such as in signal processing and communications, materials sciences, water research and in accountancy. Only in accountancy did NTU have someone with an international reputation as a "highflyer" — Professor Tan Hun Tong, a world leader in audit research. Professor Er Meng Hwa also recalls that the total number of PhD students in the mid-1990s was less than 100!

Therefore, as NTU moved into the 21st century, NUS, under President Shih Choon Fong, started to emerge into the international limelight as a significant and well-regarded institution with a strong research capacity. Professor Shih Choon Fong was one of the rare Singaporean academics who had achieved excellence in the US with his PhD from Harvard and long academic career in Brown University, Rhode Island. He was initially recruited back to Singapore as the Director of the Institute of Materials Research and Engineering (IMRE) located in NUS, but again under A*STAR direction. When he was appointed NUS President in 2000, he made a big splash by replacing six deans in one fell swoop, no doubt to clear his way for reforms to come. Under his leadership, NUS started its advance as a leading university.

In contrast, NTU and its leadership at that time did not move significantly in this direction. When NTU was created, Lord Dainton's report had advised that there should be two large public universities that would compete against each other for students and in research and so increase the level of the country's academic institutions. However, this was not the case in practice, not by chance but by design as research funds were distributed in favour of NUS over NTU by a two-to-one ratio. However, with

---

[3] Later President of the Australian Academy of Sciences.

these two contrasting approaches, such competition was not happening. Later, with the major increases of funding after 2005, the situation was to change dramatically and competition for the funds that were available was intense with NUS prevailing. As is said elsewhere, this was to change with the arrival of Guaning to the NTU presidency with his ambition to turn NTU into a globally renowned research-intensive university, as he enunciated at his inauguration. In Haresh, he found a kindred spirit to help him to move NTU forward, although the successful implementation of this aim took several more years and the coming of Bertil.

During the first decade of the 21st century, then Deputy Prime Minister Dr. Tony Tan was instrumental in persuading the Cabinet that university research must be strengthened if the country was to remain competitive in a very competitive world and region, especially with the rising giant of China. Following the earlier leap forward by Japan and Taiwan, places such as Hong Kong and Korea were racing ahead with China increasingly dominating the global market. How was Singapore's ambition to be achieved?

In developing the concept of the knowledge economy, the Singapore government established a very high-level Research, Innovation and Enterprise Council (RIEC) that brings together the 11 ministers from key ministries (who are directly involved and engaged in these discussions) plus another 11 external international experts, and it is chaired by the Prime Minister. It is very influential in driving Singapore's agenda forward. It is probably unique in having external experts having such a say in the priority setting of a nation and demonstrates Singapore's openness to ideas from across the world. It is a model that other nations could emulate to their advantage.

One way forward was to develop a really strong university sector. Through the mechanism of its five-year research and innovation plans, government funding was substantially increased some 2.5 times in 2005/2010 (see Introduction). This plan saw the establishment of the NRF, primarily aimed at supporting university research and giving a stimulus to the research-intensive university concept. It was a real scene changer. At this point, it should be noted that the concentration of effort was almost exclusively on science, technology, engineering and mathematics (STEM) subjects along with medicine and with arts, humanities and social sciences being somewhat poor relations. More recently, this gap has been recognised and a social sciences research council was formed in 2015.

NRF immediately put the universities on the front line and involved top-level science advisers from around the world, at which point Bertil joins the story when he was invited to become a member of the initial NRF Science Advisory Board in 2006, as recounted in Bertil's tale (Chapter 6). NRF essentially developed five main schemes to take its ambitious plan forward.

New Funding Opportunities — The NRF and Its "Instruments"

Very much persuaded by Bertil, drawing on the evidence of the European Science Foundation's European Young Investigator (EURYI) scheme that had, by then, evolved into the European Research Council's (ERC) Young Investigator Grants, now ERC Starting Grants within the ERC grants system, NRF introduced its own NRF Fellows scheme. The aim was to attract very bright young researchers from across the world to compete for prestigious and valuable Fellowships. In other words, this was the recruitment of the "fleetest gazelles" to Singapore. Soon after the launch of this programme, Bertil instituted the Nanyang Assistant Professorships (NAPs) — "golden assistant professors" — scheme within NTU attracting candidates of similar calibre from across the world.

A second strand of the NRF was the creation of Research Centres of Excellence (RCEs) with very substantial funding of $150 million over 10 years (with funds jointly coming from NRF and the Ministry of Education (MOE)) with the aim of establishing high-level strategic research initiatives and, crucially, being led by major scientific figures recruited to Singapore. While such "centres of excellence" schemes have been developed in many countries (Germany was one of the first), the level of support and its move to attract senior research figures make this scheme unique in size and in its far-sightedness. Each RCE was to be hosted by a local university, but with significant autonomy to pursue its own research mission and objectives. Each RCE was envisaged as being headed by a distinguished international scientist as Director, aimed at recruiting real academic "stars" to the Singapore research ecosystem. Each RCE has some 15 to 25 principal investigators (PIs), many of whom lead research teams of post-doctoral fellows, research students and supporting staff. The RCE approach essentially recruited "excellence" to the country rather than just increasing funding to existing centres, however good.

Five RCEs were selected through a competitive two-stage process between 2007 and 2010. Evaluations were conducted by MOE's Academic Research Council (ARC), a committee of distinguished international scientists and academics, chaired by Bob Brown (President of Boston University, US; former Provost, MIT; and an honorary Singapore citizen). This group has been most influential in setting the highest standards and so ensuring real excellence in Singaporean research. In addition, the Council's way of interacting with the universities' leaderships was most commendable. Moreover, now, this Council has been charged with evaluating proposals for MOE Tier 2 and Tier 3 grants. We describe both RCEs hosted by NTU in the section below. The ARC carried out its task based on international peer review and without any ingrained prejudice towards either NTU or NUS, which is important in a country with a relatively small academic community.

Third, NRF introduced its Competitive Research Programmes (CRPs) which were block grants with quite substantial funding (S$5 million–S$10 million) involving more interdisciplinarity as well as with industrial involvement, as appropriate. These are substantial funding opportunities which, at first, NTU struggled to come to terms with, but, as time went by, the university's research faculty's success eventually equalled and, at times, surpassed the success rate of NUS.

In its fourth initiative, NRF also sponsored several thematic programmes that had separate calls for proposals for each area. These included water, energy and interactive digital media, the administration of which was delegated to the relevant government agencies: the Public Utilities Board (PUB), the Economic Development Board (EDB) and the Infocomm Media Development Authority (IMDA), respectively.

The idea was to attract and import world-leading researchers to nucleate powerful research groups in key areas that, although having significant basic research, would ultimately benefit the economy.

The fifth major NRF initiative was the Campus for Research Excellence and Technological Enterprise (CREATE) programme. NRF wanted to have a quick start in rapidly moving to the knowledge-based economy on all fronts. CREATE was rather unusual as the aim was to attract major overseas universities to establish research bases in Singapore. In 2006, when the CREATE scheme was initiated, it was originally planned that the foreign universities should come and establish their research specialities in Singapore. Neither NTU nor NUS was in the picture. It was only when Bertil and others in the Science Advisory Board said that this was really not an optimal way forward for the health of Singaporean research that the CREATE scheme was modified to include collaboration between the incoming foreign university and a local university. Of course, as usual, the subjects of such proposals had to be for the long-term benefit of Singapore. Initially, three such institutions were considered for "strategic reasons" — MIT, ETH Zürich and Technion (Israel Institute of Technology) (Israel), with MIT being allocated half the available funds at the time in what was dubbed the Singapore–MIT Alliance for Research and Technology programme. Later, this scheme was extended to other eminent universities in China, Europe and the US (see below).

The official mission of CREATE is to be:

- "An international 'collaboratory' of research centres set up by top global universities and research institutes in Singapore that will:
    - Engage in cutting-edge research;
    - Be a second home that fosters deep collaborations with each other and with Singapore universities;
    - Allow students and researchers to be jointly supervised with partner universities and local universities;
    - Be a place where Singapore agencies turn to when seeking solutions to difficult problems;
    - Be a source of well-known start-ups or products or technologies; and
    - Establish a reputation as a leading research hub."

Now, the programme has attracted the likes of the *Berkeley* Education Alliance for Research in Singapore (BEARS); *Cambridge* Centre for

Advanced Research and Education in Singapore (CARES); Energy and Environmental Sustainability Solutions for Megacities (E2S2 with *Shanghai Jiao Tong University)*; Nanomaterials for Energy and Water Management (NEW with *Hebrew University Jerusalem* (HUJ)); Cellular and Molecular Mechanisms of Inflammation (NUS–*HUJ*–CREATE); Singapore–ETH Centre (SEC); Singapore–*MIT* Alliance for Research and Technology (SMART); *Technical University of Munich* (TUM) CREATE; and the Trustworthy and Secure Cyber Plexus (TSCP) with the *University of Illinois at Urbana-Champaign*. Overseas universities are given in italics.

At that time, NTU had only just started on its remarkable journey, but now is the equal of all the CREATE partner institutions! NTU has also become very much a partner of choice for these incoming institutions especially HUJ, Cambridge University and TUM. It is now anticipated that CNRS will also join the CREATE family. The CREATE institutions are all located in the specially built CREATE Tower on the NUS campus, working through locally established and registered "offshoots".

Initially, NRF imposed quite strict residency requirements on those leading each CREATE action (a minimum of six months per year in Singapore), although this regulation was softened later as such a condition was a disincentive for top researchers to be involved in the projects. In other words, coupled with A*STAR and developments within MOE (see below), this was to be Singapore's "Big Bang" in research. As eventually modified, it also helped the local universities in their aim to become research-intensive and of global renown.

While all the programmes involved some components of basic research, the ultimate justification for funding was the strategic economic benefit that would accrue to Singapore in the longer perspective. Each proposal is very much project-based, driven largely by Singapore's national priorities and with substantial financial inducements to the incoming institutions. While this has been an overall success, it shows the paradox of Singapore's "inferiority" complex in bringing in overseas universities even when NTU and NUS are shown to be top-level universities, sometimes ranked considerably higher than the incomers! The programme started in the aftermath of several unsuccessful initiatives to attract overseas universities to Singapore, among which those of Johns Hopkins University in the US, University of Warwick in the UK and University of

New South Wales, Sydney were the most notable examples. When the CREATE programme started, it was not really envisaged that NTU would play any significant part in the scheme which, as above, was aimed at MIT, ETH and Technion (Israel Institute of Technology), working mainly with NUS. As NTU's research reputation increased and the programme was opened up to other global universities, these universities increasingly linked to NTU as well as to NUS and, in some cases, worked only with NTU. For example, TUM and HUJ work very closely with NTU as does the project from Cambridge University, while the others work across the Singaporean university system. TUM CREATE has been developed into a close relationship between these two technologically-based universities, with joint PhD students and a mutual link to BMW that has formed one of our key industrial partnerships.

Thus, NRF was attracting senior researchers (through RCEs), junior researchers (through the Fellowship programme) and institutions (through CREATE).The final component of the NRF initiative was the introduction of a limited scheme to support innovation in the universities.

New Funding Opportunities — MOE as a Key Research Funding Agency

In parallel with what had happened in NRF, MOE also stepped up its funding for research. It was a co-funder, with NRF, of the RCE scheme as well as providing direct funding through "normal" investigator-led grants. This was the nearest approach to a "research council" for STEM subjects in Singapore. These were the so-called "Tier 1" grants in which MOE provides a block grant to the universities that then distribute the funds after competitive calls within the university. Such an approach, whereby funds are devolved to the university to operate on a level base between faculty members, is most unusual. It also demands that the institution has a good quality control mechanism to decide on the distribution of funds (see Chapter 17). This was and is an important criterion and both Guaning and Bertil were at pains to ensure that a fair evaluation scheme was in place.

A second and larger funding scheme is that of "Tier 2" (comparable to typical PI-led grants common in Europe and North America) that is wholly administered by MOE, using its ARC made up of high-level international academics. This not only provides good quality control through external peer review, but, in so doing, breaks free from the problems of prejudice and pro rata allocations that are so often seen in the research systems of small countries with small research communities. The key criterion is excellence. Again, as time passed and the measures taken by the Troika took effect, NTU's success rate in the Tier 2 competition started to gain parity with that of NUS — the objective of the second Dainton Report had been achieved!

More recently, in 2012, MOE instituted Tier 3 grants that provide very substantial funding arrangements. Tier 3 grants come at two levels — one at a level of $5 million to $10 million and the second at $10 million to $25 million. This funding scheme was aimed at more basic research than was the case with the CRPs, although, as ever, the ultimate aim of Singaporean research funding is to meet economic ends. NTU researchers have been particularly successful in making proposals to the Tier 3 scheme.

NTU has been successful in this competition with a Tier 3 grant linked to the Photonics Institute, led by Professor Nickolay Zheludev. Another major award at the higher funding level has been that at the heart of the Nanyang Institute for Structural Biology, led by Professor Daniela Rhodes. The RCEs have had leading faculty gain Tier 3 support such as that which supports the atmospheric genomics project at the Singapore Centre for Environmental Life Sciences Engineering (SCELSE) under Professor Stephan Schuster. Yet another Tier 3 success was that on antibiotics, in which Professor Mary Chan is the Principal Investigator. Since these initial awards, NTU has subsequently obtained several other such grants.

Other Government Funding Opportunities

There are a variety of research funding opportunities in Singapore beyond NRF and MOE and the really successful professor is able to know where to go and how to combine a variety of opportunities. These include government agencies such as EDB, the Monetary Authority of Singapore, the Ministry of Defence (MINDEF), PUB, the Building and Construction Authority and the Land Transport Authority. Such bodies tend to look for applied outcomes of research. However, on the more basic aspect of research (noting that Singapore always looks for long-term economic benefits), A*STAR itself has always sponsored extra-mural research at the universities. This A*STAR funding was important in the early years of Singapore's university research expansion, but has now become of less significance. In addition, there is the National Medical Research Council (NMRC) operating in the biomedical research area, but with a clinical emphasis. Therefore, with judicious timing and creating the right links, faculty have been encouraged to make use of these various sources of funding with which to sustain and develop their research groups, in turn leading to new discoveries and scientific advances.

NTU's Response to the New Opportunities in Research

With all of these new funding developments, it was a tremendous opportunity for NTU. Would NTU be ready for such a challenge? How would its faculty react? Would they be competitive coming from a low research base?

Bertil recalls that during his first three to four months of taking up his Provost position, he was called to meet with the then Minister for Education Tharman Shanmugaratnam. Basically, Minister Tharman said that NTU had to get its act together and that Bertil, as the new Provost, had to be able to develop a few niche areas of research in which NTU would be competitive. As described in Chapter 8, the meeting was interesting since Minister Tharman introduced the term "Tier 0", meaning that NTU should use its basic budget for research as well as for education in order to maintain and develop the quality of the faculty. This allowed Bertil and his colleagues to place "seed" money for new initiatives as well as provide "start-up" grants for new faculty recruits.

It was not only Minister Tharman who was concerned about NTU's capabilities. There was apprehension within NTU itself, and in the NRF and MOE and political circles, that NTU may not have been properly prepared and that the end result of all the new initiatives would be the channelling of funds direct to NUS, defeating the aim of having two major institutions raising standards in competition with one another. As Bertil says, "We have a saying in Sweden that when it rains gold, the poor man is he who has no bucket!" Did NTU have a big enough bucket to capture the gold?

These fears, perhaps, were realised with the first call for proposals for RCEs. In 2006, NTU had submitted proposals, none of which were even shortlisted after the first stage of a two-stage process. Lim Chuan Poh stated, publically, that this failure really was a "wake-up" call for the university, its Board, its leadership and its faculty. It was somewhat of a shock to Bertil, who was still based in Strasbourg at the time, and this outcome emphasised the big task facing him, the Troika and the university as a whole. In this first RCE allocation in 2006, NUS was awarded the Centre of Quantum Computing under the leadership of Arthur Eckhart from Oxford University, which set a very high bar for the RCE programme and created a significant challenge for NTU.

The failure of NTU in the first round was taken by many as evidence that NTU would not be in the game. Bertil recalls that when he came to Singapore in 2006 to participate in the new NRF Scientific Advisory Board (SAB), there was a lunch with the NUS President Shih Choon Fong. His discussion with the Advisory Board, according to Bertil, who at that time did not have any plans of joining NTU, was all about identifying the five areas that NUS should develop for the RCE programme and its five centres which he assumed would be at NUS!

NTU Achieves Success with Research Centres of Excellence

The RCEs, when initiated by NRF, represented, probably, the highest level of funding of such schemes anywhere in the world, being worth up to $150 million over 10 years. As described above, our first attempt had ended in complete failure in 2006 without any NTU bids making it past the first stage. Only five centres were envisaged to be created and with NUS gaining the first RCE, the Centre for Quantum Technologies (CQT, see above), the likelihood of NTU gaining such a Centre was considered implausible. In the event, NTU got its act together under Bertil's guidance and so was able to compete strongly with NUS. The second call resulted in two awards — another for NUS in cancer research: the Cancer Science Institute of Singapore (CSI). The surprise was that NTU succeeded and was able to gain support to start the Earth Observatory of Singapore (EOS). The third year saw another NUS success — the Mechanobiology Institute (MBI Singapore) with NTU gaining the fifth and final centre — that of the SCELSE. From such an inauspicious start to be awarded two of five such Centres was a considerable achievement in such a short time, especially considering the situation of NTU in 2006. Not only that but in the later calls, our proposals on water research, led by Professor Jim Leckie (Stanford University); on structural biology, led by Pär Nordlund (Karolinska Institutet); and on photonics, led by Sir David Payne (Southampton University), were all shortlisted and thus in the running for an award. To have become so competitive in such a short time was a remarkable achievement and gave encouragement to the faculty at large to submit high-class proposals to the various calls for funding that would emerge and which are detailed elsewhere in this chapter.

Next, we describe in more detail our two successful RCEs.

Earth Observatory of Singapore (EOS)

Professor Kerry Sieh, a member of the US National Academy of Sciences and a tenured professor at the California Institute of Technology (Caltech), had been attracted to NTU as a Visiting Professor and was on a sabbatical hosted by Professor TC Pan, the then Dean of Engineering. Kerry is an expert in studying the geological record to understand the geometries of active faults, the earthquakes they generate and the crustal deformation their movements produce. One of his long-standing research interests has been the subduction megathrust that has been producing great earthquakes offshore Sumatra throughout the past decade. Working with paleoseismic records (such as shown in coral reefs), one area of his special interest was the Banda Aceh region off Sumatra that had led to the 2004 Indian Ocean tsunami. Just as Haresh before him, he found that NTU (and Singapore) was an ideal base from which to study such phenomena.

However, this was in a topic not of direct economic benefit to Singapore, and Bertil and Guaning were worried that in proposing such a topic, creating new disciplines for NTU (the earth sciences) may not "fly". The proposal itself covered not only seismicity but also included volcanology and climate change and its impacts in terms of sea level rise. What it did offer was regional leadership for Singapore in the Association of Southeast Asian Nations (ASEAN) region in studying different forms of geohazards — earthquakes and volcanoes, the geometries of active faults and the earthquakes they generate as well as the crustal deformation their movements produce. Kerry's early work studying geological layers and landforms along the San Andreas Fault led to the discovery of how often and how regularly it produces large earthquakes in southern California. A few years before, he investigated Taiwan's multitude of active faults and figured out how their earthquakes are continuously creating that mountainous island.

One of Kerry's long-standing research interests has been the subduction megathrust that has been producing great earthquakes offshore Sumatra throughout the past decade. His and his students' and colleagues' paleoseismic work has led to an understanding of the repeating nature of such earthquakes. He also instigated the creation of the Sumatran global positioning system (GPS) array, a network of continuously recording GPS stations to record deformations during and in between large earthquakes, being significant threats in Indonesia and the Philippines and with climate a threat to all.

With Singapore's strong financial services sector, including insurance, the NRF/MOE panel was able to appreciate the long-term benefit that EOS would bring to Singapore as well as the intrinsic excellence of the proposal. Thus, EOS became NTU's first RCE and a "pathfinder" for the others. Early on in the application process, having cleared the first-stage assessment, Bertil, Haresh and Guaning became convinced that it would be successful and threw their full support behind Kerry.

The success of EOS could be attributed to many factors including Kerry's enthusiasm and also the fact that he was able to persuade other world-leading scientists to join the EOS team including Paul Tapponnier from Paris (a member of the French Academy of Sciences) who is an expert in neotectonics, especially of Asia, and Chris Newhall, a renowned volcanologist from the US Geological Survey, whose expertise was in the volcanoes of the Philippines. Other top scientists were recruited to the team so that it quickly developed the critical intellectual mass that would assure its success and provide an attraction for first-class young scientists such as the NRF Fellows and the NAPs.

EOS was particularly important to NTU for several reasons. First, it demonstrated to NRF and MOE that NTU could challenge and surpass NUS in major competitions — this was the first time that this had ever occurred! Second, it demonstrated our ability to attract top scientists to the university and, finally, it established a new discipline (earth sciences) within the university. NTU was becoming a much more comprehensive university! In fact, this laid the foundation for its expansion into the latest new school in NTU — the Asian School of Environment, with its strong base in the earth sciences but now expanding into other disciplines within the environmental sciences. And, nationally, it provided Singapore with regional leadership in topics with important economic and societal consequences such as climate change and its local and regional impact, and the possibility of economic disruption from volcanoes as was seen in Iceland and, locally, with the Bali eruptions of late 2017. Geohazards and climate change are now top of the international agenda and the importance of EOS has been further substantiated.

Summarising, EOS represented the first big breakthrough in research for NTU, a decade and a half after its foundation. We were on our way!

Singapore Centre for Environmental Life Sciences and Engineering (SCELSE)

Another big success for NTU in research was its second RCE — the Singapore Centre for Environmental Life Sciences and Engineering.

This was again an example of success built around attracting a top scientist to NTU to lead this activity. In this case, it was Staffan Kjelleberg from the University of New South Wales (UNSW), Sydney. As another Swede, Bertil knew Staffan as a top microbiologist whose career had been quite spectacular, becoming a full professor at the University of Gothenburg at a young age in Sweden before moving to Australia. Bertil and Staffan met up again in 2007 after UNSW had been trying to establish a campus in Singapore. This was at the time of the collapse of this endeavour.

Staffan was in Singapore to seek out research collaborators, originally looking towards NUS. Bertil persuaded him to consider NTU and convinced him that, with its strong engineering base, this would be the ideal location for a new initiative. Furthermore, as one Swede to another, Bertil said that moving from Australia to Singapore was halfway back to Sweden!

It was envisaged that the proposal would focus on bacterial biofilms with the aim of understanding the mechanisms behind their development and their role in topics such as marine biofouling or in human disease and then to seek engineering solutions. This was a whole new interdisciplinary area of study and so would put Singapore at the leading edge of such knowledge. In that sense, it was similar to EOS in its effect on both Singapore and NTU.

A key component of the proposal was in the application of genomics to the understanding of biofilms. This was at a time when Craig Venter, of human genome fame, was developing genomics as a tool to understand microbial diversity. Staffan and Bertil worked together (and with Yehuda Cohen from the Hebrew University Jerusalem), and a proposal for a RCE was submitted in 2008 and was shortlisted, narrowly failing to be funded. Convinced that this would be a success next time, the proposal was worked on and strengthened and then resubmitted in the following year, this time successfully, and NTU gained its second RCE.

SCELSE incorporates researchers from NUS, which has a 20% component of the project. SCELSE, following the model of EOS, was able to attract leading figures to its ranks such as Stephan Schuster, who joined NTU from Pennsylvania State University after a stellar career in Germany. He was identified as being one of the most influential researchers in the world in *Time* magazine's "Top 100" scientists and thinkers in 2009. He is now the scientific leader of the Genome Asia 100K project aimed at sequencing and analysing 100,000 Asian individuals' genomes to help accelerate Asian population-specific medical advances and precision medicine. Stephan is leading a study into the genomic analysis of a "forgotten" ecosystem — the urban atmosphere — and is discovering new and exciting organisms. This genomic study is really pushing the boundaries of genomics and metagenomics.

The success of SCELSE enabled NTU to bring genomics in a big way to NTU and it has become one of the foremost of such centres in Asia. One example is in the analysis of water filters in which only 5% of the species whose genomes had been identified had been previously described.

SCELSE's genomics formed the base for the coordination of several other activities in the university including a life sciences cluster bringing together SCELSE and the Lee Kong Chian Medical School, the School of Biological Science and the Nanyang Institute of Structural Biology as the NTU Integrated Medical, Biological and Environmental Life Sciences (NIMBELS) Cluster. The need for major computing support for sequencing has also been at the core of NTU's drive for super-computing provision. Thus, having SCELSE at NTU has led to other important developments of overall benefit to the university and its research endeavours.

Chapter 17

The Research Powerhouse Part 2: Systems, Structures and Quality

The year 2007 became crucial for Nanyang Technological University (NTU) in its aim of developing its research position, especially as new funding opportunities were coming on stream was also the year that Bertil joined NTU as Provost and, together with Guaning and Haresh, instituted their Troika meetings.

There was a determined push for high-level recruitment (see Chapter 14), as well as the extensive promotion and tenure reviews. This underlay actions to restore confidence in the faculty, with an expectation that research was a major part of their activities, and it aimed at creating a new mindset. We had to release the big potential that resided within NTU. One example of the depressed thinking was when new NRF calls for proposals were announced, the reaction from faculty was "Why should I waste my time in writing proposals as we know that all the monies will go to NUS anyway?" This had to change and change quickly, and through meetings and being "hectored" by Bertil, the message got home. The key message was "It is part of one's job as a faculty member to undertake research and promote this by submitting well-written and well-argued competitive proposals".

An example of the lack of motivation and confidence was when a senior faculty member, after submitting a proposal, had been told that it had been rejected but a resubmission was invited. In America and Europe, such news would be disappointing, and part of normal academic life, but would also be seen as an encouraging sign for any reapplication. Being invited to resubmit, and taking into account criticisms and comments from reviewers, one would be in a very good position to succeed at the following call. Not at NTU! Such feedback was seen as a failure, a major "loss of face" and there was no point in following up. Only after some "bullying" by Bertil was the faculty member persuaded to resubmit and was, of course, successful to a quite significant extent!

Another measure, agreed in 2007, was that young and newly appointed assistant professors needed to have support and encouragement. Therefore, NTU instituted the provision of start-up grants for them, coupled with a reduced teaching load in the first few years of their appointment. This gave a head start to the appointees and set them on the route to tenured positions. The new recruits were encouraged to seek external funds to develop their research on the back of this initial support. The Nanyang Assistant Professorships (NAPs) (see Chapter 14) had more substantial start-up grants in recognition of their status and their likely fast track to tenure. This, coupled with the NTU success in the NRF Fellows competition, boded well for the future. These developments did create some resentment from senior colleagues, as the latter had not had this seemingly privileged treatment when they joined NTU and now had to take on additional work because of the scheme.

The Troika had agreed that the Provost should take matters forward on a variety of fronts to bring NTU up to a competitive level in research. A special effort was made to bring people together to discuss, exchange and plan responses to funding calls. This not only encouraged cross-disciplinarity but also meant that the few and more experienced and successful faculty could pass on their knowledge to their more junior or less successful colleagues. By such sharing, the aim was to make NTU more competitive.

In order to take research forward, Bertil, although Provost, acted as the *de facto* Vice President (Research) from his arrival at NTU. His enthusiasm and knowledge of research on a wide front was able to inspire and guide NTU to a new level of research intensity. One of his first actions was to discuss his plans with Dr. Tony Tan, with whom he had worked with before he came to NTU as a member of the NRF Science Advisory Board.

Bertil held meetings with groups of relevant faculty whenever a new call was announced to encourage collaborative work in responding to the calls. This was a major change from the past. Up until then, Professor Tony Woo, who had been the Vice President (Research), had instituted a number of changes but, by 2007, these had not achieved the targets that the Troika had envisaged.

One major step forward was to reform and reorganise the Research Office into a Research and Support Office (RSO). The new structure was not to be a controlling function as hitherto but, rather, the accent was on "support" to provide the basis on which faculty could rely in taking their proposals forward. This included continuing to convene meetings of faculty to develop collaboration and cooperation and provide the administrative experience and advice that was so necessary, especially in understanding the funders' procedures. This has paid off in our increasing success in responding to calls and is a reflection of the dedication of the RSO director, Professor Michael Khor, who headed the RSO during most of the period covered by this book, as well as Professor Tjin Swee Chuan, who deputised for Michael while he was seconded to the NRF.

Bertil was also in charge of budget setting in NTU and he used this as a "carrot and stick" approach to inculcating the competitive "edge" necessary to succeed. Research "drivers" were put in place to determine the budget allocations to schools. Do well in research and in responding to calls for proposals and this would be reflected in increased base budgets. Each school was assessed in terms of its research publications (citations and impact) and how well it was doing with respect to attracting and mentoring graduate students. It served to start to change research priorities between and within schools and enabled them to become more competitive. School of Electrical and Electronic Engineering (EEE), School of Materials Science and Engineering (MSE), School of Biological Sciences (SBS) and School of Physical and Mathematical Sciences (SPMS) were the schools that responded most positively to these incentives and benefitted accordingly.

Interdisciplinarity and the Creation of NTU's Research Institutes

One aspect on which the Troika, Bertil in particular, was very committed was in fostering interdisciplinarity. Schools had tended to work in "silos", which meant "research silos". He set about trying to change mindsets and explained that the new trend in research was for multi-authors, working across institutions and national frontiers and, especially, across disciplines. There was also a need to maximise the potential of research on common themes across the institution. For instance, NTU was involved in energy research in many areas and in many different schools. It was common sense to bring such activities together to create new critical masses that would be even more competitive than working on one's own. This gave rise to the concept of pan-university research institutes, of which some examples are given below. The faculty involved in these institutes remained attached to their schools while, at the same time, being heavily committed as researchers in the institutes in a form of matrix management. Such a matrix arrangement is not unique to NTU. However, it enabled NTU to bring together a variety of complementary skills and interests in both an inter- and cross-disciplinary framework and this proved to be very effective in attracting significant external grant funding.

Below, we describe the key institutes that were created and are now at the heart of NTU's enhanced research reputation.

The Nanyang Energy and Water Research Institute (NEWRI)

NEWRI was created in an area critical to Singapore, as sustainable water supplies have always been a key political issue. Under the leadership of Professor Ng Wun Jern, NEWRI successfully leveraged block grants from NRF, the Public Utilities Board and the Economic Development Board to undertake a wide spectrum of research aimed at problems of remediation and recycling. Its research on the use of advanced membrane filters has been particularly significant — this was led by Professor Tony Fane who joined NTU from Australia. NEWRI brought together research interests from School of Civil and Environmental Engineering (CEE), SBS, SPMS and School of Chemical and Biomedical Engineering (SCBE) in a very successful manner, spawning interdisciplinarity and raising very substantial research funds. NEWRI was the first of the university institutes to relocate to the adjoining CleanTech Park which opened in 2010. The Park is an eco-innovation business park in Singapore aimed at the development of green technology and solutions.

Energy Research at NTU (ERIAN)

Another major institute is ERIAN. Again, this has leveraged on grants from NRF, EDB and many others. Led by Professor Subodh Mhaisalkar, ERIAN has become a pre-eminent energy research operation and, because of its success, NTU is rated number one in the world for energy research in one of the university rankings. ERIAN has been granted the use of a small offshore island (Semakau Island) to research and develop microgrids. This is NTU's Renewable Energy Integration Demonstrator-Singapore (REIDS) and it is the largest system of interconnected microgrids in Southeast Asia. The central hub of the REIDS system draws energy from the microgrids that are powered by various renewable sources including wind turbines and solar panels. It then redistributes any excess energy unused by one microgrid to another. It is a truly exciting development based on a unique piece of test bed infrastructure that most other institutions would envy. ERIAN has also worked on smart buildings, electromobility, storage batteries and alternative energy systems including a project on a "zero-energy" house for the tropics. This has placed ERIAN at the heart of using the NTU campus and other sites as test beds for original approaches to more efficient energy use. The outcome has been the "EcoCampus" concept as ERIAN not only advanced research but also became a powerful advocate for greater energy efficiency within NTU itself. ERIAN was the second of the NTU institutes to relocate to the CleanTech Park.

Institute for Media Innovation (IMI)

The third of the original pan-university institutes which were created was the IMI, taking forward NTU's interest in interactive digital media. Under its Director, Professor Nadia Thalman, one of NTU's major European recruitments, it has gone from strength to strength. It has successfully reached out into other areas such as the use of interactive media in education, especially in dealing with children with special educational needs, working with the National Institute of Education (NIE). IMI remains a centre of expertise in this area. Among its many achievements are the development of a humanised robot (Nadine) that created huge media interest and a virtual reality programme for children with special educational needs (the "Pink Dolphins" project). The creation of IMI and its success have been one of the reasons why the German Fraunhofer Institute sited its first subsidiary institute in Asia at NTU in order to create synergies in this dynamic area between both organisations. Fraunhofer Singapore aims to provide digital solutions and services, working closely with the local industry.

The Photonics Institute (TPI)

Other significant groupings have also been created in more specialist areas, of which TPI is especially noteworthy. This was a long-standing island of excellence in NTU and one on which we could build. Developing a partnership with the Optical Research Centre of University of Southampton led by Sir David Payne was a crucial factor in the development of TPI into a world leader in its area. Sir David is acknowledged as one of the foremost experts in this field in the world. Bertil had persuaded Sir David to submit an RCE proposal that only narrowly failed to be funded (see below). Convinced of the merit and importance of the area, together, Bertil and Sir David set about finding other ways to create TPI. First, we created a "mirror" of the Southampton Centre at NTU, but then developed this further, expanding it and linking strongly with local and regional industrial interests. Originally, strongly backed by the Ministry of Defence, it is a forefront activity, and leading researchers (such as Professor Nikolay Zheludev) have relocated to NTU and have won substantial competitive research funding in basic physics underpinning the Institute. Not only that, but TPI has been able to create an umbra of photonics-related industries in Singapore, to come together with TPI for their mutual benefit. Here, we have an NTU Institute linked to regional industry coupled with that in Southampton that is at the hub of a similar European industry grouping. It illustrates NTU's flexible approach of using academic and industrial partnerships coupled with interdisciplinarity and combining basic and applied sciences to create a major advanced and leading research centre.

Nanyang Institute of Structural Biology (NISB)

Starting in 2008, NTU started to develop a strong structural biology research programme. At first, this was developed around Professor Pär Nordlund, as a Visiting Professor whose own work is focused on establishing structural and mechanistic insights into disease-related proteins, with a particular emphasis on proteins in cancer, inflammation and infectious disease. Pär himself is a distinguished molecular biologist from the Karolinska Universitet. In 2009, he established a laboratory for NTU in the Institute of Molecular and Cell Biology (IMCB) in A*STAR, where the systems structural biology approach is being applied for herpes biology, lipid signalling and membrane transport processes. Locating the laboratory at Biopolis enabled a close interaction with A*STAR, creating a critical mass of expertise as well as establishing an NTU foothold in this prestigious research complex. The group has also established a platform for fragment-based ligand development in Singapore that allows for the rapid generation of high-quality chemical probes and experimental therapeutics, as well as a platform for high-throughput protein production. Although our Experimental Medicine Building had been completed on campus as part of the Medical School development, Pär preferred to remain at Biopolis working with his colleagues in A*STAR.

Building on this earlier excursion into structural biology, Bertil was able to persuade Professor Daniela Rhodes from the Cambridge Laboratory of Molecular and Cell Biology (LMB) to come to NTU. Daniela was not only a leading researcher at the prestigious LMB but she also chaired the European Molecular Biology Conference (EMBC), responsible for the European Molecular Biology Organisation (EMBO) in Heidelberg, Germany, giving her contacts in her field across Europe. With Daniela in post, we were able to establish the NISB — one of the cornerstones of NTU's development into a research powerhouse in the life and biomedical sciences. The main aim of NISB is to integrate structural biology research across NTU to address important questions in biology and human diseases. It also plays a strategic role in the NTU Integrated Medical, Biological and Environmental Life Sciences (NIMBELS) that includes both Lee Kong Chian School of Medicine and the Singapore Centre for Environmental Life Sciences Engineering (SCELSE). NISB builds on the existing strengths and facilities at the School of Biological Sciences with an excellent electron microscopy EM laboratory. Together with the Nordlund group (working with X-ray crystallography), it creates a state-of-the-art technology platform encompassing all structural methods. Professor Rhodes's specific speciality is the study of telomeres.

Learning Science — CRADLE

It is only natural that, as NTU has NIE as one of its key institutes, we should give priority to understanding pedagogy. It is no surprise that one of our key research priorities, leveraging on this pedagogic expertise in NTU, has been "learning science". Therefore, by bringing together the NIE centre of expertise plus other parts of the university with relevant experience, NTU has created a new programme, which forms one of its Strategic "Peaks of Excellence" (see Chapter 9). Very few universities have larger research programmes in pedagogy let alone putting it as one of the five key areas set out in an advanced research strategy. The major programme in this area is the Centre for Research and Development in Learning (CRADLE) that serves as an activity and technology incubator for researching and transforming learning in higher education. It was the brainchild of the late Professor Lee Sing Kong who was a former Director of NIE and later Vice President (Education Strategies) working closely with Bertil. The aim is to enhance learning by developing effective technologies, mindful learning environments and motivating activity designs that are supported by empirical research. CRADLE embraces interdisciplinary research and leverages knowledge and methods from education, psychology, neuroscience and technology design to foster theories that explain learning in all of its forms. The synergies between these disciplines are aimed at developing a new science of learning that can be an activity and technology incubator for researching and transforming learning in higher education worldwide. CRADLE links to other institutions including the Department of Psychology at Cambridge University.

The Complexity Institute

All three members of the Troika have been committed to the promotion of inter- and multidisciplinarity at NTU and many of the new institutional initiatives described here fall under this heading. A particular initiative, promoted by Bertil, and enthusiastically adopted by Guaning, has been in the area of complexity science. This interest stems from Bertil's involvement, while at the European Science Foundation (ESF), and as a founder member, in the creation of an activity called "Institute Para Limes" (IPL) ("Without Borders"). Once he left Europe, the institute foundered somewhat. Seizing the opportunity that IPL Executive Officer, Jan Vasbinder, was passing through Singapore, Bertil persuaded him to join NTU to establish IPL in Asia at NTU. Then, following a number of very successful high-level conferences, Bertil assigned funds to create another pan-university institute, this time in complexity science which was at the core of the IPL activities. He was able to track down two "elephants" to nucleate this institute. These are Steve Lansing from the University of Arizona, who has worked extensively on the topic of the complexity of water management, ecology and rice farming in Bali, and Peter Sloot, Vrije Universiteit Amsterdam, whose specialism is in information processes, applying his theories to biomedicine and the modelling of infectious diseases, especially HIV in the Netherlands and its social consequences. Using these "elephants" as "bait", the Complexity Institute has been able to attract bright "gazelles" from various schools in NTU to join the Institute.

Both the IPL and the Complexity Institute formed a close association with the iconic Santa Fe Institute in the US.

Other Initiatives

Since that initial phase of institute formation, other activities have come to the fore to which NTU has responded agilely by again breaking down silos and leveraging on expertise in interdisciplinary actions. These include the Ageing Research Institute for Society and Education (ARISE) aimed at addressing the problems resulting from the changing demographic in Singapore. It is a growing research issue for many countries, and NTU and Singapore are playing an active role in a variety of research collaborations in this area. Through ARISE, NTU has developed several international collaborations in an area of worldwide concern. Another is the Singapore Centre for 3D Printing (SC3DP). Working with the A*STAR Singapore Institute of Manufacturing Technology (SIMTech) based on the NTU campus next to the School of Mechanical and Aerospace Engineering, Professor Chua Chee Kai had amassed many years of experience in understanding the process of additive manufacturing, known as 3D printing. Leveraging the joint expertise of both institutions, NTU was able to create the SC3DP and raise substantial funding from NRF, MOE, EDB and others in partnership with the private sector. SC3DP is now an established part of the NTU landscape, links with the Advanced Remanufacturing and Technology Centre (ARTC) (see below), and is another part of the NTU foundation blocks in developing collaboration with industry.

S. Rajaratnam School of International Studies (RSIS)

Although not a new initiative, RSIS is one of the leading regional think tanks in the area of strategic and defence-related research. Named after Sinnathamby Rajaratnam (a journalist who was a close colleague of Lee Kuan Yew who became Singapore's first Foreign Minister and later Deputy Prime Minister), it is a graduate school with a significant international reputation alongside institutions such as the Brookings Institute in Washington, D.C. and the Royal Institute of International Affairs (Chatham House) in London. This graduate school, with its international profile, has undertaken a wide span of research into topics such as traditional and non-traditional security, inter-religious relations in a plural society and all aspects of societal risk. It developed itself as a world-leading academic knowledge centre on terrorist groups including Al Qaeda.

NTU at the Cutting Edge of Research and Innovation

Links with A*STAR

We are now living in a globalised world. Therefore, on the small island of Singapore, it really does make sense to collaborate and take advantage of scientific synergies and geographical proximity. Given the role that A*STAR had played in bringing leading research figures to Singapore and in funding and stimulating research, it made sense to promote a closer working relationship with A*STAR colleagues as NUS was doing. NTU took advantage of space at A*STAR while developing some of its own activities and, again, this provided a useful "glue" between the institutions.

A specific and exciting aspect of the A*STAR/NTU collaboration has been the creation of ARTC. Very much inspired by Rolls-Royce, which had led the establishment of several such similar centres in the UK located adjacent to universities, ARTC is the only one of its kind in Asia. It is physically located at the CleanTech Park next to the NTU campus. The concept of such centres is to develop strong partnerships across the supply chain, complemented by technical support from research institutes and academia. Major industrial partners come together and jointly develop core programmes with the sharing of any intellectual property that arises. They may also have their own company research programmes using the facilities, in which case the intellectual property remains solely with the company. NTU has benefitted from this three-way collaboration between a public research organisation (A*STAR) and the technology-based multinational companies that are at the core of the partnership.

Collaboration with Industry and Promoting Innovation

One of the most significant major successes of NTU research has been its close collaboration with major industrial partners. Some of these are direct arrangements, while others have leveraged yet another NRF funding scheme — that of Corporate Labs @ Universities, launched in March 2013.[1] NTU's philosophy is that by bringing such companies onto campus, it is a triple win for all concerned. The university gains financial and intellectual benefit, the company gets access to the latest research discoveries and the graduate students involved have the opportunity of working

---

[1] https://www.nrf.gov.sg/programmes/corporate-laboratory@university-scheme

in both academia and industry and so have an opportunity for career progression within the company. Furthermore, this close link is an efficient way to insert discovery into the innovation cycle and into the economy. A further benefit for Singapore is that we provide access to brains — both faculty and students for industry — which assists in anchoring the company in the local economy. The creation of such a dynamic and far-reaching portfolio of industry/university research has been due in no small measure to the proactivity, enthusiasm and commitment to such collaborations of the current Vice President (Research), Professor Lam Khin Yong ("KY"). KY has been the principal driver of this industrial collaboration, eventually bringing many hundreds of millions of Singaporean dollars to NTU's research programmes. In fact, much of our success in developing our industrial collaboration programme is due to his drive and initiative.

Rolls-Royce has been the most significant of our partnerships with its support for a University Technology Centre at NTU. Mostly, these have been at UK universities, so it is a "feather in our cap" to have such support at NTU. This relationship has lasted for over a decade and has built considerable research capacity for both parties. In 2007, Rolls-Royce established a fuel cell research facility at NTU. Then, in 2013, NRF announced its support for such arrangements through its corporate laboratories scheme. This mix of agency funds, industry and academia is what we have termed the "Triple Helix" arrangement, again something that is of benefit to all those involved, and from the funding agency viewpoint is a further "anchoring" device. The Rolls-Royce laboratory was the first such award and was worth US$75 million — a very substantial investment in NTU. By our welcome and positive link for such collaborations, we had sown the field for this success. The laboratory focuses on three areas of research: electrical power and control systems, manufacturing and repair technologies, and computational engineering for professorships.

It has to be said that the award of a corporate laboratory has been shared between the four universities in Singapore, but NTU has been, possibly, the major gainer.

Another corporate laboratory is with ST Engineering, worth US$53 million, to conduct research in the development of advanced robotics and autonomous systems in two main research areas applied to the next generation of airport management — airport precision and airside technology (such as baggage transfer systems, aerobridges and aircraft tow trucks) and in enhancing intelligence support for crisis management.

NTU now hosts a number of other corporate labs such as with the local mass rapid transit (MRT) system provider: the S$60 million SMRT-NTU Smart Urban Rail Corporate Laboratory that aims to develop solutions to enhance rail reliability and develop a more resilient urban rail system in Singapore. The MRT was in urgent need of updated technology and, hence, looked to NTU as its ideal partner. Two complementary research tracks address the development of innovative urban rail solutions. The first track focused on developing better detection methods and monitoring systems so that potential issues can be addressed quickly and accurately. The second track aims to enhance the reliability of existing rail assets by optimising maintenance and servicing processes through prediction methodologies and analytical tools.

The S$45 million Delta-NTU Corporate Laboratory for Cyber-Physical Systems addresses the development of cyber-physical systems, ranging from large infrastructure systems such as water and power distribution to emerging consumer systems including the Internet of things (IoT), an ever-growing network of physical objects and systems connected to the Internet. Another award was for the S$42.4 million Singtel Cognitive and Artificial Intelligence Lab for Enterprises (SCALE@NTU) which has the aim of developing applications for use in the areas of public safety, smart urban solutions, transportation, healthcare and manufacturing. The partners, through their collective expertise and resources, aim to accelerate innovation in the fields of artificial intelligence, advanced data analytics, robotics and smart computing.

Therefore, the total awards from this NRF scheme amounted to just under US$300 million — a really substantial investment.

Apart from those companies involved with us through the NRF scheme, NTU also developed other industrial partnerships across a range of companies including the only laboratory in Asia supported by an NTU/BMW partnership. This links into the Campus for Research Excellence and Technological Enterprise (CREATE) scheme in which we collaborate with Technical University of Munich and is an example of a three-way partnership. Another world-famous name that wanted to work with us is Lockheed Martin. A very long partnership has existed between

NTU and the big European defence contractor, Thales, and this led to an interesting three-way partnership between the university on the one hand, the company and key French universities funded through the French National Centre for Scientific Research (CNRS) on the other. As such, it was an unusual *Unité Mixte Internationale* (UMI) as most of such arrangements only involve the CNRS and universities. In addition, we have also developed industrial links with the software and social media industries.

Therefore, our industrial research collaboration scheme has been one of the key successes in NTU's drive to research intensity. The criteria for success are when the industry wants to expand and intensify after its initial engagement and it creates an intellectual critical mass in a very short time. From a university perspective, we gain substantial benefits, but it does require an element of "top-down" decision-making plus the need to convince our faculty colleagues that this is the route to take and for which they should be proud that NTU could attract such prestigious partners.

As with most universities, we have an innovation office, just as we did with the Research Support Office; this was completely reformed and reconstructed under Dr. Lim Jui, a former biomedical researcher and himself experienced in start-up activities. The innovation office was changed to a private company — NTUitive Pte Ltd. This has the mission to develop a university-wide innovative ecosystem which fosters entrepreneurship across the university's research community as well as extends to the whole student body. Remember Haresh's disappointment decades before when he first came to NTU and one sees how dramatically things have changed and developed. Under Guaning, a technopreneurship educational programme was developed offering education in this complex area. This novel programme includes the participants spending time overseas in an immersive innovation environment such as at Stanford University and its links with Silicon Valley or in other countries, including China and Europe.

So, NTU has created a two-pronged approach to taking our discoveries into the marketplace. On one side is the traditional innovation office with its incubator function and the other is with industrial collaboration and sharing the intellectual property rights that emerge from such collaborations.

An important success factor for NTU in its interactions with the industry was to create critical mass collaborations. The industrial projects had a scale such that they involved several professors from a number of schools together with post-doctoral fellows and a large number of research students. Such collaborations were very attractive to companies and it made a difference in our ability to attract them to the campus, the best example being that of Rolls-Royce.

Getting the "Gazelles" and "Calves" to Come to NTU

Doctoral Students

At the heart of a successful research-intensive university are its research students. They provide the manpower, brains and new ideas to take knowledge forward. In 2007, NTU was struggling. The outgoing Vice President (Research) Professor Tony Woo, who came to NTU from the University of Washington, Seattle, US, had introduced a coupon system in the allocation of scholarships to faculty. This was the so-called "ROAR" coupon. The underlying idea was good in that its aim was to "beef up" research by allocating the coupons to the active researchers among the faculty. The problem was in its implementation. As the coupons were only valid for two years and a typical PhD programme was for four years, it acted as a deterrent to recruitment as there was no guarantee that after two years the coupon would be renewed. Therefore, the take up of studentships fell and the financial allocation (Research Scholarship Budget, RSB) by MOE was being underused. Action was needed urgently as ROAR became a unifying complaint across the campus when Bertil, as the newly arrived Provost, commenced a "royal tour" of all the schools.

If NTU were to move to a research-intensive university, not only was action needed but the case also had to be made for increased allocations of RSB to NTU. It was agreed that we should try to ensure that each faculty member was entitled to recruit at least two research students and that we had to manage the underspending and use it for what it was intended. By ending the ROAR system and by taking this action, we were able to rapidly increase our graduate student recruitment and thus increase our research productivity. We even managed to persuade MOE to increase our RSB! The overall result has been a tripling of research student numbers to around 3,000. This means, on average, that each faculty member should be able to supervise two students. Obviously, some have more and others will have only one student, but such a ratio is at the level found in the world's leading research-intensive universities.

However, problems remain. One is that the proportion of Singaporean citizens and permanent residents (PRs) enrolled at NTU (and the other universities) falls dramatically from 80% or more at the undergraduate level to only 20% for the PhD intake. This is a national problem and MOE is now asking us to increase the proportion to at least a third while reducing the overall numbers supported across the Singaporean higher education system. The second problem is that our faculty find it very easy to go to their alma maters in China, India and surrounding countries to recruit their graduate students. The result is that we build up enclaves of students from these countries which not only "overwhelms" the local intake but also creates specific language groups and other difficulties in integrating the students into our English-speaking community at NTU. These problems will take some time to overcome.

In addition, as part of the push towards interdisciplinarity and, in order to further specific high-priority initiatives, Bertil decided to retain a tranche of studentships at the centre. This enabled the university leadership to use this RSB allocation to promote research in terms of the peaks of excellence, industrial collaborations and in furthering international collaborations with such places as Imperial College London, the Karolinska Institute, the University of Southampton and the Technical University of Munich. In these cases, NTU endeavoured to create joint PhD programmes from which its graduate students have benefitted and which remain very attractive to our top intake. A further central initiative was to create an Interdisciplinary Graduate school in which each student has to have two supervisors from two different schools.

Promoting Good Research Practice (Research Integrity and Ethics)

In moving towards a research-intensive institution, one has to have regard for the "soft" infrastructure on which such a move should be based. Initially, this did not exist in NTU and was not in place even in 2007.

On his arrival as Provost in 2007, Bertil found that NTU was deficient in many policies and actions that underpinned the research effort. For one thing, there was not even a health and safety policy and structure. NTU was also deficient in other areas such as ethics and research integrity. Again, NTU did not have a properly constructed committee to deal with all the ethical issues arising from research. Research was an afterthought. Now, we have such a complete system in place, and this has become even more necessary with new legislation in Singapore governing human biomedical research, research on involving animals and personal data protection. NTU has worked diligently to ensure that our ethical controls are rigorous and comparable to those at other top universities.

In terms of research integrity, we were again lacking policies and procedures. Bertil, having been involved in research integrity initiatives while at the ESF, was extremely conscious of these deficiencies and he invited Professor Nick Steneck, University of Michigan, US, a world-leading expert, to visit and review the situation. With Tony Mayer, a major figure in this area and a close colleague of Nick Steneck, NTU set about creating policies and procedures to promote research integrity. This included raising awareness among faculty and students, educating them in good research practice and, more recently, in instigating appropriate and robust data management. In recognition of the need for further support in this area, we have established a Research Integrity and Ethics Office (RIEO) and instituted rigorous training programmes in research integrity and ethics for the whole NTU research community, including faculty, research staff, graduate students and anyone else conducting research. In total, NTU's research community numbers about 7,000, all of whom NTU expects to conduct research to the highest standards of competence and integrity.

As part of raising awareness, NTU was able to persuade NUS and A*STAR to join it in successfully bidding to host the Second World Conference on Research Integrity in Singapore in 2010. Apart from our own funds, we also received financial support from MOE that enabled us to offer support to participants from less-developed countries. This conference was very important as it led to the Singapore Statement on Research Integrity (drafted by a small group including Tony) agreed upon at the Conference. Now, the Statement has become one of the key international foundational documents in the fostering of good research practice and underpins our own policy.

However, we did not stop there. NTU is known for its robust "zero tolerance" approach and its educational schemes to promote good practice. It continues to play its part internationally and regionally and, with A*STAR, NUS, and the Singapore University of Technology and Design (SUTD), has planned and held Singapore research integrity days for the whole local research community.

We have had some difficult and high-profile cases of misconduct to deal with. No institution can be immune and with a total research community of around 7,000 (including faculty, post-doctoral fellows, research and project officers, and students), this is only to be expected. However, now having a robust system at the best international standards, we have been able to deal with such incidents.

NTU has come a long way over the past decade or so to ensure that its research is built on very solid foundations.

Ensuring Quality — NTU's Own Assessment and Evaluation Methods

Quality control is vital and we had to ensure that NTU was only putting forward its best and most competitive proposals. We also needed a mechanism to assess all the NAP applications. With around 10 awards made each year from our own funds, we were receiving nearly 60 times that number in good applications. Therefore, after initial sifting, we needed an expert committee to make the final decisions. The same committee would also have the expertise to assess proposals being put forward for the MOE Tier 2 funding in which the numbers of applications per discipline are limited by MOE, so only our best proposals stand a chance of success. Bertil was adamant that NTU had to use the best international standards in such assessments and was able to appoint Professor Bengt Nordén, from Chalmers University, Sweden, who had chaired the Nobel Chemistry Committee, to take charge of NTU's assessment process and ensure that our research met the best international standards of excellence. A little later, in order to assess NTU's proposals for the NRF Competitive Research Projects, another committee was established to conduct these proposal evaluations, with, this time, Sir David Payne, from University of Southampton, as its chairman.

In this way, procedures within NTU have been established to provide strict internal quality control in terms of the proposals that faculty make to the Singaporean funding bodies, which also ensures that they are very competitive and, ultimately, successful.

Outcomes

The new commitment and incentives to undertake high-level research at NTU were first enunciated at Guaning's inauguration and then actively encouraged and developed by Bertil and have led to a big increase in the volume of the research output at the university. What does this mean?

We can increase quantity, but this, at the same time, provides quality. Certainly, we dramatically increased our research funding from competitive research grants so that, by 2017, the NTU research income from external sources had increased some 30 times over 10 years to a figure in excess of S$600 million. This is a truly astonishing increase. We have been able to gain the support of many agencies in Singapore, not just MOE and NRF. We have developed our strong links with the industry and so increased the relevance of our research.

Using evidence from research citation impact measurements, it can be shown how well regarded and influential our research has become. Here is the proof of our success. Over the past 10 years, the growth in citations according to normalised data from Thomson Reuters shows that we have gained the top spot in Asia, and thus in Singapore. Even when we compare this with select European universities, this shows that we are have caught up rapidly with the best in Europe and the world. Perhaps one of the most important measures of the enormous progress made by NTU is demonstrated by the change in normalised citations from 2004–2016, which shows that the rise in NTU citations has been extremely rapid. This dramatic rise is shown in Colour Plate 11 (see page 140). Other major world universities from both the West and Asia also show significant yearly increases of citations (especially as the global volume of research has increased dramatically), but the rate of increase of NTU citations has been much more rapid. This is a unique accomplishment that shows that the changes made to the NTU research system had worked exceptionally well and in such a short time. In more general terms, it is encouraging that universities under the right management and leadership, together with political and financial support, can change quickly. This argues against the common perception that universities are either unable, unwilling or very slow in reforming themselves and responding to change. Perhaps this is the most important lesson from the NTU story.

It has been an intensive period and one that required hard work and dedication not only from ourselves in a leadership role but also from all our faculty colleagues. It has also demonstrated the wisdom of our recruitment policies, capturing high-flying senior researchers on the one hand and being attractive and a beacon for the very bright young researchers on the other.

NTU has managed to change the research agenda. From the RCE bid failure in 2007, and the "wake-up" call, it is hard to imagine that it has been possible to move forward so rapidly that, 10 years later, NTU is number one in Asia, which is a truly remarkable journey.

This is because NTU has been able to reform the whole system of which research is an integral part. Research has been emphasised from the start as a key priority. The Provost and his team were charged with such reforms in order to create a research-minded culture. Now, NTU is able to compete and succeed and we have fulfilled the original objective of long ago in the Dainton Report to achieve parity with NUS. Now, our two great universities can compete with each other based on mutual respect and esteem.

Chapter 18

Ranking and Reputation

The US News and World Report ranking of US universities was the first ranking system established but confined to institutions in the US. Top universities regarded the rankings with disdain, but the media and parents lapped it up eagerly. This trend spread to world university rankings only in the last 15 years or so. It is hard enough to compare universities within the same country, so to compare them internationally is really sticking one's neck out.

The history of world rankings and that of the NTU Troika story parallel each other, both starting in 2003. The first ranking results, created by the Shanghai Jiao Tong University in China (Academic Ranking of World Universities, ARWU), were published in 2003. This was followed quickly by the Quacquarelli Symonds (QS) rankings system, published first under the auspices of the Times Higher Education (THE) weekly newspaper and later independently. The THE, later, came up with its own separate system. Thus, those from Shanghai and QS are the longest running in which the QS is probably the one which has developed the best all-round indices to measure university performances. One major difference is that the ARWU is still very heavily historically reputation-based, while QS measures current indices. Therefore, one is able to track changes from year to year and identify trends at both the individual institution level as well as regionally.

Rankings have their critics, but they are now an accepted part of academic life, especially for funders, top managements, policy makers, parents and students. Thus, we have had no choice but to pay attention to them. Sometimes, it is the headline number that is taken into account rather than the details that go to make up the actual ranking position. Of course, overall rankings do not demonstrate the particular strengths of an institution. For example, the University of Rhode Island in the US, sometimes unkindly described as the "High School after High School", hosts its Graduate School of Oceanography, one of the leading oceanographic institutions in the world. One cannot say that an institution ranked at 50 is quantitatively and qualitatively better than a university ranked at, say, 55. However, it is clear that anyone ranked in the top 25 has achieved a level of excellence far above one, say, ranked at 100 and certainly one ranked at 200.

Prior to rankings, the only "measure" of a university, outside normal disciplinary knowledge, was that of its reputation, however defined. This was a "static" system as reputations are a reflection of history rather than the *actualité*, and this is the basis of the Shanghai ARWU system. Well-known universities could not "lose" and neither could new excellent institutions "win" nor be recognised except by a limited "word of mouth" recommendation. Inevitably, this is a slow way of building a reputation. Now, rankings can provide a picture of the university concerned combining a variety of pieces of information to reflect more rapid changes, no better exemplified than that of NTU, followed by *École polytechnique fédérale de Lausanne* (EPFL, Swiss Federal Institute of Technology Lausanne) in Lausanne, Switzerland.

So, what is "reputation" and is it "real"? How easy is it to make and gain a reputation, and how easy is it to lose it? One may surmise that it is harder to gain a reputation and get a brand name recognised than the inverse. It is difficult to see the Ivy League or Oxbridge losing reputation. Again, the question has to be asked as to why it is wrong to develop ranking systems even if one can argue about which metrics provide the most valuable and realistic information. The introduction of rankings means that a range of information is available. There is a reputational element within ranking methodology with the weighting of such surveys varying between different ranking systems and based on many thousands of academic opinions (it should be noted that in such surveys, those taking part are self-selected).

Rankings have become especially important in Singapore, which likes to see such "quantitative" measures, whatever they may mean in reality.

In fact, Singapore is somewhat of a slave to measures such as key performance indicators (KPIs). For NTU, the importance of rankings is that the choice of university is very much determined by parents. They want to be assured that their child (or children) is going to an institution that has achieved international recognition. When there was a large gap between NUS and NTU in rankings, parents would frequently query why they should encourage their offspring to attend the lower ranked institution. Once NTU started to close the gap between itself and NUS, this question became easier to answer. The very real outcome for NTU became our increased ability to recruit Singaporean top students and enter into a virtuous spiral as top students in turn get better jobs, our reputation is enhanced and the story continues.

Were the perceptions about the academic system and individual institutions better or worse before rankings and how have rankings changed universities and their behaviour? Certainly, before rankings, there was no measure or semi-quantitative comparison available, and there was an opacity in the system that meant that younger institutions or "challenger" institutions might not have had the visibility that they deserved. At the same time, established universities across the world with a top-level reputation were never challenged.

For an ambitious and reforming institution such as NTU, rankings have provided a means for our achievements to be recognised regionally and across the globe. Upon gaining autonomy, the first challenge for the new Board of Trustees was to establish the vision and mission for the university so that the entire university has a clear sense of direction. After lengthy discussions, the Board of Trustees approved the NTU vision and mission statement, declaring that it should be "a great global university founded on science and technology, nurturing leaders through research and a broad education in diverse disciplines".

In this book, we demonstrate that the NTU community has indeed achieved this vision and this is now reflected in our high ranking, whatever system is used. In 2003, when rankings were first created, there was a large gap between us and NUS. In the eyes of the government and the public, NTU was once probably regarded as its "poor" relation. Yet, the Dainton Report to the Singaporean government, which led to the creation of NTU, had said that Singapore needed at least two institutions of high standing to compete against each other and mutually drive up standards in both education and research. This was also Guaning's message in his inaugural address. It was imperative that NTU developed so as to compete effectively both for the top students in the university entry cohort and in research. Recognising this need, Bertil, as the incoming Provost, was urged to close the rankings gap with NUS. Coming from Europe, Bertil was initially sceptical about the value of rankings, but the importance accorded to rankings by the Board of Trustees and Singaporeans quickly changed his mind. Closing the "NUS gap" has now been achieved nearly a decade after Bertil's arrival and now both NTU and NUS are at number 11 in the QS World University Rankings in 2018/19. In 2007, no one would have believed that this was achievable and certainly not within this short time period. This is a great achievement both for NTU and for Singapore itself, which should be immensely proud to have two universities in the top 15 of world universities. In fact, NTU is now ranked ahead of many eminent institutions in Asia, Europe and North America. The country's success with both NUS and NTU, now accepted as world-leading institutions in such a small country, is a reflection of the commitment to the knowledge society that has been the mark of government policy throughout the period that we discuss in this book. It makes Singapore a unique place.

So, the story of NTU's unique, very rapid rise and its recognition in world university ranking systems have been, probably, the most unexpected of outcomes for Singapore and, globally, in the very conservative world of the upper echelons of higher education. It is certainly doubtful whether the gap between us and the other world-leading universities could have been closed without the substantial reforms that we initiated in NTU and certainly not with such rapidity. In early chapters, we have quoted Lim Chuan Poh saying, after the first round of calls for the Research Centres of Excellence (RCEs) initiative (with its substantial funding of US$150 million per project), that NTU had not been awarded a single project. Not only that, none of its proposals had even been shortlisted for the second stage of the process. He considered that this was a "wake-up" call for the university leadership and this led to the radical and major reform on the research front initiated by the Troika.

The importance of promoting competitive first-class research, with its concomitant good publications and high citation rates, helped attract leading multinational companies to partner with us. The other chapters recount how this was achieved, with these reforms eventually feeding through into the rankings, and so began our rapid rise. Once a university is on the move, in this way, it achieves international recognition, which in turns leads to the ability to attract the very highest quality staff from around the world, leading to even more high-quality research, and so the cycle continues with gathering momentum. Therefore, our rankings progress has fed back into creating the reputation which was the achievement of the Board's vision. Bertil for one, steeped in the European tradition of scepticism about the importance of rankings, was very doubtful about the priority attached to rankings by the Board of Trustees, but he is now convinced by the evidence of the impact of a high ranking in these global league tables.

We have discussed the general university ranking system, but one should also look in greater depth at some of the indices. It is particularly gratifying to look at NTU's progress through normalised citation impacts. These are in a sense "real" figures in that they are based on the citations that our research generates. We have achieved almost exponential growth to become the leader in the Asian part of such rankings and we are now catching up with the likes of Imperial College London, University College London, ETH Zürich in Switzerland and institutions in the US and elsewhere. In the 2018 QS World University rankings, NTU was behind only the top four American institutions (Massachusetts Institute of Technology (MIT), Stanford, Harvard and the California Institute of Technology (Caltech)) and then the UK universities (Cambridge, Oxford, University College London and Imperial College London), followed by The University of Chicago and ETH Zürich in Switzerland. Although this represents the highest ranking that NTU has achieved, it has moved rapidly upwards in other ranking systems (even when these, THE and the ARWU (operated by Shanghai Jiao Tong University), are much more heavily reputation-based and, therefore, conservative and largely historic). Altogether, the rankings have demonstrated that NTU is probably the most rapidly upwardly mobile institution globally.

NTU now ranks in the top 50 of world universities in the THE ranking and is now around 75 in the very conservative ARWU. When we embarked on the NTU journey, NTU was in the group ranked between 300 and 400 and it seemed inconceivable that NTU would advance so much in this conservative ranking system. In Asia, NTU has achieved top status in bibliometric comparisons, as shown in normalised citation measurements. When one looks at the *Nature* Index, which is a measure of the productivity of research in a range of high-impact journals, we rank 32nd overall in a list that includes the biggest and most significant national research institutes such as the Chinese Academy of Sciences and the Max Planck Society in Germany. In chemistry (from across the board in NTU), we ranked fifth. In physical sciences, we ranked 27th, again a very creditable achievement and the story will continue as success breeds success.

If we look in greater depth at rankings, and especially disciplinary ones, then the NTU progress and achievements are particularly impressive. We have held the top spot among young universities worldwide (a young university is one established within the last 50 years). Here, our main "competitor" has been the Hong Kong University of Science and Technology (HKUST), which is the equivalent of NTU in that city and was also founded in 1991. In chemistry (across the university as a whole), NTU is ranked number three, and yet the School of Physical and Mathematical Sciences, which includes chemistry, was not established at NTU until as recently as 2005. In materials sciences, we rank in second place, and in engineering, still at the heart of NTU, we rank in fourth place, behind only MIT, Stanford and Cambridge. In 2007, and for some years thereafter, NTU was rated below NUS, embarrassing for us but not surprising as the research portfolio belonged with NUS, even though this was in our core set of disciplines! Finally, in the topic of artificial intelligence (AI), now one of the hottest of hot topics, NTU ranks in second place and is in a world-leading position alongside Microsoft, the Chinese Academy of Sciences and Carnegie Mellon University in the US.

What are the consequences of this high ranking? As we have stated, Singapore attaches considerable significance to such seemingly "quantitative" measures, and this is reflected in our standing with the government, senior administrators, politicians, parents and students. Most importantly, it changes the perceptions of NTU in comparison with NUS and overseas universities. For parents, NTU is no longer seen as a poor relation and the default option for their children. Without such public measures, it would be difficult to explain to parents that we have closed the gap and passed

NUS as no one would have believed that this was remotely possible. As we have found, perceptions based on old reputations, once embedded, are difficult to change. Rankings provide the evidence of such change and movement. Not only do rankings help our general student recruitment but they also have a particular impact on those rated as the top students within any age cohort.

On another front, the high ranking has made NTU much more visible on the international stage. It is now seen as a desirable partner by other universities based on what Sir Keith O'Nions (former Rector of Imperial College London) has said is "mutual academic esteem". In turn, this means that we can attract and employ top scientists and scholars from across the globe, both at the senior level, nucleating research groups around themselves, as well as at the junior (around 10 years after gaining one's doctorate) assistant professor level.

Of course, with such recruitment success and our high profile and visibility, we have rising academic stars who, in turn, may be "poached" by other institutions, but that is the price of success. In a way, one may say that without having such "stars" on our academic books who will be the subject of "poaching", we would have failed.

NTU's success story has been recognised all over the world and is seen as a model of development to emulate for new and old institutions in Asia and emerging economies. Its leadership is in high demand and invited to academic meetings to relate the NTU "story".

Quality will always prevail and we have striven for the very highest academic standards, and through rankings and indices this has been demonstrated to the world. We do not have to say it — the evidence is there for all to see.

We end this part of our story with a quote from Phil Baty, the Editor-in-Chief for the THE World University Rankings, who said, "NTU is the outstanding success story of World University Rankings.... It has moved up this prestigious league table an extraordinary 108 places in the last three years making it the best performer in the top 200 (universities) in recent times.... NTU is an exceptional achievement as a case study that stands out for the rest of the region and the world." The same rankings described NTU, in 2016, as the "world's fastest rising youngest university". Nevertheless, the story must continue and we have to maintain this elevated position. As with any similar achievement, getting to the top is one thing, sustaining one's position is another matter entirely, and so actions have to be continually maintained and intensified, as well as being modified to meet a changing environment. However, we can now face this future from "the high pastures near the summit of the mountain".

Appendix 3 provides a summary of NTU's rankings in 2017 at the conclusion of the Troika era, both general and discipline-specific.

Chapter 19

Communicating with and Serving the Society

One of the difficulties encountered by NTU during its rapid progress over the past 15 years to become a leading research-intensive has been the general public's perception of the universities in Singapore and NTU in particular. This derives substantially from the previous perceptions of NTU as being the old "Chinese" *Nantah* or, indeed, the Nanyang Technological Institute (NTI)/early NTU period when the institution was concerned, principally, with educating engineers rather than being one of the world's leading universities with its extensive portfolio of academic activities. As we have previously stated, the reform process started in 2003 under Guaning's presidency. As always, public perceptions change much more slowly, but now, 15 or so years later, Singaporeans recognise and are proud of the high standing of NTU.

The Singapore public has traditionally regarded universities as teaching institutions catering for all those who, for largely financial reasons, were unable to go to North America, Europe (especially the UK) or Australia for their university education. Also, higher education was viewed as the door to wealth creation and improved lifestyle rather than being valued for its own intrinsic academic value. So, as NTU evolved over the past 15 years into becoming a leading research-intensive university (based on the Humboldtian philosophy), public perceptions lagged behind the new reality, especially as research was not seen, necessarily, as being a priority for the universities or even Singapore.

Therefore, this was the challenge in terms of our communication and public persona. It seemed, at times, like trying to "sell ice cream to Inuits" — especially those in their parkas in Singapore's offices when, in the 2000s, the air condition temperatures seemed to be just above freezing point!

How were we going to get our message out to the public? Another example of the problems faced was that the high-level opening of our Energy Research Institute (ERIAN) as well as its partnership with Robert Bosch GmbH, both attended by ministers, led to articles in the local press in which, after two sentences about the event, it then described, at greater length, similar activities at NUS. No matter what NTU did, reporters always referred to NUS while reporting events at NTU. It was very frustrating. Again, this was a reflection of the old perceptions about NTU and the unassailable position of NUS in Singapore which had become embedded in local English-language journalism, although the Chinese-language newspaper was more positive.

Therefore, we had to inform the public about and "sell" the idea of the "new" NTU. We had to inform them about our new research capacity and the output from it, which was relevant to the economic health of the country, and we had to communicate with the student community, and especially with their parents. In many parts of the world, there is a lot of pride in the activities of the local university. We had to create a situation in which Singaporeans would take pride in the achievements of their own Nanyang Technological University however "ulu"[1] it was. This is where our rapid rise in the rankings (see Chapter 18) became a very useful "tool" in changing perceptions. When the NTU rankings started to rise, the first reaction from the public was that there must be something wrong with the rankings themselves! Later, as NTU continued to climb the world rankings, this scepticism slowly turned to pride in this Singaporean achievement.

Another challenge was to raise the visibility and reputation of NTU globally. This was to make it known and attractive to other universities as a partner, to the major industry that we were open for business and

---

[1] "Ulu" is used in Singlish from Malay denoting a remote, distant place or "in the boonies" to quote the American vernacular.

collaboration, and to ensure that our recruitment process would bring top talent to the institution.

First, we had to have professional staff to really spin-up our communications and we were lucky to be able to recruit Dr. Vivien Chiong (a leading Singaporean professional communicator and an alumna of our own Wee Kim Wee School of Communication and Information) to build a top-class information and communications department. Vivien, in particular, has knowledge of academia, was completely familiar with the Singapore "system" and had experience in written, spoken and visual media. She recruited, in turn, a dynamic young team that was also expert in communicating using all the modern tools of media. Vivien and her team have won and accumulated over 50 prizes for communication excellence. The introduction of *HEY!*, a "with it" magazine designed specifically with students in mind, was another achievement. *HEY!* is now probably one of the best student magazines in the world.

Another hard copy initiative was *Pushing Frontiers*, our research periodical. Dr. Chiong also enlivened the President's annual academic talk with amusing introductions, including a film of the President (Bertil) as the "secret biker" on campus and, on another occasion, having his speech delivered to him (on the podium), by drone. These happenings rapidly went viral on social media.

Of course, the storyline was one of positive and exciting growth and change and, with NTU rising rapidly in the rankings, NTU communications had a great story to tell and sell. This contrasted with earlier days when stories in the press about NTU tended to be either negative or played down our success.

Vivien and her team have updated NTU's communication approach and have used mainstream and social media to great effect. Again, an important modern means of communication, but it also demonstrated that NTU was no longer the "staid old lady" in the "far west" of the island.

With this much improved public persona, NTU attracted more attention than the other universities and its leadership featured more frequently in the news. The main target, however, remained both students and parents, and Bertil and the NTU leadership team made themselves available to this important community. Bertil has always considered that, in this regard, his top priority had to be interaction with the "tough" Singaporean mothers when dealing with student recruitment. This has resulted in our increasing share of top students and has demonstrated that NTU has crossed a barrier in recognition and acceptance. NTU is now seen as an exciting place at which to study and work.

However, this was not the only thing that has occurred in projecting the image of a fast-moving and engaged modern institution. This started with NTU's involvement in the annual Singapore Chingay Parade, then our hosting of the first Youth Olympic Games, culminating in the now much appreciated NTU Fest. When faced with these opportunities, the Troika embraced them with enthusiasm and saw that they could be a way to break down society's preconceptions about the university.

So, what is "Chingay"? The word is an Anglicisation of the Hokkien dialect pronunciation of *zhuangyi* parade (妆艺大游行) that means "parade of the decorated miniature stages" or floats. To quote from its website, Chingay is "the largest street performance and float parade in Asia". Derived from old Chinese customs and deity processions, Chingay is part of Chinese New Year celebrations and it has now become an annual national event with participants from all the communities and is a major Singapore expression and celebration of its multiculturalism. In 2009, NTU entered a float which featured a fire-breathing dragon (Tong Liang Fire Dragon), combining the skills of the Schools of Art, Design and Media (ADM) and the engineering schools, which won the award for the best float. An estimated 150,000 spectators attended the 2009 Chingay Parade, which was broadcast to Singapore and Southeast Asia. Therefore, our first big venture into such community engagement brought NTU's name to the attention of many people.

The second big event to draw attention to NTU was the first ever Youth Olympic Games when NTU was selected to host the Olympic Village. With its residential campus, sports facilities both on the main campus and within the National Institute of Education (NIE), this was a very significant endeavour. It meant that a large part of the campus had to be fenced off and guarded for security reasons for the duration of the Games in 2010. But, it again demonstrated NTU's ambition to be a significant part of Singapore society helping with national societal aims.

A few years later, in 2014, NTU mounted its first NTU Fest. Students first proposed such an event and, encouraged by the new Student Life initiative, this really took off. The aim was fund-raising to support students from low-income origins with additional means. NTU rented the Padang (a large open space at the centre of the downtown area) promoted a "fun run", had carnival stalls and imported pop stars from Korea (K-pop) for entertainment. Getting K-pop groups was a major achievement as, at the time, these were the most celebrated bands in Asia and were the prime representatives of the cutting edge of Korean trendy "super-culture". It was a major carnival staged by NTU and held at the heart of Singapore. Again, NTU was no longer a "staid old lady", but represented the best of Singapore's younger generation in a burst of creativity — a very important change of perception. Of course, we took advantage of the whole scene to have stalls featuring our teaching and research. With an estimated attendance of more than 10,000, we had really reached out to the community. A year later, NTU staged a second edition — this time at the exciting new developments of Marina Bay. Of course, this was particularly significant because it was one of NTU's contributions to the celebration of Singapore's 50th anniversary as an independent state and NTU played its full part in these celebrations. As President, Bertil played an enthusiastic role in these occasions, but it was a much "harder sell" to get many of his senior colleagues to be equally enthusiastic. Coming out of "ivory towers" to engage with the general public is often difficult for academics across the world!

Today, NTU is recognised because apart from teaching — the fundamental *raison d'être* of all universities, which, by definition, reaches into and supports society — there is research and now there is the "third mission" of serving society. NTU sees all three missions as fundamental to its role as a key part of Singaporean society. NTU provides top-level education delivered by high-level professors recruited from the world's best, producing well-educated Singaporean citizens, most of whom become "practice professionals" as engineers, managers, accountants and auditors, civil servants, journalists and media professionals, designers and artists, and, now, doctors for Singapore's ageing population. NTU undertakes high-impact research leading to innovation and working not only with the world's leading technologically-based multinationals but also with "home-grown" industry, business and infrastructure providers such as SMRT, ST Engineering, the Civil Aviation Authority of Singapore, the Public Utilities Board and Keppel Corporation. For example, NIE, a key part of NTU, reaches out to and provides support to all corners of the much-admired Singapore school system.

Through its alumni, of which NTU now has over a quarter of a million, the university is able to be an active part of Singaporean society.

Also, NTU must pay attention to its immediate neighbours in Jurong. As we describe in the chapter about the campus, we have excellent facilities and, although they primarily provide for the students and staff, we have the capacity to invite in and share with our neighbours. The three all-weather pitches that we have, plus tennis and basketball courts, are able to take a very high usage and it is pleasing to see that people from the surrounding areas are using these facilities, not to mention the jogging track. There is a bridge across the expressway so that the local population can enjoy the quiet contemplation area of the Yunnan Garden. Nevertheless, we have to do more. In 2017, Bertil initiated a local community engagement initiative to start to develop activities of particular relevance and benefit for our neighbours. His message was always that NTU should be proud of its neighbourhood in Jurong and that Jurong should be proud of NTU.

With all the many activities that are described here, we believe we have overcome the old stereotypical view of NTU and have shown to Singapore that we are part of and major contributors to its well-being and that we are proud of being part of Singapore's position as a world leader in teaching and research excellence as well as being considered to be "cool"!

Chapter 20

The University in a Tropical Garden

NTU is a substantial organisation with a large residential component. In fact, it is possibly one of the world's largest residential universities by virtue of the numbers involved. At the height of any semester, there will be 17,000 or more students plus about 1,000 faculty and senior staff and their families living on campus (in comparison, NUS has about 10,000 residential students in its University Town). With the influx of non-residential students and other faculty and staff, this rises to around 40,000 people on campus each day. This is the population of a small town, so the President of NTU is also the "mayor" of the NTU "town" and ultimately responsible for its well-being and that of all the people on site. Put this into a tropical green campus of 200 hectares covering a series of rolling hills and valleys and you have NTU's Yunnan Garden campus in the west of the island of Singapore. Therefore, NTU has to provide not only its academic facilities but also the living areas as well as shops and food outlets, a clinic and a day care centre plus transport to service this community.

Anyone visiting NTU's main campus will be impressed by its excellent architecture and its green environment. No matter from which entrance one approaches the campus, one's overriding impression is of tropical greenery with many species of birds and small animals. There are also other larger beasts around at night including monkeys, wild boars and a variety of snakes and other reptiles. Indeed, even in one's modern office, you can have golden orioles and woodpeckers outside the window. It is rated among the 15 most beautiful campuses in the world in *Travel and Leisure*. Located in Jurong, in the west of the island of Singapore, it is frequently regarded as "remote" by Singaporeans who are strangely deterred by the 25 kilometres or so between downtown and Jurong. Hence, it is often referred to as an "ulu" place.

The 200-ha (500 acres) site was originally gifted to the Nanyang University (*Nantah*) by the Singapore Hokkien Huay Kuan (新加坡福建会馆) — the clan association of the people of southern Fujian province. It was originally even larger at 523 acres, having lost some land to the Pan-Island Expressway (PIE) and public housing estates. The original entrance arch to *Nantah*, now a national monument under the charge of NTU, is 1.5 kilometres away from the boundary of the campus across the PIE behind a sports stadium. The replica of the Chinese-style entrance arch was built in 1995 in Yunnan Garden.

Contrary to common impression, the Yunnan Garden campus was not named after the Chinese province of the same name. The land that the Singapore Hokkien Huay Kuan donated was a plantation south of the western hills of Singapore. The plantation was named Yun (云 cloud) Nan (南 south) Yuan (园 garden), meaning south of the clouds that tended to gather near the hills in the afternoon often resulting in heavy rain. The Chinese garden on the NTU campus also took on the name Yunnan Garden (云南园) from the name of the campus. The garden was constructed as part of the old *Nantah* in 1954 and is an area of pavilions, lawns, trees and other plantings and a place of peace and contemplation. A bridge across the expressway connects the university with the surrounding community; it is used by residents of the housing estate on the other side. More recently, the whole garden has been upgraded with new planting, waterfalls and many other features to enhance the enjoyment of the area. Yunnan Garden also contains the *Nantah* Founding Memorial, another national monument that records the principal donors to the original Nanyang University. An embankment leads to what is now the Chinese Heritage Centre, yet another national monument which was the original Nanyang University Administration Building. Into this embankment are inserted eight huge Chinese characters that read "自强不息, 力求上進" (zi qiang bu xi, li qiu shang jin), translated as "to thrive in adversity, to strive and improve oneself constantly". The Heritage Centre is not only a national monument but is also a registered museum. Both Yuannan Garden and the museum, as well as other iconic buildings such as that of the School of Arts, Design and Media (ADM) and the Hive Learning Centre, are frequently used by bridal couples as backgrounds for their wedding photographs!

Again, as mentioned in the history chapter, the Japanese architect Kenzō Tange was commissioned in 1981 to design an academic structure that would use the topography in an innovative way. Thus, the academic buildings consist of two spines with spurs running off on either side. The North Spine was built first for Nanyang Technological Institute (NTI) and opened in 1985, but it was not until 10 years later that the South Spine was added to complete Tange's vision. Near the junction of the two spines is the NIE campus. NIE has its administration in the shape of a giant V, built around 2000. That was also the last time NTU did campus planning. Given its ideal combination of facilities, this became the site of the Olympic Village when Singapore hosted the inaugural Youth Olympic Games in 2010. NTU provided the residential and practice facilities.

NTU has been fortunate to inherit this marvellous site and an excellent infrastructure on which we have been able to build on both literally and metaphorically. Recently, in 2020, the donation of the land to *Nantah* and ultimately to its successor NTU was memorialised by the naming of the Schools of Humanities and Social Sciences building next to the Chinese Heritage Centre as the Singapore Hokkien Huay Kuan Building, with the road alongside Nanyang Lake renamed Tan Lark Sye Walk in honour of the founder of Nanyang University (*Nantah*).

During the period covered by this book, there has been a huge investment in NTU's academic infrastructure. The move to become a more comprehensive university brought in its wake the need for a major expansion of the academic buildings, infilling and extending the original Tange concept.

One building a little apart from but close to the junction of the two spines is the Nanyang Auditorium that can take audiences of up to 2,000 and is used for convocations as well as for many other events and concerts.

In 2002/2003, a magnificent new building was erected to house the School of Biological Sciences (SBS) with a Central Atrium that can be used for exhibitions, conferences as well as serve as a large examination hall. It includes an extensive Traditional Chinese Medicine (TCM) Clinic that attracts clientele from across the island. Outside the Atrium and connecting to Nanyang Auditorium is the Quad which was built at the same time as the SBS building after consultation between Guaning and James Tam, the Dean of SBS at the time. Within the Quad is a ring of class plaques, a tradition started by Guaning in the year 2005 connecting the old *Nantah* alumni to the new NTI/NTU alumni. Each graduating class since the 2005 Convocation has organised a class gift campaign collecting donations, no matter how small the amount, to donate as a gift to the university to benefit their juniors. A bronze plaque marks the presence on campus of each graduating class. For those already graduated, the plaque was laid at alumni reunion events. The ring is complete from 1960, the first *Nantah* graduating class, to 2019, with a break of three years, 1982–1984, where instead of the class plaque, one finds a bronze plaque explaining the merger with University of Singapore (SU) to become NUS and the creation of NTI and NTU.

At the same time as the SBS building was being constructed, its neighbour the Research Techno Plaza building was also being erected during Cham Tao Soon's presidency. This building has been used by the Nanyang Technopreneurship Centre and hosts many joint laboratories with the industry. The building has an oversized atrium making for poor utilisation of space. This atrium had elicited negative comments from MOE as well as the 2005 QAFU External Review Panel. Further up the road, another new building was constructed for the School of Chemical and Biomedical Engineering. This was followed shortly thereafter by the iconic School of Art, Design and Media building situated in a wooded valley right in the heart of the campus. It was designed by Singapore Architect Timothy Seow. This building consists of three intertwining blocks that form a natural extension of the landscape. The highlight of the building is the verdant-turfed roof that blends with the ground contour. Apart from its visual impact, the turfed roof is a functional space accessible via sidesteps along the roof edge, thereby allowing the rooftop to be a scenic outdoor communal space. Environmentally, it helps to lower the roof temperature and in the surrounding areas and, locally, is referred to as "NTU's ski slopes" by one homesick Swedish Provost/President!

The School of Physical and Mathematical Sciences, established in 2005, took some time to settle on the building design. In the end, it took reference from the then new chemistry building at Oxford. Construction was completed in 2007. The last of the three new schools mooted in 2003 to get its building was that for the Schools of Humanities and Social Sciences located next to the Chinese Heritage Centre.

Finally, with the advent of the Medical School, the latest academic building is the Experimental Medicine Building (EMB) with its flipped classrooms and group-learning facilities as well as well-appointed laboratories, which includes a suite of magnetic resonance imaging (MRI) scanning machines. The EMB abuts closely to the adjacent military training area.

Consistent with the Blue Ribbon Commission Report, two new learning centres have been added, the Hive and the Arc, which are referred to in the education chapter. The Hive, designed by London 2012 Olympics architect, Thomas Heatherwick, is a futuristic and environmentally sustainable building formed by a series of linked round towers with balconies of greenery and with an internal space illuminated by natural light.

On the east side of the academic area is the residential part of the campus, not just for students but also for staff. These are built into the hills and valleys with, on an isolated hill, the President's Lodge and associated villas for senior staff. One limitation with which the university has to contend in any further developments is a height restriction due to the flight path for military aircraft taking off and landing at the nearby Tengah Air Base.

Some distance from the academic centre within the faculty residential area is the university's executive education centre (the Nanyang Executive Centre, NEC) serving as a site for conferences and residential courses and a hotel for visitors adjacent to a campus clubhouse and the sports facilities. The sports complex includes an Olympic-sized swimming pool, two large artificial grass pitches catering to a variety of sports, a modern and fast running track built to top international standards, an old sports hall, as well as the magnificent new all-wood Sports Hall — The Wave, opened in 2017 and which can accommodate an audience of up to 3,000. Because of having the all-weather pitches, which can carry heavy usage, it has become a centre for student activities as well as provides the local community with access to top-quality sporting facilities. Not least important, and built as one of Bertil's initiatives, there is a blue-surfaced jogging track along the perimeter of the campus on which one could see the third President jogging and more recently power walking!

To feed the large NTU community, one needs food outlets and these have to be multi-ethnic to cater to the large and varied international community. Here, one sees all varieties of Asian and Western food establishments including the ubiquitous McDonalds, Subway and Starbucks! Cuisine is a reflection of culture and it vividly illustrates the multi-ethic and multinational character of the university. In addition to facilities, including shops, on the main academic part of the campus, there are numerous food outlets linked to the student residential halls (open to everyone, including the general public).

Because of the location, *Nantah* and NTI were both residential campuses. When Guaning embarked on building three new schools and increasing enrolment by 6,300, there were commensurate plans for student residences to maintain the ratio that half the students could stay on campus. However, during the boom years of 2006–2007, before the financial crisis of 2008, the building industry in Singapore was overheating and the government instructed government projects to be put on hold. NTU was forced to stop new construction projects and as a result, the existing residential halls became very crowded with three to a room being quite common. After the 2008 crisis, the industry cooled down and projects could resume.

Meanwhile, in 2008, Koh Boon Hwee and Guaning initiated a Campus Master Plan exercise with a committee chaired by Edmund Cheng, then on the Board of Trustees and an architect and property developer. The committee visited Princeton, Cornell, Harvard, Yale, Washington University in St. Louis and Stanford to learn from the efforts of others. This Master Plan was intended to guide NTU campus development for the foreseeable future, the first time such a plan had been developed. Previous Master Plans were all more short term in nature, including the original design for NTU by Tange and the Master Plan for NIE. Now that NTU had its own strategic vision, we needed a Campus Master Plan to support the strategic plan.

Proposals from renowned architects were shortlisted and evaluated in a design competition. Guida Moseley Brown Architects from Canberra was selected. The NTU Campus Master Plan was approved in 2010 by the Board of Trustees to guide the future development for at least the next 20 years.

NTU was expanding and needed the infrastructure to match, so building started again in 2011. This would substantially increase the already substantial student accommodation so that NTU would become even more of a residential university in support of undergraduate education, as well as enhance other aspects of the university (including the shops and food outlets).

NTU has now enhanced its provision for student accommodation, adding nine new halls to the existing 14 halls, expanding staff housing and adding a second large graduate student hall, all built into the tropical hillsides of the campus. The food courts in the North and South Spines were revamped and a small shopping mall was constructed together with student lounges. Some S$1.8 billion has been invested in campus development over this period. Now, NTU is running out of space for new buildings and has had to use infills to add much-needed additional academic facilities as well as demolish and rebuild some of the older buildings. A new Business School Building is being built in one of the few remaining areas available for development. The A*STAR Singapore Institute of Manufacturing Technology had been located at NTU in two buildings. With some relocation to the A*STAR centre at Fusionopolis, one building has become available for NTU and provides much needed additional space, principally devoted to supercomputing and a new site for the Innovation Centre.

We have come to a limit of what can be done on the Yunnan Campus without destroying its unique character as a green, tropical centre of learning.

During the period covered by this book, there has been one other major development adjacent to the campus. This has been the creation of the CleanTech Park. The aim is to attract activities, both commercial and academic, linked to various aspects of "green technology" — in other words an eco-business centre. NTU itself has moved two of its pan-university institutes to locations in the park. These are the Nanyang Environment and Water Research Institute (NEWRI) and Energy Research Institute (ERIAN), and as energy and water technologies groups, they are ideal tenants for the park. In addition, the Advanced Remanufacturing Research Centre, driven very much by A*STAR and NTU and inspired by the significant involvement of Rolls-Royce, is located in the park. This business park mutually reinforces the ecocampus concept to which NTU had committed itself.

The EcoCampus

In this regard, the university has taken many steps to reduce its carbon footprint and be a leader and an example of the efficient use of energy in a tropical setting. In the first decade of this century, air conditioning was centrally controlled and set at temperatures so low that Bertil would say that, in Sweden, it is freezing cold outside but warm inside, whereas, in Singapore, it is warm outside but freezing cold inside! Now, steps have been taken to control energy use with more realistic temperature setting with room-by-room control and movement-activated lights in common areas. The roofs of the buildings in the academic complex are now covered with solar panels that generate about 5% of the university's energy. NTU is committed to sustainability and this is one of its research peaks of excellence and a major research activity attracting very substantial research funds. Therefore, we have to lead by example and the EcoCampus (the concept is shown diagrammatically on page 139, Colour Plate 1, Figure 4) is just such an initiative. The aim is a lofty one of becoming the "greenest" campus in the world to match our tropical greenery! It is a flagship for ERIAN and incorporates both the Yunnan Garden campus and the CleanTech Park, so it is an extensive area that acts as a test bed. From a baseline of 2011, the aim has been to reduce energy use by 35% by 2020 (the Singapore national target under the Paris Agreement is 36%), an ambitious but achievable target as, at the time of writing, NTU has achieved 25% energy savings and reaching our target is certainly attainable. So, starting in 2011 and formally launched in 2014, this has been both a research and management success. This is no mean achievement given the varied and often energy-demanding activities that make up a university.

However, NTU is not just a single campus university as it has developed sites elsewhere in Singapore at one-north and with the major Medical School second campus at Novena.

Novena Campus

With the establishment of the Lee Kong Chian Medical School, a site was needed for the school adjacent to our partner hospital — the Tan Tock Seng Hospital in the district of Singapore known as Novena and, thus, this has become our second and very significant campus.

Tan Tock Seng, and now the Medical School, is located in what has become "Health City Novena" — an incredible concentration of integrated medical and healthcare operations. There are not only Tan Tock Seng Hospital and the Lee Kong Chian Medical School (housed in spectacular new buildings) but also the National Skin Centre and the National Centre for Infectious Diseases with, alongside, the private Mount Elizabeth Hospital.

The Medical School consists of three buildings. The first is the heritage building, originally a hostel for medical students (built in the old "colonial" style) that subsequently became residential quarters for nurses and is now the headquarters building of the Medical School. The auditorium is in a new Annex to that building, the Toh Kian Chui Annex. This Annex, although architecturally modern, has a glass side that reflects the nurses' home to provide a very attractive architectural entrance to the school. Next to it is a 20-storey building (the Clinical Science Building) that is equivalent to six football pitches (such comparative measurements are now the norm!). It is equipped with the latest information technology (IT)-enabled teaching and with consulting rooms and operation theatres in which the teachers can observe the students in action. Of course, the Medical School is split between Novena and the main NTU Yunnan Garden campus where it has its research laboratories. This is the Experimental Medicine Building (EMB) with advanced research laboratories and flipped classrooms including a large "learning studio". To this end, the dual-campus model with the EMB adjacent to the School of Biological Sciences has served to promote opportunities for interaction and convergence to better drive basic medical science research efforts.

one-north

First, an explanation about one-north. Why this name? It is because Singapore lies one degree north of the Equator. The name is now given to a high-technology centre halfway between Jurong and the city centre. It has become home to the two enormous A*STAR centres for its life sciences institutes — Biopolis — and its physical sciences and engineering institutes — Fusionopolis. Both house A*STAR institutes as well as other organisations' laboratories, including pharmaceutical companies and others. It has attracted other high-profile institutions such as the French business schools, ESSEC and INSEAD. It is fairly close to the main NUS Kent Ridge campus as well as to the CREATE Tower. Thus, it has become an important pole for technology and learning in Singapore. During the late 1990s, with this major development in the offing, it was realised that NTU needed to have a presence in this prime research and development (R&D) zone in Singapore.

The result is the NTU building next to Biopolis. Designed and constructed towards the end of Cham Tao Soon's presidency, NTU@one-north focuses on continuing education activities as it is convenient for part-time and evening students coming from downtown, especially being located fairly close to two mass rapid transit (MRT) lines. Part of the building has been devoted to the Alumni Club and the rest houses not only continuing education but also the Confucius Institute, the United Nations Singapore Sustainable Development Solutions Network (SDSN) and the French National Centre for Scientific Research (CNRS) in its joint operations with NTU in Singapore. For more than 10 years, it also housed the European Union Centre in Singapore.

Not Everything Goes Smoothly

Despite the massive investment to create our new vibrant campus, not everything goes smoothly. In the early days, before health and safety was instituted and enforced, the then new School of Chemical and Biomedical

Engineering (SCBE) building was constructed without water sprinklers installed in classrooms as there was a misguided belief that teaching areas did not require such anti-fire devices that were confined to research areas. This is a classic case of lack of consultation with users. Similarly, in the new School of Physical and Mathematical Sciences (SPMS) building, some laboratories needed retro-fitting because their original design and assumed use did not match!

Although opened in 2003, the one-north building is not well designed and is both inconvenient and wasteful of space, even though NTU has carried out some upgrades. One colleague, on first visiting the building in 2007, returned to the main campus to ask when was this dreadful 1970s building going to be demolished, only to be told that it had just been opened!

By the time the latest developments have come on stream, such mistakes are now, fortunately, rare. However, when the new EMB building was constructed, it was planned to have a bridge across a road to link EMB with the School of Biological Sciences (SBS) building so as to create a life sciences "mini-campus". The bridge was constructed, but ended in a solid wall! Again, this has now been solved, but only at the price of increased costs and building disruption.

Despite the provision of many food outlets, it has been difficult to sustain the presence of moderately high-end catering due to an obsession that all the shop and food outlets should provide a commercial return. While not directly subsidising these commercial operations, one needs to take into account that these outlets provide a service to our NTU town and also have to cope with rather extreme variations in footfall. At the height of the semester, there will be around 40,000 people on campus, but in the recesses, this declines to about 5,000 or so.

Another aspect of servicing this small town is the need for transport. Ever since NTU was established, the Yunnan Garden campus was served by two public bus services from the Jurong West Bus Interchange with the MRT at Boon Lay. This frequently resulted in long queues of students waiting for buses at peak times. Then, in 2010, the MRT service was extended to connect to Tuas at the extreme Western end of Singapore Island where the new industrial estate is. Therefore, we implemented a free shuttle bus service to link the campus to the new Pioneer MRT station. Eventually, the transport problem may be solved as there is a long-term plan over the next decade or so to extend the MRT entering into the campus with NTU having its own station(s). This is great, but we have to see how this will affect our unique campus environment. However, with such a transport connection, we shall really be in business and NTU will no longer need to envy places such as the University of Birmingham, UK, and The University of Hong Kong that have their own stations next to the campus!

Having embarked on its multi-billion dollar development plan, the campuses of NTU are places of which we can be very proud, and few universities can equal the size of our investment. NTU has now become not just an isolated campus in the far West of the island for engineers, but it is now a presence in two other important quarters (Novena and our building in one-north) and has increased its visibility to the Singaporean community at large by its physical presence and its intellectual contributions.

Chapter 21

A Great Global University: Taking NTU to the World

When one goes back to Guaning's inauguration address in 2003 and to the 2005 QAFU Report for the initial reference to Nanyang Technological University (NTU) endeavouring to "go global", the QAFU report recommended that NTU should establish a clear statement of its vision and mission, and assuming that an ambitious statement would emerge, it also recommended that NTU should pursue international alliances. Of course, with the coming of autonomy and the reforms introduced by the Troika, coupled with the proactive Board of Trustees, there was every incentive to open up the university to the world, while still remembering its core mission of educating Singaporeans to the highest level as well as conducting top-quality research.

Soon after the granting of autonomy and the creation of the Board of Trustees, its vision and mission statement established the ambition to become "a great global university". So, from 2005, NTU had to think on a wider and global horizon.

Once NTU embarked on its present course, it was natural that its faculty recruitment would need to be international. With the further development of NTU as a research-intensive university, this process accelerated and from 2007 onward it has been a major part of NTU's talent search. The conditions for the Research Centres of Excellence (RCEs) demanded that projects should be led by world-leading researchers drawn from the best institutions, which is why NTU ended up with people such as Kerry

Sieh, Paul Tapponnier, Staffan Kjelleberg and Stephan Schuster, and they, in turn, brought in other international experts. At the more junior level, the NRF Fellows and the Nanyang Assistant Professorship (NAP) have been recruited from across the globe.

Naturally, the great bulk of the undergraduates are from Singapore, but students from other countries also come to NTU either paying for themselves or with Singapore government support (in return for a bond to work in Singapore after graduation). For postgraduates, it is different and elsewhere we discuss the problem of getting Singaporeans to undertake PhD studies. Thus, there is a need to recruit the best students from wherever they originate. Traditionally, NTU has been able to attract good students from Singapore's Association of Southeast Asian Nations (ASEAN) neighbours as well, and at times too well, from the giants of China and India. Led by the Chairman of A*STAR, there has been a concerted attempt to recruit students from what are termed "non-traditional countries" with a generous scholarship — the Singapore International Graduate Award (SINGA). Thus, we have been able to attract students from Eastern Europe, the Central Asian "Stans", the Middle East and elsewhere.

This was given a boost with NTU and National Institute of Education (NIE) hosting the International Physics Olympiad in 2006 at which several Nobel Laureates attended, notably C. N. Yang. The CN Yang Scholar's Award was personally authorised by him and he officiated at the scheme's launch.

Taken together, NTU boasts over 70 nationalities represented among our faculty, research staff and students. It is no mean achievement and NTU is justly proud of its "United Nations" and ambiance as all contribute both intellectually and culturally to this vibrant community.

NTU has established both student exchange schemes and research collaborations, including the joint supervision of students, with many academic institutions around the world especially in Europe, North America and Australia.

In the chapter on education, we refer to the schemes for student exchange and global immersion as part of the holistic education which NTU students receive. Experiencing overseas culture along with education on such exchanges is part and parcel of the rounded education that

NTU gives its students. It is well on track to achieve the target that 80% of all students should be enrolled in the global immersion programme by 2020. Interestingly, Sweden is a very popular country for Singaporean student exchange and this has nothing to do with Bertil as this trend preceded his arrival at NTU! We have already referred to the Renaissance Engineering Programme that incorporates one year of study at one of our partner institutions.

In terms of research collaborations, these are again developed through the coming together of mutual interests of faculty in both places, although there is also a top-down strategic approach at work as well. No matter how much leaderships of institutions desire collaboration, it will only work when faculty perceive that it is in their own interests to use such arrangements to further their own research. Ideally, the model that NTU has adopted with great success is that when strategic interests of the institutions are aligned, then the next step is to promote one or more workshops which delve into the details of each other's programmes and stimulate faculty to come together. The next step is to arrange for informal joint supervisory activities of PhD students with students working in the laboratories of the partners. This really embeds collaboration and enables both parties to then mutually explore funding opportunities which can support the widening and deepening of the collaboration. Ultimately, this may also require the establishment of more formal arrangements, especially in PhD supervision with joint and double PhD agreements being signed.

Which institutions should we partner with?

From statistics available on collaboration, it is clear that "like" prefers to work with "like". So, the major extramural activities of Stanford University tend to be with MIT and Harvard and then Cambridge University in the UK. As NTU is now up with the elite universities of the world, it is natural that collaboration with institutions such as MIT and University of California, Berkeley in the US, Cambridge University and Imperial College London in the UK, ETH Zürich in Switzerland, Karolinska Institutet (KI) in Stockholm, Technion (Israel Institute of Technology) and the Hebrew University of Jerusalem in Israel, Technical University of Munich in Germany and Tsinghua University in Beijing will be very important. At the same time, NTU needs to collaborate the disciplinary leaders wherever they are. For instance, the University of

Strathclyde, Glasgow, is ranked in the upper 200s and yet hosts major activities in pharmaceutical engineering and industrial manufacturing, and in the recent UK Research Excellence Framework, it even outperformed and outranked Cambridge University in physics due to its expertise in quantum physics. Similarly, Technion (Israel Institute of Technology) and the Ben-Gurion University of the Negev in Israel are ranked well below NTU and yet have areas of expertise with which it is important for NTU to collaborate. These are a few examples, but NTU boasts very many research collaborations, and PhD supervision, with most of the leading institutions in the world. It truly is a global player and a "wanted" and desirable partner.

In looking at the NTU portfolio of working links and collaboration, based as always on mutual academic esteem, it really is a listing of the top universities from the four continents of Asia, Australia, Europe and North America and with institutions in the countries that lead the league table in research and education.

Another recommendation from the 2005 QAFU was that NTU should seek to establish a grouping of the leading technology- and engineering-based institutions around the world. Guaning took up this challenge and embarked on a series of journeys to meet with the Presidents of these universities in Europe, the US, China and India. He met with his counterparts in these institutions including David Baltimore, President of California Institute of Technology (Caltech); G. Wayne Clough and Jean-Lou Chameau, President and Provost, respectively, at Georgia Institute of Technology; Ralph Eichler at ETH Zürich; Sir Richard Sykes and Sir Roy Anderson at Imperial College London; Ashok Misra and Devang Vipin Khakhar, successive Directors of the Indian Institute of Technology, Bombay (IITB); and Zhang Jie at Shanghai Jiao Tong University (SJTU).

Having persuaded them of the value of creating an alliance, this eventually became the Global Alliance of Technological Universities (GlobalTech). Its starting membership was NTU, Imperial College London, ETH, Caltech, Georgia Tech, IITB and SJTU. It held its first meeting (launch meeting) in April 2009 at NTU with Guaning as its first Chairman as well as being the host. The Alliance aims to address global societal issues for which science and technology could be the solution. These issues include biomedicine and healthcare; sustainability and global environmental change; security of energy, water and food supplies; security; and changing demographics/population. Ad hoc meetings are arranged on topics of mutual interest to the members of the Alliance. In addition, it is able to address and speak about issues of global concern from the position of representing some of the world's leading engineering and technological institutions. When Guaning stepped down from the NTU presidency and Bertil succeeded him, Bertil was elected as the second Chairman of the Alliance. During this period, NTU provided the Alliance's secretariat under the energetic direction of Professor Er Meng Hwa.

The membership has changed somewhat over the past decade with Caltech and ETH withdrawing, but with the Technical University of Munich (TUM), the University of New South Wales (UNSW) and Carnegie Mellon University (CMU) joining. These eight members form a strong network of common interests and, to quote from the website, "Leading universities from all over the world clearly have a role to play in forging a global approach, especially in research and education, to address global challenges such as climate change, population growth, ageing population, pandemics, and food and water security."

In 2016, Bertil stepped down from the GlobalTech Alliance and the chairmanship was passed to Professor Wolfgang Herrmann, the then President of TUM, whose institution also took responsibility for the secretariat. Thus, starting with NTU's initiative, there is now an established and ongoing network which can speak with a powerful voice about world problems and key higher educational issues.

Thus, a lot of effort was made to take NTU to the world, but there were also initiatives to take the world to NTU. One such initiative to put NTU on the global stage has been through what we have termed "Global Dialogues". This was a way of branding what NTU had been doing for some time. In 2005, under Guaning's presidency, NTU created its own Institute of Advanced Studies (IAS) led by Professor K K Phua, the founder of the World Scientific, a worldwide scientific publishing company with its headquarters in Singapore. World Scientific is the publishing company for the Nobel Foundation as it publishes all the memoirs of Nobel Prize winners. Supported by NTU with substantial additional support from the Lee Foundation, the IAS has been able to organise and support very high-level international scientific meetings, bringing very many Nobel laureates to Singapore and to NTU. Bertil's own high-level connections in the Nobel Foundation have also been a great asset in this endeavour. So, NTU is very visible on this particular world platform. The IAS is advised and guided by a committee of world-renowned scientists, including 11 Nobel laureates and a Fields Medallist. Mr. George Yeo, Former Minister for foreign Affairs in Singapore, is currently the Patron of the IAS. The Institute, probably the best known of such institutes in the Asia-Pacific region, has helped to forge interdisciplinary research and close collaboration between NTU and major centres of research around the world, and it has inspired numerous talented youth through its many programmes and allowed them to interact closely with eminent visitors and speakers around the world. The multidisciplinary topics include physics, chemistry, engineering, biomedical imaging, materials science, maths, liberal arts and urban planning.

Related to the IAS is the International Union of Pure and Applied Physics (IUPAP) which now has its headquarters in NTU. IUPAP is the physics union within the Paris-based International Council for Science (ICSU).

Another activity, inspired by Bertil and strongly supported by Guaning, was to create the Para Limes series of meetings to which reference has already been made in the description of the Complexity Institute in Chapter 17. Originally started by Jan Vasbinder in the Netherlands, Para Limes is an operation to bring very high-level speakers together in international meetings on cross-disciplinary subjects (hence Para Limes — without boundaries). Para Limes organised a series of such meetings on complexity topics starting in 2009. Another topic dealt with has been disruptive balances — the major planetary risks which society is facing today. Again, this activity within Global Dialogue has done much to raise NTU's worldwide reputation and visibility.

Yet another initiative to both raise the profile of NTU and to bring the world to NTU was the first of the Times Higher Education (THE) World Academic Summits. This first meeting was held at NTU in 2013 led by Bertil and the THE Chief Knowledge Officer Phil Baty. It brought together the Presidents of universities from around the world. Its list of speakers was most impressive including not only Bertil as well as Lim Chuan Poh (then Chairman of A*STAR) from Singapore but also Professor Jean-Lou Chameau, by this time at Caltech, US; Sir Keith O'Nions, Imperial College London; Professor Ed Byrne, then President, Monash University, Australia, and later President, King's College London; Professor Ihron Rensburg, President, Johannesburg University, Republic of South Africa; with the final keynote being delivered by the multiple Oscar winner, Lord David Puttnam, Chancellor of the Open University, UK.

Clearly, with all its exchanges, research collaborations and alliances, coupled with its extremely diverse community of students, scholars and researchers, NTU has come a long way from what NTU was in the 1990s as described by Haresh in his tale. That was when the concept of international collaboration seemed far distant from the core of NTU and there was a lack of appreciation of the benefits that such collaborations could bring.

NTU can now truly be counted among the leading academic institutions of the world and can truly be said to be fulfilling its mission and vision of being a great global university.

Stage IV

Peaks Ahead

Chapter 22

Unfinished Business — Future Challenges in an Uncertain World

As we have already related, Singapore has a first-class education system and produces excellent and very bright students. There is strong governmental and political support for the education system overall, including the higher education sector. Singapore, through its commitment to the knowledge-based economy and society, is one of the most advanced in the world. It is a wealthy country with top-notch universities. So, what and where are the problems?

A sensitive policy issue for Singapore will be its global positioning vis-à-vis China and the US. The country has always prided itself as being the crossroads for the East and West. It has developed strong links with China in terms of research (NTU's involvement in the Guangzhou science initiative is one such example), while at the same time having very significant and long-term research collaboration with Europe and North America. The increasing tension and great power rivalry between China and the US provides a significant challenge for Singapore to maintain such a balance. This will be a continuing challenge for Singapore as tensions rise in the South China Sea.

At the same time, Singapore has seen itself to be a "small, smart country", akin to those of Scandinavia. Now, it is considering forming a more formal consortium with such countries and Israel to encourage collaboration as well as learn from each other.

Singapore is both a young country and young in terms of research and has a thriving higher education sector. It does lack long-standing academic traditions and tends towards pragmatism above more philosophical considerations. This thinking permeates the population at large and so, few Singaporeans go into academia as a career. This reflects a mindset in the population of "super-pragmatism" in which students complete a double-degree programme as fast as possible and then enter employment.

At most, around one quarter of the post-graduate research students are from Singapore and, thus, there is an insufficient Singaporean input to sustain a predominantly Singaporean academic base. Of the Singaporeans who have entered academic life, many will be working abroad and may not necessarily wish to return to Singapore to continue their academic career. This means that the country will be dependent on the import of expatriate experts from both East and West for a long time into the future. The government is aware of the problem and the Ministry of Education is endeavouring to close the gap, but this will take time.

Bertil recounts that as the Chair of an A*STAR panel interviewing candidates in a talent search, the panel identified an outstanding student who, when questioned as to her ambition after her research degree, answered that she wanted to work in the Singaporean civil service. It never seemed to cross her mind that she should look for opportunities elsewhere, including academia, and become a professor. This probably reflects the Chinese good luck wish, which is "to wish you a good job in the civil service"! Perhaps research is too "young'" in the country, having, as we report elsewhere, only "taken off" in Singapore since 1991. So, research as a professional occupation, especially in a university, may not be seen as a "legitimate" job. There is also the tendency to equate an academic job just with teaching rather than to fully embrace the Humboldtian philosophy which includes research.

There is also some public scepticism about the success achieved by Singaporean universities especially NUS and now NTU, which may be described as an "academic inferiority complex". And yet, the rest of the world is impressed with what Singapore and its universities have achieved. In fact, today, some 10 years on from when the NRF announced the CREATE scheme to import overseas universities to Singapore to conduct research, one may wonder whether such a scheme could be justified today given the leading status of NUS and especially NTU. Maybe one of the problems is that a significant proportion of the Singaporean "establishment" has been educated abroad. Still, about one fifth of top students elect to go overseas, to the US and the UK in particular, for their university education and have parents who can afford to support them. It is a case of what is said in the Bible (Luke 4:24) that "no prophet is accepted in his own country".

To attract young people into research and the possibility of an academic career means that there have to be incentives such as more lucrative rewards including good salaries and job security through tenure and promotion schemes plus help with the Central Provident Fund (CPF, the Singaporean social security system), which is an important consideration for Singaporeans as it links to housing, healthcare as well as pensions.

Another challenge is the lack of a seminar culture within the university, and that is despite top-level recruitment from institutions where such a culture is deeply embedded. Even with highly rated scientists or even Nobel Prize laureates as speakers, it is difficult to get attendance from faculty and students (including the top students) at seminars outside one's immediate research area and there is a lack of appreciation of the benefits of broadening one's knowledge and experience. It is difficult to encourage interdisciplinarity of which a seminar culture is part. For junior research staff and post-graduate students, it is often seen by the supervisor as being a waste of time. Broadening one's horizons is not seen as a priority. Have the imported supervisors gone "native" in this respect? In other words, supervisors/mentors frequently look on their PhD students not as the young intellectuals of tomorrow, but as today's "measuring slaves"! This also creates and reinforces the silo mentality which the Troika has striven hard to remove in NTU, but has, so far, failed.

Turning to innovation, this is another challenge that Singapore and NTU must face as identified in Haresh's tale where he relates the difficulties that he had in the 1990s in getting faculty and students to understand the need for innovation and entrepreneurialism. The professor with the most *Nature* papers or students with the top grades may not always be the best innovators or entrepreneurs. Every country sees the linear relationship of basic research leading to strategic and applied research leading to innovation, patents, start-ups and hence companies and jobs. As is generally known, this is a simplistic view as the system has many feedback loops and does not have a clear flow. However, in Singapore, there is certainly a strong commitment to this linear system and a generally rather utilitarian view of research. Generally, research projects having a large critical mass only have a 15 or so years' history. It has never had a tradition of "blue skies" research and no natural champions for it. Politicians need to have a demonstrable economic output from research so that it has become easier to embrace engineering and computer sciences rather than the other natural sciences. Again, if one considers the development of new drugs, which normally has a 10- to 15-year lead time with clinical trials, this has to be set against the just over 50 years' history of independent Singapore so that such developments seem exceedingly long put into the context of the country's history.

While the "system" recognises the importance of innovation and development, the lack of an entrepreneurial tradition means that Singaporeans tend not to go into innovation. In turn, this means that there are not so many indigenous companies able to take up innovative ideas from research, and the lack of this industrial uptake capacity means that it is left mainly to the technologically-based multinational companies to fill this gap. There are major exceptions to this scene, but it generally holds true. NTU has tried to address this through courses, including providing a Master's degree in "technopreneurship", and a technology transfer and incubator arrangement (NTUitive), but the challenge remains.

This has become a possible long-term threat to the research funding system and there is always the possibility that there could be significant cutbacks in research funding in the future. After the extremely rapid expansion of funding and research in Singapore, from which NTU has greatly benefitted, it is likely that, in the medium term, Singapore will start to resemble what might be termed "normal European-style research support" although still with increases in its research budget. Adjusting to such a new level of research support is a challenge for the future.

As far as NTU is concerned, its extremely rapid development and leap into the top tier of universities worldwide now require consolidation and a move into a "steady state". Its commitment to the new learning pedagogies will need to be renewed and updated as technological and social changes occur. NTU will continue to need to have seed funding at its disposal to recruit the brightest and best young faculty from around the world through the Nanyang Assistant Professorship scheme. Also, it will need to continue to invest in the process of competing strongly for the top-level, prestigious funding schemes available in Singapore such as CREATE and the new Research Centres of Excellence (RCEs), as well as attracting senior professors from around the world to lead new initiatives. The level of PhD recruitment, despite the concerns about whether one can recruit sufficient Singaporean entry to a research career, needs to be maintained in order to bring in new ideas and brainpower. This is key to a sustainable research future (one notable example of the wisdom of this approach is the continuing success of CERN (the European Organisation for Nuclear Research) which, over decades, has been due to the constant "churn" of young research students joining its experimental teams). Continuation of NTU's partnership with major technologically-based multinational companies has been a particular success story for NTU and one in which the university has created a significant international reputation.

Finally, universities are changing fast in both education and research with increased transparency, the commitment to "open" research and a global unease about academic career development and the factors used to determine tenure and promotion. One university, Utrecht University, has publicly abandoned using impact factors in appointment and promotion decisions. This is likely to be an increasing trend which creates its own set of challenges.

All of this will require an academic entrepreneurial spirit that has characterised the rise of NTU into the ranks of the most highly rated research-intensive universities working fully within the Humboldtian concept of bringing education and research together.

Together, these represent major challenges for the future, but we, as the Troika, have every confidence that the base that we have laid in both education and research will, with enlightened stewardship by our worthy successors, sustain NTU well into the future.

To conclude, we hope that this book will be an inspiration for people working with universities and academia from different angles. Everything done in Singapore or NTU cannot be easily implemented elsewhere, but, hopefully, there are some raisins in the cake baked at NTU that can be applied to other universities with an ambitious agenda to climb the ladder of academic excellence and prestige.

Appendices

Appendix 1: Singapore/Nanyang Technological University (NTU) Timeline of Events

Year	Event
1819	Stamford Raffles acquires Singapore for Britain from the Sultan of Johor
1905	Straits Settlements & Federated Malay States Government Medical School founded, later renamed the King Edward VII College of Medicine in 1912
1929	Raffles College founded
1949	King Edward VII College merges with Raffles College as University of Malaya in Singapore
1950	Teachers' Training College founded
1955	***Nanyang University (NU, Nantah) founded by the Chinese community***
1959	Singapore attains self-government, the People's Action Party led by Lee Kuan Yew wins landslide
1962	University of Malaya in Singapore becomes the University of Singapore (SU)
1963	Federation of Malaysia (including Singapore) formed
1965	Singapore leaves Malaysia to become an independent country with Lee Kuan Yew as Prime Minister
1980	Minister for Education: Dr. Tony Tan Keng Yam (June 1980 to May 1981 and 1985 to 1991)

1980	***Nanyang University (NU) and University of Singapore (SU) merged to form the National University of Singapore (NUS)***
1980	Polytechnics for skilled workers and technicians initiated
1981	***Nanyang Technological Institute (NTI) founded to train practice-orientated engineers***
1981	***President of NTI: Cham Tao Soon (until 1991)*** ***Chairman, NTI Council: Michael Fam***
1981	Minister for Education: Dr. Goh Keng Swee
1988	**NUS School of Accountancy transferred to NTI, eventually becoming the Nanyang Business School (NBS) at NTU**
1990	Goh Chok Tong becomes Prime Minister, succeeding Lee Kuan Yew
1991	***NTI and Institute of Education merge to form NTU***
1991	National Science and Technology Board (NSTB) formed (until 2000)
1991	First National Technology Plan (now the Research, Innovation and Enterprise Plan)
1991–2002	***First President of NTU: Cham Tao Soon (until 2003)*** ***Chairman, NTU Council: Michael Fam***
1992	Minister for Education: Lee Hock Suan
1993	***Chairman, NTU Council: Koh Boon Hwee***
1995	***NBS inaugurated from the renamed School of Accountancy***
1996	***Institute of Defence and Strategic Studies (later renamed the S. Rajaratnam School of International Studies (RSIS)) established headed, by S. R Nathan***
1996	***Su Guaning appointed Council Member, NTU (until 2002) — First Troika member linked to NTU***
1997	Minister for Education: Teo Chee Hean
1999	S. R. Nathan becomes President of Singapore (until 2011)
2001	NSTB and institutes become the Agency for Science, Technology and Research (A*STAR)
	Bertil visits President Cham Tao Soon at NTU
2002	Su Guaning meets Haresh Shah at Stanford University
2003	***Second President of NTU: Su Guaning (until 2011)***

2003	Minister for Education: Tharman Shanmugaratnam
2004	Lee Hsien Loong becomes Prime Minister
2005	***Haresh Shah appointed Senior Academic Adviser to the President — Second Troika member to arrive***
2006	***Autonomy granted to Singapore universities with Nanyang Technological University (Corporatisation) Act*** ***Chairman, NTU Board of Trustees: Koh Boon Hwee***
2006	***Haresh Shah appointed NTU Trustee, Chairman Academic Affairs Committee***
2006	National Research Foundation (NRF) established in the Prime Minister's Office under Dr. Tony Tan **Bertil becomes a member of the NRF Science Advisory Board**
2007	***First Troika meeting Aptos, California***
2007	***Bertil Andersson appointed NTU Provost — third member of the Troika arrives***
2008	Minister for Education: Ng Eng Hen
2011	Dr. Tony Tan becomes President of Singapore (until 2017)
2011	Minister for Education: Heng Swee Keat
2011	***Final Troika meeting 2010 Lee Kong Chian School of Medicine initiated in partnership with Imperial College***
2011	***Third President of NTU: Bertil Andersson (until 2017)***
2015	Minister for Education (Higher Education and Skills) and then Minister for Education (from 2018): Ong Ye Kung
2018	***Subra Suresh appointed Fourth President of NTU***

Appendix 2: Nanyang Technological University (NTU) Facts and Figures

Key Research Centres and Institutes

- Delta-NTU Corporate Lab
- Earth Observatory of Singapore
- Singapore Centre for Environmental Life Sciences Engineering
- Nanyang Environment & Water Research Institute
- Institute for Media Innovation
- Energy Research Institute @ NTU
- Nanyang Institute of Technology in Health & Medicine
- Centre for Research and Development in Learning
- The Photonics Institute
- Institute of Catastrophe Risk Management
- Institute on Asian Consumer Insight
- Maritime Institute @ NTU
- Nanyang Institute of Structural Biology
- Nanomedicine Institute @ NTU
- NTU-BMW Future Mobility Research Lab
- Singapore Centre for 3D Printing
- Singtel Cognitive and Artificial Intelligence Lab for Enterprises @ NTU
- SMRT-NTU Smart Urban Rail Corporate Lab
- Rolls-Royce@NTU Corporate Lab
- ST Engineering-NTU Corporate Lab
- Active LIving for the ElderLY (LILY)
- Advanced Remanufacturing & Technology Centre (ARTC)
- Skin Research Institute of Singapore

Some of NTU's International Academic Partners

Europe

- CEA: French Alternative Energies and Atomic Energy Commission
- CNRS — Centre National de la Recherche Scientifique
- ETH — Eidgenössische Technische Hochschule Zürich

- Fraunhofer-Gesellschaft
- Imperial College London
- Karolinska Institute
- King's College London
- Medical University Vienna
- Technical University of Denmark
- Technische Universität München
- TNO (The Netherlands Organisation for applied scientific research)
- Université Grenoble Alpes
- University College London
- University of Bristol
- University of Cambridge
- University of Edinburgh
- Sorbonne University
- University of Southampton

North America

- California Institute of Technology
- Carnegie Mellon University
- Cornell University
- Georgia Institute of Technology
- Massachusetts Institute of Technology
- Northwestern University
- University of British Columbia
- University of California, Berkeley
- University of North Carolina at Chapel Hill

Asia and Beyond

- Australian National University
- Chinese Academy of Sciences
- Fudan University
- Hebrew University of Jerusalem
- Hong Kong University of Science and Technology
- Indian Institute of Technology Bombay

- Korea Advanced Institute of Science and Technology
- Kyoto University
- National Taiwan University
- Peking University
- Seoul National University
- Shanghai Jiao Tong University
- Technion-Israel Institute of Technology
- The University of Hong Kong
- Tokyo Institute of Technology
- Tsinghua University
- University of New South Wales
- University of Tokyo
- Zhejiang University

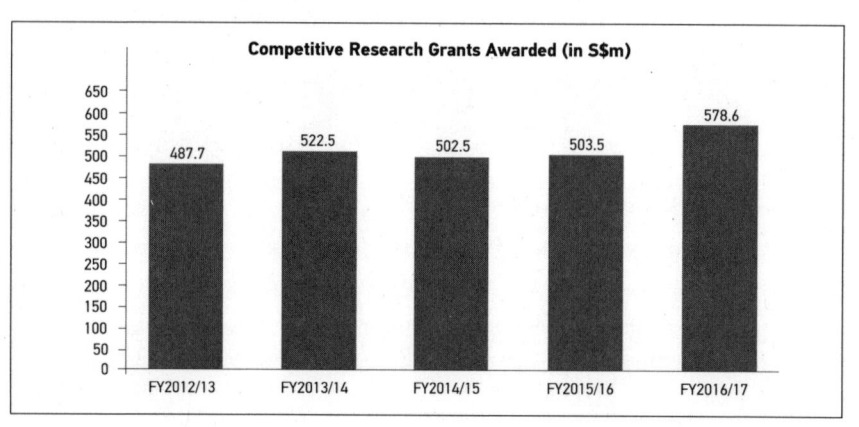

Competitive Research Grants Awarded (in S$m)

FY2012/13	FY2013/14	FY2014/15	FY2015/16	FY2016/17
487.7	522.5	502.5	503.5	578.6

Above figures include RSB and Tier 1

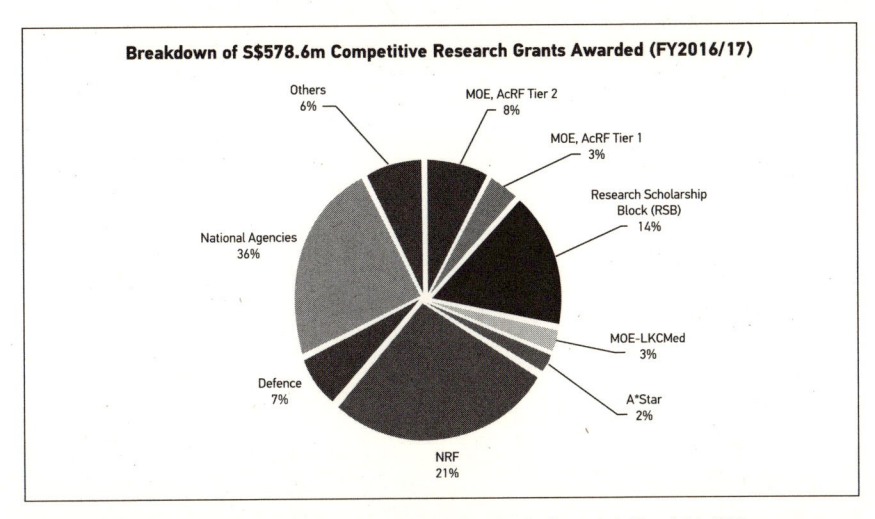

Breakdown of S$578.6m Competitive Research Grants Awarded (FY2016/17)

- Others: 6%
- MOE, AcRF Tier 2: 8%
- MOE, AcRF Tier 1: 3%
- Research Scholarship Block (RSB): 14%
- MOE-LKCMed: 3%
- A*Star: 2%
- NRF: 21%
- Defence: 7%
- National Agencies: 36%

MOE AcRF: The Ministry of Education's (MOE) Academic Research Fund (AcRF) encompasses three tiers of research grants, with Tier 1 grants being the smallest.

NRF: NRF grants, awarded by the Singapore government, include Competitive Research Programme (CRP), NRF Fellowship and Proof-of-Concept grants.

Major Industrial Research Partners

- AIA*
- AXA*
- Alstom
- Bae Systems
- BMW*
- Carl Zeiss*
- CNRS*
- Crystalsol GmbH
- Delta Electronics*
- Det Norske Veritas
- DRTech (Defence Research and Technology Office)*
- Dyesol Limited
- ELID Technology International
- ENGIE
- European Aeronautic Defence and Space Company*
- Finmeccanica

- Fraunhofer-Gesellschaft*
- German Aerospace Centre (DLR)*
- Huawei Technologies Co Ltd
- Hyundai Engineering & Construction*
- IBM
- Infineon*
- Inspur
- Kemira Oyj
- Lockheed Martin*
- Johnson Matthey*
- LightLab Sweden AB
- Lushang*
- MediaTek Inc
- MicroVision*
- Nitto Denko Corporation
- NXP Semiconductors NV
- PTT Global Chemical (PTTGC)
- Robert Bosch*
- Rolls-Royce*
- Royal Philips
- Saab*
- Sembcorp Industries
- SGL Carbon
- Siemens Pte Ltd*
- Singapore Power
- SLM Solutions*
- Sportmaster*
- ST Engineering*
- ST Kinetics*
- ST Microelectronics*
- SOLID ASIA*
- SONY
- Tencent*
- Thales*
- The International Table Tennis Federation (ITTF)*
- Toray Industries Inc
- Toshiba*

- Vestas*
- Volvo
- World Entrepreneurship Forum
- Xenon Technologies (XT)

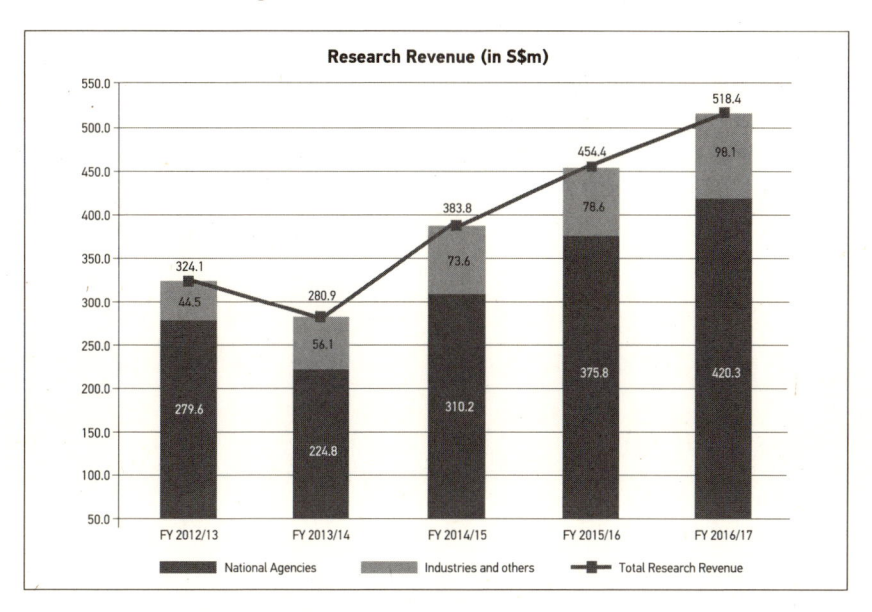

Research Revenue (in S$m)

FY	National Agencies	Industries and others	Total Research Revenue
FY 2012/13	279.6	44.5	324.1
FY 2013/14	224.8	56.1	280.9
FY 2014/15	310.2	73.6	383.8
FY 2015/16	375.8	78.6	454.4
FY 2016/17	420.3	98.1	518.4

Enrolment by College (AY2017–18)

College	Undergraduates[2]	Graduate students[2] Coursework	Graduate students[2] Research	Graduate Diploma[2]
Engineering	10,331	1,253	1,641	—
Science	3,844	47	634	—
Nanyang Business School	3,855	575	71	—
Humanities, Arts & Social Sciences	4,772	668	306	—
NIE	504	1,478	218	438
Medicine	447	—	35	—
Others[1]	—	317	393	—
Total	23,753	4,338	3,298	438

[1]Others include the Interdisciplinary Graduate School, Nanyang Technopreneurship Centre and S Rajaratnam School of International Studies.

[2]There are 819 part-time undergraduate students; a total of 594 graduate research and 2,264 coursework students take part-time programmes. Figures are correct as at 11 Sep 2017.

Graduates from 2013 to 2017

Year	Bachelor's	Master's	Doctorate	Total
2013	6,562	2,410	549	9,521
2014	6,079	2,461	572	9,112
2015	5,799	2,244	575	8,618
2016	5,981	2,484	621	9,086
2017	6,247	2,708	677	9,632

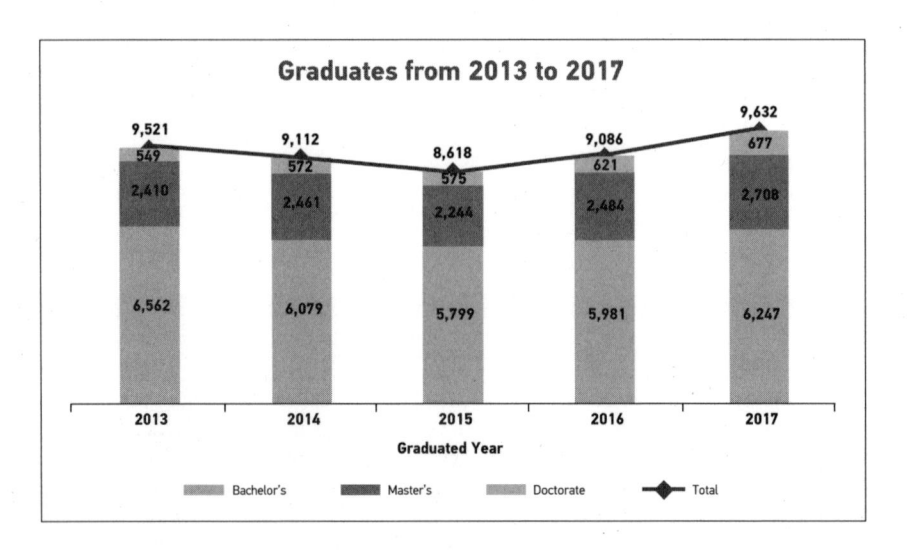

Faculty and Staff

NTU has a total faculty and staff population of 8,311* (as at 1 Jul 2017).

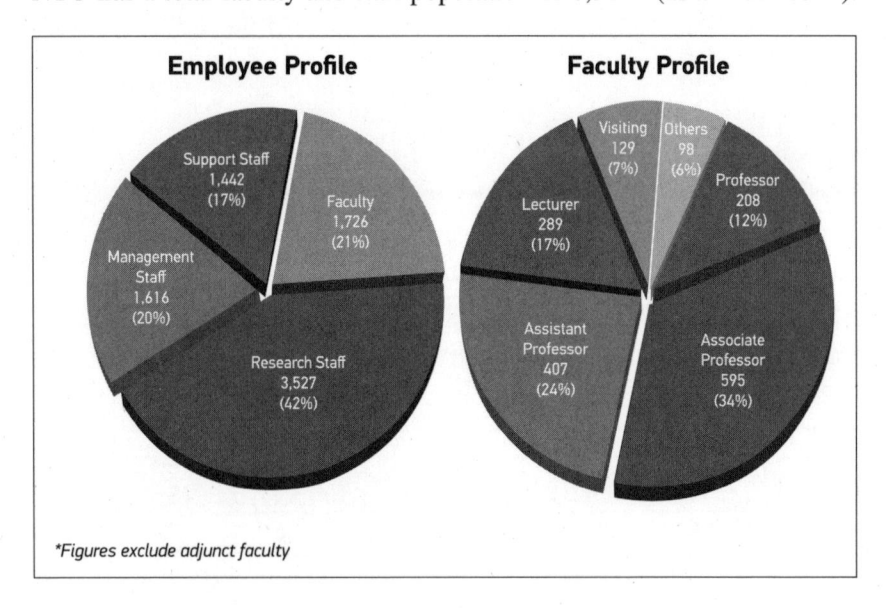

Employee Profile
- Faculty: 1,726 (21%)
- Research Staff: 3,527 (42%)
- Management Staff: 1,616 (20%)
- Support Staff: 1,442 (17%)

Faculty Profile
- Professor: 208 (12%)
- Associate Professor: 595 (34%)
- Assistant Professor: 407 (24%)
- Lecturer: 289 (17%)
- Visiting: 129 (7%)
- Others: 98 (6%)

*Figures exclude adjunct faculty

Alumni

- 222,504 university alumni representing 154 nationalities
- 47 overseas alumni associations: **Cambodia, China** (Anhui, Beijing, Chongqing, Fujian, Gansu, Guangdong, Guangxi, Guizhou, Hainan, Hebei, Heilongjiang, Henan, Hong Kong SAR, Hubei, Hunan, Inner Mongolia, Jiangsu, Jiangxi, Jilin, Liaoning, Ningxia-Qinghai-Xizang, Shanxi, Shaanxi, Shandong, Shanghai, Sichuan, Tianjin, Xinjiang, Yunnan and Zhejiang), **Europe, Gulf Cooperation Council, India** (Northern, Central and Southern), **Indonesia, Malaysia, Myanmar, Philippines, Taiwan, Thailand, United Kingdom, United States of America** (USA-East and USA-West) and Vietnam (Hanoi and Ho Chi Minh City).

Lyon, Our Mascot

"Lyon the lion" symbolises the University's values of strength, courage and fearlessness. As the embodiment of the NTU spirit, it not only brings the University community together, but also inspires student teams to give their best performance at inter-varsity and other competitions. Designed by an NTU student, it made its debut in August 2013.

The NTU Flower

Dendrobium Nanyang is a pristine white orchid with a burst of purple at the heart of the bloom, signifying pure energy and a caring heart. The hybrid was created by students and teachers of Temasek Primary School as part of an orchid hybridisation programme developed at NTU's National Institute of Education. The exquisite white petals represent the qualities that embody the university spirit – passion, tenacity, fortitude, leadership, innovation and entrepreneurship.

Appendix 3: NTU Rankings 2017

- In the **7th QS World University Rankings (WUR) Top 50 Under 50** ranking published in July 2017, NTU continued to be **ranked first** position for the fourth consecutive year among the world's young (under 50 years) universities.
- In the **14th QS World University Rankings (WUR)** published in June 2017, NTU moved up two places to be **ranked 11th** position in the world and first position in Asia. NTU made improvements across four of the six metrics that QS uses to rank universities and made the biggest gains in employer reputation and citations per faculty. For normalised citations per faculty, NTU ranked first position in Singapore.
- In the **9th QS Asian University Rankings (AUR)** released in October 2017, NTU had risen from 18th position to **first position in Asia** with its citations per paper (CPP) indicator rank rising from 84th position to first position since 2010.
- In the **Times Higher Education (THE) "The World's Fastest Rising Young Universities"** published in March 2015, NTU was **ranked first** with its meteoric rise of 108 places in the rankings in just four years. THE had shortlisted 15 universities which are less than 50 years old from its top 200 World University Rankings and measured their rise since 2011. NTU's growing international reputation and its continued solid performance in terms of citations, teaching environment and research were the several key factors that led it to the top spot.
- In the **6th THE Top 200 Under 50** rankings released in April 2017, NTU ranked **third position** in the world and **second position** in Asia order rank.
- In the **THE, WUR 2017/2018** published in September 2017, NTU had moved up two places to **52nd** position in the world and ranked **seventh position in Asia**. NTU had moved up by 122 places, making it the fastest-rising young university in the world since 2010.
- In the **5th THE Asian University Rankings (AUR)** released in March 2017, NTU **ranked fourth** position in Asia. The fourth position was higher than the seventh position in the THE WUR 2016 Asia

order rank, which was released in September 2016. NTU research citations per paper indicator rank continued to be the leader in Singapore since 2014.

- In the **4th US News Best Global Universities Ranking 2018** results released in October 2017, NTU's overall rank jumped up by 19 places to **55th** position in the world and **second position in Asia**. For the subject rankings, NTU had **four subjects ranked in the top 10 in the world**. The four subjects were **materials science (first position in the world), chemistry (second position in the world, first position in Asia and Singapore), computer science (third position in the world, second position in Asia and first in Singapore), and engineering (fourth position in the world and third position in Asia)**.
- In the **15th Academic Ranking of World Universities (ARWU)** released in August 2017, NTU's overall ranking moved up 12 places to **rank 111th** position. In the **2017 Shanghai Ranking's Global Ranking of Academic Subjects** results, NTU had **five subjects ranked in the top 10 in the world**. NTU's **nanoscience and nanotechnology and energy science were ranked first position in the world (first in Asia), telecommunication was ranked third position in the world (third in Asia), instruments science and technology was ranked fourth position in the world (fourth in Asia), and electrical and electronic engineering was ranked sixth position in the world (first in Asia)**.
- In January 2017, NTU was ranked as the **fifth most-cited university for engineering research output that was among the top nine universities globally in engineering** by Essential Science Indicators of *Thomson Reuters*.
- In the **5th Nature Index** published by Nature Publishing Group in 2017, NTU ranked 35th position in the world, seventh position in Asia and first position in Singapore. NTU's **chemistry ranked 17th position in the world**.
- In the **7th QS World University Rankings by subject** published in March 2017, NTU **engineering and technology, natural sciences and social sciences by faculty area rankings were ranked fourth, 17th and 22nd position in the world, respectively**. For specific subjects ranking, NTU has **two subjects ranked in the global top**

10: electrical and electronic engineering (sixth in the world and first in Asia) and materials science (seventh in the world and first in Asia). See table below for the remaining NTU subjects that are ranked in the top 50:

No.	Subject	Specific Subject Rank 2017	No.	Subject	Specific Subject Rank 2017
1	Electrical and Electronic	6 (1)	11	Environmental Sciences	23 (3)
2	Materials Science	7 (1)	12	Hospitality and Leisure Management	25 (3)
3	Mechanical, Aeronautical and Manufacturing	11 (3)	13	Statistics and Operational Research	32 (6)
4	Communication and Media	14 (2)	14	Business and Management Studies	36 (5)
5	Chemistry	16 (5)	15	Art and Design	40 (7)
6	Chemical	17 (7)	16	Mathematics	43 (9)
7	Education	18 (3)	17	Linguistics	44 (10)
8	Computer Science and Information Systems	20 (6)	18	Biological Sciences	44 (5)
9	Accounting and Finance	21 (3)	19	Physics and Astronomy	47 (12)
10	Civil and Structural	22 (8)			

Note: ( ) refers to Asia order rank.

- In the **Financial Times' (FT) Global MBA Ranking** published in January 2018, the NTU **Nanyang Business School's Master of**

Business Administration (MBA) was in the 22nd position. For the Asia-Pacific alone, NTU's Nanyang MBA rank moved up three places to **third position**. The average weighted annual salary three years after graduation is US$126,000, up from US$119,000 in the previous year. In terms of offering good value for money, NTU's Nanyang MBA came in 26th from 38th position globally.

- In the **Financial Times' Global Executive MBA (EMBA) ranking** published in October 2017, NTU's **Nanyang Business School's EMBA was ranked 30th position in the world and seventh position in Asia**.
- In the **global ranking of full-time MBA programmes published by** *The Economist* **(EIU)** in October 2017, NTU's business school has maintained the rank of **top business school in Singapore for the 14th consecutive years**. NTU was ranked **78th position in the world and second position in Asia**.
- In the **2016 Global "Go To" Think Tank rankings published by the University of Pennsylvania's Think Tanks and Civil Societies Programme (TTCSP)** in January 2017, NTU research centre, **Institute of Defence and Strategic Studies (IDSS), ranked 36th position for the Best University Affiliated Think Tanks in the world and ranked eighth position in Asia order rank**.

Appendix 4

Growth of Singapore's National Investment in Research and Innovation

National Technology Plan 1991	S$2 billion
National Science & Technology Plan 1995	S$4 billion
Science & Technology Plan 2000	S$6 billion
Science & Technology Plan 2005	S$13.5 billion
Research, Innovation & Enterprise Plan 2010	S$16.4 billion
Research, Innovation & Enterprise Plan 2015	S$19 billion
Research, Innovation & Enterprise Plan 2020	S$25 billion

Bibliography

1. Wilhelm von Humboldt, *"The Limits of State Action"*, 1851.
2. Ministry of Education, Singapore, "Report of the Inaugural Meeting of the International Academic Advisory Panel", 6–9 August 1997.
3. Massachusetts Institute of Technology, "Strategic Review of the National University of Singapore and the Nanyang Technological University", 16 June 1998.
4. Ministry of Education, Singapore, "Report of the Second Meeting of the International Academic Advisory Panel", 10–13 January 1999.
5. Lee Kuan Yew, *"From Third World to First: The Singapore Story: 1965–2000"*, Straits Times Press, 2000.
6. Committee to Review the Governance and Funding Structures of NUS and NTU, "Fostering Autonomy and Accountability in Universities", 20 June 2000.
7. Ministry of Education, Singapore, "Report of the Third Meeting of the International Academic Advisory Panel", 8–11 January 2001.
8. Ministry of Education, Singapore, "Report of the Fourth Meeting of the International Academic Advisory Panel", 13–16 January 2003.
9. Ministry of Education, Singapore, "Report of the Committee to Review the University Sector and Graduate Manpower Planning", 20 May 2003.
10. Ministry of Education, Singapore, "Report to DPM Dr. Tony Tan and Minister Tharman Shanmugaratnam's Trip to the US", 11–16 April 2004.
11. The International Panel to Study the Establishment of a Research-Intensive Science and Technology Institution in Singapore "Building a Foundation for Research Excellence", 1 December 2004.

12. Ministry of Education, Singapore, "Report of the Fifth Meeting of the International Academic Advisory Panel", "Autonomous Universities — Towards Peaks of Excellence", 11–14 January 2005.
13. Steering Committee to Review University Autonomy, Governance and Funding, "Autonomous Universities, Towards Peaks of Excellence", 4 April 2005.
14. Miller, C. *et al.*, A Report of the Commission Appointed by Secretary of Education Margaret Spellings, "A Test of Leadership — Charting the Future of US High Education" 2006.
15. Mary Turnbull, "*A History of Modern Singapore 1819–2005*", NUS Press Singapore, 2009.
16. "Singapore Statement on Research Integrity", https://wcrif.org/guidance/singapore-statement.
17. Cham Tao Soon, "*The Making of NTU — My Story*", Straits Times Press.
18. Michael M. Crow and William B. Dabars, "Designing the New American University", Johns Hopkins University Press.
19. Su Guaning, "International Collaboration as a Catalyst for Change: The Case of Nanyang Technological University, Singapore 2003–2017" in "Successful Global Collaborations in Higher Education Institutions", edited by Abdulrahman Al-Youb, Adnan H. M. Zahed and William G. Tierney, Springer Open (eBook), 2020.
20. Peh Shing Huei, "*Standing Tall: The Goh Chok Tong Years (Volume 2)*", World Scientific Publishing, 2021.

Index

Academic Ranking of World Universities, 245
Advanced Remanufacturing and Technology Centre (ARTC), 234
Ageing Research Institute for Society and Education (ARISE), 233
Agency for Science, Technology and Research (A*STAR), 4, 27, 37, 38, 59, 61 85, 94, 97, 142, 148
Appointment, Promotion and Tenure (APT), 73, 77
Art, Design and Media, 22
ARWU, 246
Asian School of Environment (ASE), 23, 107, 222
Association of Southeast Asian Nations (ASEAN), 272
Australian National University (ANU), 54

Berkeley, 99
Berkeley Education Alliance for Research in Singapore, 214
Biopolis, 268
Blue Ribbon Commission, 150, 169, 171

Blue Ribbon Commission on Undergraduate Education, 92
Blue Ribbon Commission Review of Undergraduate Education, 93
BMW, 237
Board of Trustees, 27, 28, 66, 74, 76, 77, 82, 86, 95, 96
Bob Brown, 213
Boston University, 213
Brookings Institute, 234
Brown University, 210
Building and Construction Authority, 217

California Institute of Technology (Caltech), 33, 97, 249, 274, 275, 277
Cambridge Centre for Advanced Research and Education in Singapore, 214
Cambridge Laboratory of Molecular and Cell Biology, 231
Cambridge University, 232, 249, 273
Campus for Research Excellence and Technological Enterprise (CREATE), 94, 214, 237, 268, 285

Carnegie Mellon University (CMU), 250, 275
Cellular and Molecular Mechanisms of Inflammation, 215
Centre for Environmental Life Sciences Engineering (SCELSE), 107, 108, 217, 220
Centre for Quantum Technologies (CQT), 219
Centre for Scientific Research, 238, 268
Centre national de la recherche scientifique, 208
CERN, 285
Chalmers University, 187, 242
Cham Tao Soon, 17, 19, 20, 23, 25, 38, 39, 47, 56, 58, 262, 268
Chinese Academy of Sciences, 250
Chinese Heritage Centre, 260
Chingay Parade, 256
Civil Aviation Authority of Singapore, 258
CleanTech, 235
CleanTech Park, 229, 265, 266
CN Yang Scholars Programme, 165, 166
Committee for the Expansion of the University Sector in Singapore (CEUS), 71, 191, 192
Complexity Institute, 107, 276
Confucius Institute, 268
Corporate Labs @ Universities, 235
Centre for Research and Development in Learning (CRADLE), 171

Dainton, 28, 247
day care, 259
Defence Science and Technology Agency (DSTA), 5, 36, 37, 39, 65, 96

Defence Science Organisation (DSO), 27, 34–37, 39, 56, 96
Delta-NTU Corporate Laboratory for Cyber-Physical Systems, 237
Deng Xiaoping, 9, 113
Dr. Tony Tan, 3, 24–27, 29, 51, 58, 94, 211, 226
Dr. Tony Tan Keng Yam, 20, 39
Dr. Vivien Chiong, 255
Duke–NUS Graduate Medical School, 194
Duke University, 190

Earth Observatory of Singapore (EOS), 101, 107, 183, 220
EcoCampus, 266
École Polytechnique Fédérale de Lausanne (EPFL), xxvii, 246
Economic Development Board, 11, 142, 213, 217
Energy and Environmental Sustainability Solutions for Megacities, 215
Energy Research Institute at NTU (ERIAN), 101, 107, 229, 266
Er Meng Hwa, 6, 28, 72, 97
ESSEC Business School, 268
ETH Zürich, 70, 249, 273, 274, 275
European Molecular Biology Organisation (EMBO), 54, 184, 231
European Research Council (ERC), 186
European Research Council's (ERC) Young Investigator Grants, 212
European Science Foundation (ESF), 56, 61, 70, 81, 186, 233, 241
European Union, 57
European Union Centre in Singapore, 268

European Young Investigator Awards (EURYI), 57, 185, 187, 212

Fraunhofer Institute, 230
Fusionopolis, 268
Future Healthcare, 101, 102
Future Learning (Understanding, Learning, Teaching), 107, 109

George Yeo, 15
Georgia Institute of Technology, 274
GERD, 3, 11
Global Alliance of Technological Universities (GlobalTech), 195, 274
Global Asia, 107
Global Dialogues, 275
Goh Chok Tong, 19

Harvard, 151, 210, 249, 273
Health City Novena, 267
Healthy Society (Healthy Living, Active Ageing), 107, 108
Hebrew University of Jerusalem, 223, 273
Hive Learning Centre, 261
Hong Kong University, 189
Hong Kong University of Science and Technology (HKUST), xxvii, 250

Imperial College London, 99, 147, 151, 157, 165, 185, 194, 195, 196, 200, 249, 251, 273, 274, 277
Indian Institute of Technology, Bombay (IITB), 274
Infocomm Media Development Authority, 213
Innovation Asia, 101, 102
INSEAD, 268

Institute for Media Innovation (IMI), 102, 229
Institute of Advanced Studies (IAS), 275
Institute of Technology in Health and Medicine (NITHM), 103
Institute of Technology (MIT), 249
Institute Para Limes (IPL), 233
Interdisciplinary Graduate School, 103
International Academic Advisory Panel (IAAP), 10, 21, 96, 98
International Council for Science (ICSU), 276
International Union of Pure and Applied Physics (IUPAP), 276

Johannesburg University, 277
Johns Hopkins University, 215
Jurong, 260, 268, 269

Karolinska, 192
Karolinska Institute, 184, 185, 192, 194, 220, 231, 273
Kenzō Tange, 18, 261
Keppel Corporation, 258
King's College London, 277
Koh Boon Hwee, 5, 28, 39, 48, 58, 59, 77, 86, 87, 91

Land Transport Authority, 217
Lam Khin Yong, xviii, 72, 107, 116, 124, 236
Learning Science — CRADLE, 232
Lee Foundation, 197, 275
Lee Hsien Loong, 11, 37, 115, 116
Lee Kong Chian School of Medicine (LKCMedicine), 22, 108, 123
Lee Kuan Yew, 7–11, 14, 16, 28, 29, 46, 53, 113, 117
Lim Chuan Poh, 26, 27, 59, 85

Linköping, 56, 91
Linköping University, 20, 38, 55, 60
Lockheed Martin, 237
Lord Frederick Dainton, 16, 18, 210
Lund University, 54

Maastricht University, 151
Mao Zedong, 113
Massachusetts Institute of Technology (MIT), 25, 26, 84, 99, 151
Max Planck Society, 209, 250
Mechanobiology Institute (MBI Singapore), 220
Michigan State University, 185
Minister for Education, 11, 49
Ministry of Defence (MINDEF), 34, 36, 39, 96, 108, 217
Ministry of Education (MOE), 10, 11, 19, 25, 26, 59, 61, 71, 82, 83, 89, 91, 94, 96, 141
MOE's Academic Research Council (ARC), 213
Molecular Biology (LMB), 184
Monash University, 277
Monetary Authority of Singapore, 217

Nanomaterials for Energy and Water Management, 215
Nantah, 14–19, 28, 95, 114
Nanyang Assistant Professorships (NAPs), 212, 226
Nanyang Business School, 18
Nanyang Environment and Water Research Institute (NEWRI), 101, 107, 228, 266
Nanyang Institute of Structural Biology (NISB), 184, 217, 231

Nanyang Institute of Technology in Health and Medicine (NITHM), 108, 193
Nanyang Integrated Medical Biological and Environmental Life Sciences (NIMBELS), 108
Nanyang University (*Nantah*), 9, 10, 13, 83
National Centre for Infectious Diseases, 267
National Institute of Education (NIE), 19, 72
National Medical Research Council (NMRC), 218
National Research Foundation (NRF), 3, 27, 28, 51, 58, 94, 141, 185
National Science and Technology Board (NSTB), 3, 38
National Skin Centre, 267
National University of Singapore (NUS), 4, 10, 14, 23–28, 37, 39, 70, 79, 83–85, 95, 98, 99, 114, 259, 268
New Media, 101, 102
New Silk Road, 101, 102, 107
New Undergraduate Experience, 148
Ng Eng Hen, 21
Nobel, 75, 81, 189
Nobel Chemistry Committee, 187, 242
Nobel Committee, 54
Nobel Foundation, 55, 275, 276
Nobel Prize, 283
Northwestern University, 165
NRF Board and its Science Advisory Board, 61
NTU Education, 106, 170
NTU Fest, 257

NTU Institute for Health Technologies (HealthTech NTU), 103
NTU Integrated Medical, Biological and Environmental Life Sciences (NIMBELS), 232
NTU-NIE Teaching Scholars Programme, 165

Open University, 277
Oxford, 249
Oxford University, 219

Para Limes, 276
Pennsylvania State University, 223
People's Action Party (PAP), 8, 9, 11, 83
Poona, 41
Princeton University, 151
Promotion and Tenure (PT), 91
Provosts and Deans Group (PDG), 124, 143, 178
Public Utilities Board (PUB), 213, 217, 258
Pune, 70, 72

QAFU-ERP, 92
QS World University Rankings, 28
Quality Assurance Framework for Universities (QAFU), 24, 47, 87, 88, 90, 93, 95, 99, 154, 159, 173–176, 179, 182

Renaissance Engineering Programme, 164
Research and Support Office (RSO), 227
Research Centres of Excellence (RCEs), 94, 212, 271, 285
Research, Innovation and Enterprise Council, 211
Research Integrity and Ethics Office (RIEO), 241
Robert Bosch GmbH, 254
Rolls-Royce, 235, 236, 239, 266
Royal Institute of International Affairs (Chatham House), 234

School of Art, Design and Media, 21, 98
School of Biological Sciences (SBS), 22, 60
School of Chemical and Biomedical Engineering (SCBE), 22
School of Civil and Environmental Engineering (CEE), 21
School of Electrical and Electronic Engineering (EEE), 21
School of Humanities and Social Sciences (SHSS), 22, 23, 97
School of Mechanical and Aerospace Engineering (MAE), 21
School of Physical and Mathematical Sciences (SPMS), 22
Scientific Advisory Board (SAB), 51, 94
Secure Community (Preventing, Adapting, Resilience), 107, 108
Semakau, 229
Shanghai Jiao Tong University, 114, 245, 249, 274
Shih Choon Fong, 210, 219
Singapore Centre for 3D Printing (SC3DP), 234
Singapore Centre for Environmental Life Sciences and Engineering (SCELSE), 101

Singapore–ETH Centre, 215
Singapore Hokkien Huay Kuan, 260, 261
Singapore International Graduate Award (SINGA), 272
Singapore Management University (SMU), 20, 24–27, 85, 149
Singapore–MIT Alliance for Research and Technology, 215
Singapore Statement on Research Integrity, 241
Singapore University of Technology and Design (SUTD), 164, 165, 191
Singtel Cognitive and Artificial Intelligence Lab for Enterprises (SCALE@NTU), 237
Sino-Singapore Guangzhou Knowledge City (SSGKC), 116
SMRT, 258
SMRT-NTU Smart Urban Rail Corporate Laboratory, 237
Southampton University, 184, 220
S. Rajaratnam School of International Studies (RSIS), 22
S. R. Nathan, 46, 49
Stanford, 28, 43, 45, 46, 65, 84, 99, 249
Stanford University, 6, 35, 42, 44, 47, 50, 69, 73, 188, 220, 238, 273
ST Engineering, 236, 258
Stockholm University, 55–57
Subra Suresh, 26
Sustainable Earth, 101
Swiss Federal Institute of Technology Lausanne, 246

Tan Kah Kee, 14, 15
Tan Lark Sye, 14

Tan Tock Seng Hospital (TTSH), 198, 199, 267
Technical University of Munich, 185, 237, 273, 275
Technion, 148, 273
Temasek Laboratory at NTU, 108
Tharman Shanmugaratnam, 26, 49, 144, 218
the Arc, 263
The Complexity Institute, 233
The Hive, 263
The Photonics Institute (TPI), 230
The University of Hong Kong, 270
The Wave, 263
Thomas Heatherwick, 158, 263
Thomson Reuters, 243
Times Higher Education (THE), 245
Times Higher Education (THE) World Academic Summits, 276
Timothy Seow, 262
Traditional Chinese Medicine, 262
Trustworthy and Secure Cyber Plexus, 215
Tsinghua University, 273

Umeå University, 54
Undergraduate Research Experience on Campus, 153
United Nations Singapore Sustainable Development Solutions Network (SDSN), 268
University College London, 99, 249
University of Arizona, 185, 233
University of Birmingham, 270
University of British Columbia, 165
University of California, Berkeley, 45, 151, 165, 273
University of California, Los Angeles (UCLA), 185

University of Gothenburg, 222
University of Michigan, 241
University of New South Wales (UNSW), 215, 222, 275
University of Pennsylvania Wharton School of Business, 20
University of Poona, 42
University of Rhode Island, 246
University of Singapore, 16
University of Southampton, 230, 242
University of Strathclyde, 273
University of Sydney, 194
University of Warwick, 194, 215
University Scholars Programme, 165, 167
URECA, 154
Utrecht University, 285

Vrije Universiteit Amsterdam, 185, 233

Wee Kim Wee School of Communication and Information, 18
Wharton Business School, 24

Xi Jinping, 116

Yale, 151
Yonsei University, 189
Youth Olympic Games, 256, 261
Yunnan Garden, 15, 258–260, 266, 269